Genazzano:
The Chosen Town
of the
Mother of Good Counsel

THE MOTHER
OF GOOD COUNSEL
OF GENAZZANO

—————— João S. Clá Dias ——————

With a foreword by
Plinio Corrêa de Oliveira

WESTERN HEMISPHERE CULTURAL SOCIETY, INC.

DECLARATION

In obedience to the decrees of the Holy See, and specifically the decrees of Pope Urban VIII on March 13, 1625, and June 5, 1631, we submit everything we have written here or in other works to the judgment of the Holy Church. When we narrate prodigious facts or use the word "miracle" or analogous words or when we apply the adjective "blessed" to persons not beatified by the Church, we do so only following the customs that prevail among the faithful and in no way do we intend to anticipate the judgment of Holy Church.

The Author

ACKNOWLEDGMENTS:

The author is thankful to Mr. José Manuel Jimenez and Mr. Nestor José da Silva Fonseca for their excellent collaboration in the research and selection of documents used in this work and for their editorial suggestions.

The photographs of Genazzano that illustrate this work were taken by the author during his visit to the region.

Translated from the original Portuguese by Mr. Philip Moran Sr.

Western Hemisphere Cultural Society, Inc.
P.O. Box 417, Sunbury, Penn. 17801

Library of Congress Catalog Card Number: 91-68343
ISBN: 1-8810-0803

Contents

CONTENTS

Approbation

The present work was submitted to renowned Dominican theologian Fr. Antonio Royo Marín's keen and competent scrutiny. He expressed his favorable opinion in the letter transcribed below.

My dear friend,

With much delight and great spiritual joy did I read your historical work on Our Lady of Good Counsel, venerated in the Italian town of Genazzano, which you kindly sent to me for a doctrinal and literary examination. I consider it to be perfect and irreproachable in both respects. Your extensive knowledge of the most solid and reliable sources of information; the seriousness of your historical research of the changing fortune that has been visited upon the image in the different times and places where it has been venerated, beginning with its apparition more than seven centuries ago in the Albanian town of Scutari and its prodigious crossing over the sea to Genazzano; the countless miracles of all kinds worked in connection with this most devout image of Mary, many of which loftily resist the requirements of the most severe historical analysis; your strictly Catholic interpretation of events; and still more, the suave unction and tender Marian devotion that your lines exhale; all endow your precious study with such charming quality that the reader untiringly devours pages on end without realizing it, completely subdued as he is by the marvelous narrative presented to him as a plentiful spiritual banquet. Add to this the splendid album-like presentation, rich in magnificent photography that offers views of the village and surrounding landscape, and one may forecast, without need of prophetic insight, the great success that awaits the editions in the English and Portuguese languages and any future translation as well. My dear Juan, would it be too much to begin planning an edition in Spanish, which would be joyfully welcomed, not only in Spain, but also in the twenty Latin American nations that speak the same language of Cervantes?

I will close by saying, my dear friend, that I could not adequately tell you how much I enjoyed reading your beautiful work nor express the great spiritual benefit it afforded me, increasing my devotion to Mary, the Immaculate Virgin and Mother of Good Counsel. I will henceforth remember you and your beautiful book when, calling to mind the blessed image of Genazzano, I devoutly pronounce the sweet invocation Mother of Good Counsel in my daily recitation of the Litany of Loreto. May She "turn her eyes of mercy toward us" for as long as our pilgrimage on earth lasts and, above all, may She "show unto us the blessed fruit of her womb, Jesus" in the ceaseless day of eternal bliss.

With warmest regards from your faithful friend,

Antonio Royo Marín, O.P.

Madrid, September 15, 1988
Feast of Our Lady of Sorrows

Fr. Antonio Royo Marín was professor of Moral and Dogmatic Theology for twenty years at the famous University of Salamanca, Spain.

While a student in the seminary of Madrid, which he entered in 1933 during the ill-fated period of communist domination, twice he was on the verge of martyrdom as he came close to being gunned down by agitators. Once the "crusade of liberation" was over, he entered the Dominican Order and completed his theological education in the University of Saint Stephen, in Salamanca, and in the Angelicum, in Rome. Later he was given the title of Preacher General for his Order and spent several years traveling throughout Spain in that capacity, drawing multitudes with his eloquence and ardor. He began his writing activities during his period as a professor at Salamanca. He has authored twenty-four works on Catholic theology and doctrine, totaling more than half a million copies in different editions, printings and translations.

His fruitful dedication was acknowledged not long ago when His Holiness John Paul II bestowed on him the medal Pro Ecclesia et Pontifice, an award instituted by Pope Leo XIII for those who have excelled in the defense of the Church and the Papacy.

In September of 1988, Professor Plinio Corrêa de Oliveira, author of the foreword, visited the shrine of Genazzano to thank the Mother of Good Counsel for his sixty years of anticommunist Catholic militancy.

Foreword

SEVERAL reasons prompted my joyful agreement to write a foreword for this book at the request of its author, whom I dearly esteem. Foremost, it is a book about Our Lady, whose greatness I have not ceased to exalt throughout my life and will continue to exalt until my last moment.

Secondly, the author of the work is one of my most dedicated collaborators in the great fight in which the Brazilian TFP (as well as each of the other autonomous 15 TFPs) is engaged—a struggle against the fundamentally atheistic and pantheistic egalitarianism* that is increasingly dominant in contemporary society.

There is yet a third reason—a strictly personal one, which I cannot pass over in silence.

---

* The atheistic character of egalitarianism is brilliantly demonstrated by Saint Thomas Aquinas when he states: "We must say that the multitude and distinction of things come from the intention of the first agent, Who is God. For He brought things into being in order that His goodness might be communicated to creatures, and be represented by them; and because His goodness could not be adequately represented by one creature alone, He produced many and diverse creatures, that what was wanting to one in representation of the divine goodness might be supplied by another. For goodness, which in God is simple and uniform, in creatures is manifold and divided; and hence the whole universe together participates in the Divine goodness more perfectly, and represents it better than any single creature whatever" (*Summa Theologica*, I, q. 47, a. 1).

In 1967, as a part of my daily routine, I began to read a book about Our Lady of Good Counsel.* How I came upon it I do not recall, but I read it very late at night while lying in bed awaiting the onset of sleep after days filled with arduous effort.

The reading of that book brought me a gentle and discreet spiritual joy—something infrequent for me. I felt this even when the author digressed on some matters very indirectly related to the subject of his excellent book. Those movements of my soul were, however, so discreet that I paid little attention to them. Nevertheless, the recounting of the impressive facts which constitute the history of the invocation and painting of Our Lady of Good Counsel led me to ask a friend with contacts in Italy to obtain a picture of it for me.

Shortly thereafter I fell seriously ill, so much so that I was hospitalized and underwent a serious operation. While recovering with promising speed, circumstances of a different nature caused my soul distressing concerns.

It was at this time that some friends brought the requested picture to me in the hospital. I must say that I had virtually forgotten about Monsignor Dillon's excellent work by then.

The friends who had gathered around my hospital bed unwrapped the picture. I gazed at it with natural and respectful attention when—wonder of wonders!—something most indescribable happened. It absolutely could not be called a miracle. The picture had not been sensibly altered; the figures and colors of Our Lady of Genazzano and the Infant Jesus she held in her arms were unchanged.

---

* He refers to *The Virgin Mother of Good Counsel* by Monsignor George F. Dillon, apostolic missionary in Australia, in its French translation, *La Vierge Mère du Bon Conseil* (Bruges: Desclée de Brower, 1885).

However, I had the surest impression that the figure of Our Lady gazed at me with moving kindness, while it expressed (in a way I do not know how to explain) something that in a serene and irrefutable way luminously resolved the problems of my soul, which were far more tormenting than those of my body. I did not mention this to any of those present at the time. When I commented on the occurrence later, two friends who had been present affirmed that they had perceived no change in me but only in the image that gazed at me with merciful love.

Since then, I have been bound to the image of Our Lady of Genazzano by an indescribable debt of gratitude. To fulfill that debt, I began to relate the incident to my courageous and devout battle companions. Later, at the behest of the Augustinian Fathers of Genazzano, I decided to recount the story in the magazine that they publish in the city of the Mother of Good Counsel.*

*   *   *

Having said this, let me state the essential facts about that august image.

Religion was seriously threatened in fifteenth-century Albania. On one hand, the fervor of the Catholic populace was declining; on the other, hordes of Mohammedan invaders were assaulting the country, intent upon destroying the Catholic faith to its very roots. To prevent this catastrophe, Divine Providence raised up a hero comparable in courage and faith to Charlemagne's peers or the outstanding warriors of the Crusades and the Spanish-Portuguese Reconquest. His name was Scanderbeg. While he lived,

---

* "Una Dichiarazione," *Madre del Buon Consiglio*, Genazzano, July-August 1985, p. 28. We have reproduced this text on pages 122-123.

performing heroic and glorious feats, Albania resisted. When he died, Albania's resistance crumbled—a fitting punishment for a population steeped in lukewarmness.

In addition to Scanderbeg, and far superior to him, there was another pillar of shaken Christendom in Albania: a fresco of Our Lady then known as "Our Lady of Good Services." (This title is analogous to Our Lady Help of Christians, a devotion that has spread throughout the Catholic world.) Since the picture was located in a shrine near Scutari, Albania's capital, it was feared that this source of so many precious graces for even so lukewarm a people would fall into the hands of the Mohammedan invaders.

This was precisely the fear felt by two devout Albanians, Georgio and De Sclavis, worthy representatives of the country's faithful remnant.

The solution to this predicament was not long in coming. Before the very eyes of astonished devotees, compatriots of the great Scanderbeg, the fresco slowly detached itself from the wall. It rose and began to move in the direction of the Adriatic Sea and never varied in its course. At the same time, Our Lady made the two Albanians understand that she wanted them to follow her image. With a faith and moral fiber like that of Scanderbeg, they did not hesitate. They walked miraculously over the water until the image reached most Catholic Italy.

Consider the synthesis of events narrated to this point: a world falling victim to its own moral and religious crisis rather than to the strength of a terrible enemy; two faithful who believe and continue to hope against all hope; then a stupendous miracle that crowns their perseverance.

These facts merit our attention even in their details and are related further on by the author, João Scognamiglio Clá Dias, in a fluent style, full of piety and enthusiasm.*

---

* See Chapters 4 and 5.

These qualities of soul are evident throughout the text, with the savory repetition of divers concepts contributing to this.

Even up to our days, a recurring characteristic can be observed in the anecdotes about the devotion to the Mother of Good Counsel of Genazzano: the faithful who come to her feet beseeching her assistance are in the midst of bewildering and distressing trials. Such was the situation shared by Georgio and De Sclavis, the two heroes chosen by Our Lady to be her mortal escorts in crossing the Adriatic, and an elderly Italian woman, Petruccia, whose brave soul was proportional to theirs.

Indeed, while the Albanians followed her image across Italy, Our Lady suddenly disappeared from their sight. It had gone to fill the soul of Petruccia with heavenly consolation at a time when she was at the height of trial and adversity.

It is opportune to say a word about this woman, a great example of the strong woman of the gospel, who was chosen by Our Lady to build the most blessed shrine where her image has been exposed for the veneration of countless faithful for five centuries.

Petruccia was a devout, rather well-to-do widow. She had been favored with a vision in which the Blessed Virgin entrusted her with the mission of restoring the church of Our Lady of Good Counsel in Genazzano, which had fallen nearly into ruin.*

To that end, Petruccia sought out the charity of the faithful of the town. Their response left much to be de-

---

* A bas-relief has been venerated in this church since the fourth century under the invocation of Our Lady of Good Counsel. Petruccia began her reconstruction with one of the side chapels that is dedicated to Saint Blaise; it is against the principal wall of this chapel that the venerated fresco from Scutari came to rest.

sired, so the alms she collected fell short of what was required to finish the work on the church. Not lacking in courage, she decided to apply the remainder of her inheritance to the reconstruction project. Even this proved insufficient, leaving the work far from completion. This failure provoked sarcasm from the very population that had been so lukewarm in its response to her pleas for financial help. Petruccia, despite her eighty years, remained enthusiastic, nevertheless, trusting firmly in the help of the Blessed Virgin.

What an immense and marvelous surprise it was both to her and the townspeople when on the evening of Saturday, April 25, 1467, a cloud of striking appearance drifted down upon the village. Emanating from the cloud was the sound of equally striking and beautiful music. Slowly, the fresco of Our Lady separated from the cloud and positioned itself on the altar that Petruccia had ordered in anticipation of the church's complete restoration.

Blessed Petruccia's earlier vision was confirmed. The Blessed Virgin obviously desired the completion of the work. From then on, the townspeople, who ran in awe to pay homage to the image, contributed most generously to the quick and final reconstruction of the church.

There, while the faithful today venerate the picture of the Blessed Virgin and Child (marvelously transported from Scutari by angels), the mortal remains of Blessed Petruccia sleep the sleep of peace awaiting her final resurrection.

The two Albanians, baffled by the painting's disappearance and ignorant of its appearance in Genazzano, were wandering about Italy in futile search of their lost treasure.

When news of the events taking place in Petruccia's village finally reached them, they hastened there. One can easily imagine their wonder and rejoicing upon finding the heavenly painting. They attested that the picture that excited all Genazzano was one and the same as that formerly venerated in Scutari, and thus their mission as witnesses was fulfilled. Both Georgio and De Sclavis remained in Genazzano and each eventually married. To this day, descendants of Georgio still live in the town.

It is self-evident that the mission of the two Albanians was intimately connected with that of Petruccia. Under the maternal direction of the Blessed Virgin, all three struggled and overcame all manner of obstacles and trials until the glorious completion of a common goal.

*   *   *

We can draw from this story a lesson for our own century, corrupted like fifteenth-century Albania by the religious and moral decadence which is the starting point for all other forms of contemporary decadence.

In 1917, the Blessed Virgin appeared to three shepherd children of Fatima. She entrusted them with the duty of communicating her message of justice and mercy to the world: If mankind did not convert and if the world was not consecrated to her by the Holy Father in union with all the bishops simultaneously in their respective dioceses, the world would be ravaged by terrible punishments. Impiety and immorality would thus be duly chastised and, consequently, vanquished. "Finally," the Blessed Virgin concluded, "my Immaculate Heart will triumph."

It stands to reason that during that time of trial, Divine Providence will not fail to raise up strong and generous souls in the Church, somehow making His designs known to them and using them in one way or another to obtain His victory.

When the events predicted at Fatima are spoken of, attention is focused mainly on the future punishments and on those who will suffer them. Indeed, the privileged devotees of the Blessed Virgin that she will raise up seem all but forgotten.

**Jacinta and Lúcia,
two of the seers of Fatima.**

*IN the environs
of the nearby village of
Aljustrel, an unpretentious
sculptural ensemble
represents the apparition of
the Angel of Portugal,
who gave Holy Communion
to the three shepherd
children under the shade of
a holm oak that still
stands at the site.*

Who will they be? My own conjecture is that they will be in the minority but will be recruited from among persons of the most varied nationalities and social conditions from all corners of the globe. Each one, according to the manner and degree chosen by Mary Most Holy, will be the recipient of admirable graces, will face terrible obstacles, and will at times consider himself to have failed completely. Yet, on the day of the great triumph, each will be marvelously convoked to take part in the glorification of the Blessed Mother of God and to live during at least the first days of that glorious Marian era eloquently foreseen by Saint Louis Marie Grignion De Montfort, the great seventeenth-century apostle of Mary Most Holy.*

I have those souls of fire in mind as I write this foreword. Thus, I would be pleased if my words incline them to an attentive reading of this excellent book of João Clá Dias, through which they may be led to beseech more courage during the great trials they will encounter, courage they may surely obtain.

PLINIO CORRÊA DE OLIVEIRA

---

* Saint Louis De Montfort was born in 1673 in Montfort-sur-Meu, France. Ordained in 1700, he entered heaven in 1716. Leo XIII declared him blessed on January 22, 1888, and Pius XII canonized him on July 20, 1947.

CHAPTER 1

Mother of Good Counsel

THE beautiful and noble church of Our Lady of Good Counsel (so dedicated since its origin), recognized for its harmonic and distinctive architectural style, arches skyward in Genazzano, Italy, amidst an atmosphere of centuries-old peace and blessings.

The present shrine was built between 1621 and 1629 by the Augustinian Friar Felice Leonceli of Cave to replace the old church built by Blessed Petruccia. According to Friar Leonceli, the ancient church was "very deformed, not well ordained, and without lighting." Only its quattrocentro portal remained intact.

Later, in 1840, the façade, which was on the verge of ruin, was rebuilt by Father Fanucchi, an architect who had the good taste to adopt the style of the fifteenth century, thus keeping the whole in harmony with the ancient portal. In 1956, rich mosaics were added to the new façade. In the interior, at the head of the left aisle, is a small chapel especially built to enshrine the miraculous fresco of the Mother of Good Counsel.

The painting, executed on a thin crust of plaster and measuring about 16.5 inches high by 12 inches wide, depicts Mary Most Holy holding the Infant Jesus in her arms with ineffable maternal affection. Both are crowned by a simple rainbow. The fresco's colors are soft, and the lines of both admirable faces are finely drawn.

"*O Magnum Mysterium!*" sings the Church in the Matins responsory for Christmas. If it were not for the virtue of faith, who, looking at the child, could affirm that God and man are hypostatically united? Seriousness and sweetness, majesty and innocence are marvelously expressed in the countenance of the Infant. The straight nose calls to mind the infinite uprightness of the One Who is the Sun of Justice. His expressive eyes (slightly almond-shaped with soft, luminous chestnut color and greenish tones) radiate peace, unlimited kindness, and infinite wisdom.

The Infant's red-ocher tunic agreeably attracts one's gaze. Embroidered on the collar are harmonious and enigmatic designs. Is this inscription merely decorative, or is it perhaps a phrase in an unknown language suggestive of His mission? His right arm encircles the noble and delicate neck of His Mother in a gesture of intense affection. His left hand securely grasps the upper portion of her dress as if saying, "Thou art all Mine!" So touching is this divine embrace and so emphatically focused is the Divine face on that of His Blessed Mother, that the right eye is slightly diverted from the normal line.

The Divine Infant's face, while proper to that of a child, does not express any of the superficiality so characteristic of that phase of life. On the contrary, like an ocean of seriousness, all the profundity and breadth of understanding, all the force and strength of will, all the elevation and nobility of feeling, shine forth in Him. He is fully aware of what His Mother represents and of the interior paradise she offers Him.

With a gaze that is all-embracing, the Infant contemplates the past, present, and future. He analyzes the whole work of creation, in all its variety and splendor. He sees Lucifer's revolt and the *praelium magnum*, the great battle in which Saint Michael casts Satan and all the rebellious angels into hell.

After considering the trial of the angels, He looks upon that of men, seeing the sin of Adam and Eve, with all its consequences: the breaking of the covenant between Creator and creature and the necessity of the redemption of the human race. The disobedience offended God in His infinite majesty. It was thus necessary that the redemption be made by one who possessed equally infinite merit. This is the divine mission of the Infant Jesus, to redeem mankind, to establish the new covenant, in perfect conformity with the designs of the Eternal Father: "I came down from heaven, not to do my own will, but the will of him that sent me" (John 6:38).

Like a new Isaac, He desires to obey ardently and completely. Was not the sin of our parents precisely one of disobedience? He takes on the holocaust resolutely and lovingly, despite painfully finding Himself in the Garden of Olives repeating the prophetic words of the Psalmist: "What profit is there in my blood?" (Ps. 29:10).

This internal state of contemplation notwithstanding, He wishes to manifest here all His satisfaction, all His happiness, at being in the arms of His Blessed Mother. Thus He demonstrates the necessity of having recourse to that Mediatrix so that, amidst the storms and sufferings of this life, one may have the indispensable strength and courage to imitate Him Who is "the way, and the truth, and the life" (John 14:6). The Infant seems to say to each of us, "If you want something of Me, ask for it through the intercession of My Mother and you will be heard.'' The words ''universal mediation of Mary'' could very well be inscribed above the halo of the holy fresco of Our Lady of Good Counsel, for the God-Man Himself finds protection and shelter in the virginal arms of Mary.

The Infant presses His face ever so slightly against that of His Mother and receives, in turn, her ineffable affection, veneration, and tenderness, an exchange represented with special adroitness by the inclination of their heads toward one another and by the intimacy of their gazes.

The mysteries of this union made Saint Bernard exclaim: ''Admire therefore these two marvels, and choose which of them thou wilt admire the more, whether the gracious condescension of the Son, or the glorious exaltation of the Mother. Each of them oppresses our mind, each of them passes our comprehension. That God would obey a woman is a condescension without parallel; that a woman should command God is a glory beyond compare.''[1]

Could it be that the artist's intention in painting the faces so close together was to symbolize the grandeur and profundity of the mysterious union between the Mother and the Son, the archetypical union of Jesus and Mary? One needs only to analyze the facial features of the Mother of Good Counsel, the rose-color of her face, the straight line of her nose, her arched eyebrows, the golden color of her hair, the inclination of her neck, to conclude that she is the Mother of that Son who so much resembles her.

But why paint the Infant Jesus and Mary so close together? Because the Son is the Creator of this sublime Mother, and the Mother, the most perfect of creatures, carried this Divine Infant in her virginal womb.

All the while, even at the moment of adoring her Son most fervently and wondering about His thoughts, this Mother still regards the faithful kneeling at her feet. As Mediatrix of all graces, she welcomes their prayers and presents them to God Our Lord.

Who has ever held in his hands a treasure equal to this, the Infinite? At the same time, who was ever more desirous than Our Lady of attracting others to share their treasure?

In contemplating this fresco, one sees that the kaleidoscope of paradoxes of the relationship of Our Lady with her Divine Son is endless.

There is an intimacy and a depth of relationship in this union of Mother and Son that surprises and attracts. The union of soul, reflected in their shared gaze, generates in both of them a tranquility and steadfastness in affection, an affection that seems to make them truly sense the blessed delight of this mutual understanding, of this togetherness!

*S*et aside this text
for a moment
and contemplate the fresco
once more.

At the same time, this deep, calm, serious, and intimate gaze is not exclusive. The faithful who kneel before the image are attracted to enter into the friendliness and serenity of this gaze. Mother and Son are ready to receive with kindness all the devout faithful seeking help, mercy, and protection. The sacred warmth radiating from both faces makes the faithful feel understood and loved for the noblest aspects of his soul.

If the reader sets this text aside for a moment and once again contemplates the fresco, letting himself be enveloped by the heavenly atmosphere that Mother and Son create, he will perceive that, beyond the painting's pictorial and artistic qualities, the graces of the presence of Our Lady and the Infant Jesus emanate from the faces. They are graces very few can resist, graces that may be felt knocking at the door of one's soul or, perhaps, already inside and bringing an assuaging rest. At times it is the Mother's face; at times it is the gaze of the Son; at yet others it is the fresco as a whole that will impart courage amidst difficult situations, consolation in sufferings, calm in afflictions, confidence in hours of anxiety, courage when one must advance, prudence when one must retreat. It is a gaze that can bring down a miracle from heaven when all human resources have been exhausted.

Venerating the sacred picture, we recall the words of Saint Alphonsus De Liguori who, a great devotee of the Mother of Good Counsel, habitually worked with a picture of the Virgin of Genazzano on a table in front of him:

"In fine, O sovereign Princess, from the immense ocean of thy beauty the beauty and grace of all creatures flowed forth as rivers. The sea learnt to curl its waves, and to wave its crystal waters from thy golden hair, which gracefully floated over thy shoulders and ivory neck. The crystal fountains and their transparent depths learnt their tranquil and steady flow from the serenity of thy beautiful brow and placid countenance. The lovely rainbow, when in full beauty, learnt with studious care its graceful bend from thy eyebrows, thus better to send forth its rays of light. The morning star itself, and the sweet star at night, are sparks from thy beautiful eyes. . . . The most delicious milk and sweetest honey are distillations from the sweet honeycomb of thy mouth. The scented jasmine and fragrant Damask rose stole their perfume from thy breath. . . . In fine, O Lady, every created beauty is a shadow and trace of thy beauty.

"And thus I wonder not, O sovereign Princess, that heaven and earth place themselves under thy feet; for such are they, and thou art so great, that to be only under thy feet enriches them. . . . Thus did the moon rejoice when the evangelist Saint John saw her under thy feet, and the sun increased in splendor when it clothed thee with its rays of light. . . .

The Title of
Mother of Good Counsel

The residents of Genazzano called the image that came miraculously to their city, *Maria del Paradiso*, because they believed it came directly from heaven or because of its marvelous beauty. Some called it *Madonna della Piazza* because it appeared in the square where Petruccia was trying to reconstruct her dream of a church. The image was still known by the simple invocation of Madonna of Genazzano.

However, the Augustinian friars continued to call their convent and church by the name of Santa Maria of Good Counsel. That title, attributed to the Virgin by Saint Augustine and others, was that of the bas-relief venerated in the ancient chapel since time immemorial.

The multiplicity of invocations lasted until the seventeenth century when the one of Good Counsel was generalized. The Popes, in their documents, always used that title. Finally, the Liturgy consecrated it definitively with the Mass and Office of the Mother of Good Counsel.

"O gracious and beautiful heaven, more vast than the heavens themselves, for they cannot contain God, who is immense, but he concealed himself in thy womb."[2]

Many and powerful are the miracles brought about through that heavenly fresco of the Mother of Good Counsel, witnessed by saints, popes, Catholics of all walks of life, and even by unbelievers. May the account of some of these incidents in the following pages strengthen the reader's faith. May he benefit from those graces, poured out with maternal abundance, with a queen's magnificence, over all those who piously and trustfully know how to say the sublime words, "O Mother of Good Counsel, pray for us!"

CHAPTER 2

The Town
of Genazzano

GENAZZANO, once the dominion of the Colonna family, is an authentic example of a fortified medieval town. Due to frequent wars, either against barbarians and infidels or between feudal lords, medieval cities were constructed in localities that would render a siege by enemy forces difficult while at the same time making defense easy. These cities were encircled with thick walls and guarded by stationed sentinels. Best use of space necessitated narrow streets, at times steeply inclined due to the nature of the terrain. More than anywhere else in Europe, the mountainous landscape of Italy displays cities resembling eagles' nests dominated by high towers and elegant campaniles. With the passing of time and the pacification of the contending parties, construction spread outside the walls and thus today we have the resultant arrangement of edifices.*

The general view of the town seemed to me very picturesque. Seen from a distance, that accumulation of modest, unornamented houses—it is a town of country folk—presents all the qualities of the country life of times past. The stone houses with sturdy roofs are simple and old, or, better said, ancient, since so many centuries of laborious existence grant them an undeniable respectability.

The onslaught of time has modelled the town and was evident in all the buildings: here a town wall eroded by the inclemency of the weather; close by, a dilapidated house wall; further on, stairs worn down by the footsteps of generations. Taken as a whole, almost nothing about the buildings or their surroundings

---

* Juan Miguel Montes is one of the many devotees of the Mother of Good Counsel of Genazzano. A native of Chile, he has lived in Peru, Ecuador, and England. He is presently the director of the bureau in Rome that represents the 15 TFPs. The April 1986 edition of the Brazilian monthly magazine *Catolicismo* published his beautiful detailed commentary on the village of Genazzano, a fruit of his frequent pilgrimages to the shrine there. We are pleased to be able to reproduce here some of his remarks about this attractive town. It would be difficult to find more adequate commentaries than his to accompany the photographs presented here.

would denote great richness but, rather, a dignified well-being lived under the influence of religion and Christian civilization.

What if someone decided to renovate and paint all of this, leaving the walls smooth, shining, and like new? What if somebody paved these undulating and unpredictable streets? What if all the businessmen installed illuminated signs throughout the town? I took care to quickly cast aside thoughts of such possibilities, so befitting modern Vandals. Let us leave Genazzano as it is, time-worn but picturesque and respectable with its happy and unpretentious populace.

Indeed, the town displays what could well be called the "art of being poor" for, walking through it to the shrine, I saw poverty and art at each step. I first discovered such art on a section of the ancient wall at the very entrance to the town. Although built with an evident practical purpose, artistic creativity was not absent. There is a simple and gracious stone arch, above which a shield bearing the arms of the city adorns the curved wall. Battlements surmount the whole. A well-kept pavement free from the geometrical monotony of modern designs runs beneath the arch to provide access to the enclosed fortified area.

The streets are narrow, winding, and of irregular pattern. One might almost conclude that the inhabitants of Genazzano were horrified at straight lines. There are paths and constructions that were not planned but, rather, resulted from the walking to and fro of many generations, arising spontaneously, organically, in accordance with necessities and possibilities. A house is built because there is an empty space; a street is opened respecting the position of the house; a wide or narrow staircase spans the different levels between streets; an arch buttresses two neighboring structures and simultaneously plays an aesthetic role. Must everything be straight and symmetrical?

Without the monotony of planned urbanism, the town acquired extremely varied and picturesque traits. It rose from the work of generations throughout the centuries, each generation contributing its work and creativity. The effort of everyone is present here, giving the town a personality of its own. All the townspeople derive a sense of belonging from that environment which reflects the characteristics of everyone and every lineage.

It is impossible to describe in detail a town wherein each angle is different, each house an ingenious individuality, each street a surprise generated and modified throughout the centuries, each inhabitant a curious synthesis of the past and present—and all are in perfect harmony.

Tourists with much money and little time have neither the sensibility nor patience to appreciate a town like this. However, there are persons of good taste who travel the world over seeking out these little architectural and urban jewels,

Town gate, and wall eroded by the elements.

Worn stairs,
in silent witness to
generations of footsteps.

Narrow,
winding streets

*of irregular
pattern.*

The townspeople derive a belonging from that environment

which reflects the characteristics of everyone and every lineage.

A dignified well-being lived under the influence of religion and . . .

. . . Christian civilization.

Opposite page:
Above left.
Twelfth-century bell tower. Saint Paul's Church.
Above right.
Bell tower of the shrine of Our Lady of Good Counsel.
Below left.
A watchtower rising from the city walls.
Below right.
Saint Blaise's archway.

This page:
Above right.
Roman Gate.
Center right.
Typical passage ways in Genazzano.
Below right.
Fountain by the Roman gate.

cut and polished by successive generations that, typically poor and for the most part uneducated, nevertheless possess great riches in talent and creativity.

Steep slopes, endless steps—everything forced me to make my way slowly on the climb toward the shrine. Undoubtedly, this town was not made for people in a hurry. I took advantage of the walk to observe the richness of the surroundings and to imagine the multiplicity of states of spirit that could be formed in each of those corners. I was enchanted to discover that there was no need to be pressed for time. Contemplative slowness: How much good it would bring to today's hurried world.

*   *   *

Having rested from the exhaustion of the contemporary hustle and bustle with this interesting and rich description and with this analysis of a few of the multiple aspects of such a picturesque town, let us enter the Shrine and examine the fresco of the Mother of Good Counsel close up.

CHAPTER 3

The Fresco Miraculously Suspended in the Air for Five Centuries

THE fresco is more than seven centuries old, but the exact date and place of its origin, as well as the artist who conceived it, are unknown. Could it be the work of angelic hands? Did it come directly from Paradise? These questions may first take one aback, but attentive observation and analysis of the effects the original painting, or even a copy, produce on those who contemplate it, renders the hypothesis of a miraculous origin more tenable.

When the fresco is observed close-up, the freshness of the colors create the impression that the artist, be he human or angelic, has just finished his work and placed a protective crystal covering over it. Reality, however, is quite different! Translated by angels from the Albanian city of Scutari all the way to Genazzano, the fresco has unexplainably remained suspended in the air close to the wall of the chapel in the church of Our Lady of Good Counsel for over five hundred years.

Three Prodigious Aspects of the Holy Fresco

The permanence of the fresco with the stability of its colors is the first prodigy. It is well known that even paintings of the great masters, despite being painted on thick walls and placed in appropriate and well-sheltered places, begin fading with the passing of time. This devout painting, on the contrary, was executed on a thin layer of stucco about the thickness of cardboard. Nevertheless, until today its colors retain their freshness without ever having undergone any restoration.

The second, and even more impressive, prodigy is that since its arrival in Genazzano on April 25, 1467, the holy image has remained suspended in the air without any means of support to maintain it in its extraordinarily stable condition. It is unfortunate that the altar that shelters it was not built with a concern for displaying such a wonderful miracle. However, several declarations made under oath by highly reliable witnesses attest to this fact and can be found in the historical chronicles of the Shrine.

Suspended in the Air
for Five Centuries

The most important documents proving the perpetual miracle are stated in Chapter 3: The holy fresco arrived in Genazzano and it remains there until today, facing one of the walls of the church without being affixed to it in any way. Important conclusions reached by some of the main historians of the shrine are quoted: Friar De Orgio, Father Buonanno, Monsignor Dillon and Bishop Addeo.

Friar De Orgio ■

"Brought by angelic hands, it was found suspended on the rough wall of the new church. Three new and very exceptional prodigies occurred then. . . . The heavenly painting was supported by divine virtue an inch away from the wall without in any way touching it. This miracle is even more wonderful when we consider that the aforementioned image is painted with brilliant colors on a very fine layer of plaster that detached itself from the church in Scutari, in Albania. [Finally], a fact confirmed through experience and observation is that when the holy image is touched, it yields" (op. cit., p. 20).

Father Buonanno ■

"All of these marvels [of the holy image] are summarized in one word: in the continuous miracle of until today finding this image in the same place and in the same way as it was when it was left there by a cloud on the day of its appearance, in the presence of all the people who had the happiness then to see it for the first time. It landed a short distance from the floor, approximately one inch from the new and rough wall of the chapel of Saint Blaise; and there it remained, suspended without any support'' (op. cit., p. 44).

■ Monsignor Dillon

''Although the Office of the Feast of Our Lady of Good Counsel states distinctly that the sacred Image appeared on the wall of the church of the Augustinians—*mirabiliter apparuisse in pariete*—yet a constant tradition mentioned by many writers exists, to the effect that it stood at first near, and in no manner touching the wall. There is nothing contradictory in these statements; for it could well have occurred that the holy Image did not rest at once upon the wall, though it afterwards may have touched it above or below. The archivists Cajetan and Calistus Marini already mentioned, who took such pains to examine every circumstance connected with the Translation and the Apparition, have not noticed the matter, nor has it been alluded to by the advocate, who placed the arguments in favour of the one and the other before the Sacred Congregation of Rites, in 1789. It is, however, perfectly certain; 1) that the Image has never been removed from the position it so miraculously selected; and 2) that many who have had to examine it, through the course of ages, have stated that they believed it to rest isolated without any support whatever'' (op. cit., pp. 233-234).

■ Bishop Addeo

''The material on which the miraculous image was painted is what is commonly called 'plaster,' detached from the respective wall'' (op. cit., p. 118).

There is yet a third and no less extraordinary miracle: the variations in the physiognomies and colors of the image. Various talented artists have tried their utmost to reproduce the venerable painting. Their efforts were doomed to failure since the colors of the fresco change, especially in the faces of Our Lady and the Divine Infant, at times taking on the hue of golden wheat or becoming rose-red. Besides such a portent as this, the facial expressions also vary, ranging from soft sadness to radiant joy.

The Surprising Facial Changes of the Image "Answer" the Prayers of the Faithful

It is no simple matter to capture the portrait since the countenances change so often. Whatever the most excellent brush or photographic equipment can produce is still far from reality, as many artists and photographers attest. These changes, seen by so many of the faithful and authors who have written about the Shrine, are perpetual miracles at the disposition of all the needy who visit the Mother of Good Counsel.

How many afflicted faithful who have approached her with faith and piety have been caressed with interior consolations! It is not unusual that each one verifies the alterations in color and expression taking place in the fresco. The Mother of Good Counsel and Infant Jesus seem to smile as if to affirm to those in need that which they have already felt interiorly: "My children, be not troubled. The cause of your anguish will be resolved." At such moments, it is easier to understand the profundity of those words of Father Thomas de Saint Laurent when he writes of confidence:

"O Voice of Christ, mysterious voice of grace that resoundeth in the silence of our souls, Thou murmurest in the depths of our hearts words of sweetness and peace. In response to our miseries, Thou repeatest the counsel so often given by the Divine Master during His mortal life: 'Confidence, confidence!' "[3]

An Eyewitness Account of the Crowning of the Image, November 17, 1682

Throughout the passing centuries, several commissions were set up by ecclesiastical authorities to analyze the miracles pertaining to the fresco. Here is a sample of the declarations and testimony taken over four hundred years.

Father Master Friar Fulgencio Recitelli, an eyewitness to the crowning of the image by the Chapter of Saint Peter's on November 17, 1682, made the following statement five days later:

"The Chapter of Saint Peter's sent a canon with two crowns of gold, one

Top. *View of the central nave of the Basilica of Our Lady of Good Counsel today. In the background is the chapel of the holy image.*

Right. *Solemn coronation of the holy image of Genazzano by the Chapter of Saint Peter's in the name of Pope Innocent XI, on November 17, 1682 (fresco at the shrine of Genazzano, 1885, by Prospero Piatti).*

for the Blessed Virgin and the other for the Infant. On Tuesday of the current month, the canon, in the presence of His Excellency the Constable and many other knights who had accompanied him, as well as a multitude of people, removed the silver-ornamented crystal that protects the image. In so doing, he marveled at noting that the painting, which was done on a fine crust of plaster, touched the wall only on the upper edge above the head. The rest of the painting had no support whatsoever. This is so much so that when the canon touched the faces of the image the plaster yielded like a piece of fabric. Everyone assembled was quite amazed, for they knew that a piece of plaster could not naturally stand alone. Thus it was firmly judged that the painting was held in place miraculously. In order to position the golden crowns, it was necessary to tie cords around them and suspend them in place from nails in the wall above the image since they could not affix them to the Madonna's forehead."[4]

"Mary Most Holy Granted the Grace I Was Seeking, as the Painting Appeared Joyful and Rose-colored"

Canon Andrea Bacci, a famous shrine historian known for his zeal in propagating devotion to Our Mother of Good Counsel, addressed a letter to Friar Angelo Maria De Orgio[5] in which he relates the observations he made when visiting Genazzano to venerate the blessed image in 1734:

"With all my heart and with an extraordinary interior tenderness, I asked the most clement Mother of Good Counsel for the great grace I desired and that meant so much to me. Halfway through the litany, I clearly saw that the image had become radiant and ruddy like a crimson rose. I was convinced I had not been mistaken when, as I was leaving, one of the religious present told me that Mary Most Holy had undoubtedly granted me the grace I had interiorly requested because the holy image looked joyful and the colors had intensified. Indeed, upon my return to Rome, filled with a lively confidence of having been heard, I suddenly received the longed-for grace. It came in such a fullness that all at once the difficult vexations that had been troubling me cleared up, and a great peace and serenity of soul came over me. I considered myself the happiest and most blessed man on earth."[6]

An Illustrious Artist Observes Several Miraculous Aspects of the Painting

A famous Genoese painter, Luigi Tosi, reported the observations he and six priests made on June 11, 1747. On this occasion, the artist closely examined the painting without the protective crystal covering. It was his intention to paint as faithful a copy as possible for his native city. As we shall see later, in Chapter 9, this copy became famous for miracles performed through her mediation. A document regarding that examination was drawn up and its authenticity attested to by those present, namely, Father Master Friar Guglielmo Pancotti, Prior of the Augustinians of Genazzano; Andrea Bacci, canon of Saint Mark's; Friar Bartolomeo Daglio, Augustinian Provincial of Lombardy; Friar Giambatista Maria Fossati, sacristan; Father Antonio Maria Madureyra; and Lorenzo Jacopini, treasurer of His Excellency Lord Colonna. The document reads:

"First, the aforementioned artist, Signor Luigi, having knelt before the Holy Image and after having well contemplated, regarded, and many times most attentively studied it, has clearly seen and publicly asserted that of all the copies made of this so prodigious and holy image at different times up until now, whether painted on paper or engraved on copper, none properly resembles it; and that it will always be most difficult (indeed, more than difficult) to find a painter, no matter how skillful, to whom could be given the merit and glory of executing a painting or copy of her portrait because the features and lines both of Mary and of the Infant, Whom she so graciously and lovingly holds close to her breast and face, are so fine, delicate, graceful, amiable, and singular that the whole seems rather an angelic than a human work.

"Second, the same Signor Luigi, an acknowledged authority on ancient and modern images of Mary as a worthy student and disciple of the celebrated Solimene,[7] observed, asserted, and concluded that the holy and miraculous image, of which we speak, is neither of the Greek style, nor of the Gothic style, nor the style of our past centuries, nor of modern style. Possessing such a fineness and exquisiteness of taste, it requires thoughtful observation, even of the minutest delineations, in order to succeed in executing as close a copy as art and mastery of painting can achieve. Whence he has publicly affirmed that an artist much superior to man or, at least, some holy man, must have delineated and painted it. Indeed, this is so much so as to be impossible to know or determine whether the image is truly painted or if it is an image miraculously, and with celestial colors, impressed on or impregnated in the simple plaster crust that is the sole support of so great a treasure.

"Third, he candidly admitted that, scarcely having seated himself before the altar about the nineteenth hour, that he might more easily make the longed-for copy, the forms (of the Child and Mother) suddenly became so confused to him that without being able to form any idea or image of the original, he knew not where to turn, nor what to decide, nor how to commence. In a moment, however, he felt inspired to prostrate himself. He had no sooner bent his knees before the holy image, humbly and devoutly and with great reverence and devotion, than his mind became serene and the concept of the original was impressed in his imagination. He was thus able to successfully begin to copy it. The effort took almost two days to complete, during which time he worked almost always on his knees.

The Image Frequently Changes Both in Countenance and Color

"Fourth, the same painter, Signor Luigi, has observed and considered, and in the presence of us all, affirmed that this holy and miraculous image changes very frequently, both in countenance and color. In fact, about the nineteenth hour, the holy image, being uncovered[8] and we, all the undersigned, being present, have seen it with a visage joyful, sweet, and amiable, albeit of a pale color as is usual. Then, at the twentieth hour, all of a sudden, it changed countenance and color, appearing to the eyes of all those present, with a new air of majesty, and with a face so lit up, rosy, and brilliant that her cheeks seemed as two fresh vermilion roses. This unexpected, most visible, and most powerful alteration filled the minds of all present with such great amazement and tenderness that one among us, so emotionally touched, started to shed a tender and copious flood of tears, being forced thereby to depart from the chapel and the holy altar. The abovementioned and virtuous Signor Luigi, almost as if lost, knew not where to lay hand upon color or brush to continue the work he had begun. Afterwards interiorly inspired, however, and encouraged upon hearing the comment of the priests that when the holy image appears ruddy, brilliant, and joyful, it was then an excellent sign, according to the many observations made in past times. Encouraged then in this wise and animated suddenly by that amiable countenance, he copied such fine delineations and exquisite delicacies of the holy image that his copy can be said to be, among all the copies, most like the original.

"Fifth, he himself also observed repeatedly and with exactness that as the holy image changes its aspect, so also does it change the gaze and brilliance of its pupils. If it shows itself pleasant and serene, the eyes become majestic and joyful; if it is pallid and faded, so also appear the virginal pupils; if with a visage inflamed, brilliant and rose-like, then the eyes appear more pleasant, joyful, and lucid, and even more open. Besides these prodigious changes, we, the undersigned, saw others with amazement and great tenderness. Whence it is to be concluded that the holy image is a work rather divine than human.

"Sixth, Signor Luigi also observed, considered, and believed that the stripes of different colors above the diadems upon the heads of the Virgin and Son are not ornaments of a canopy or awning, as some have judged in the past, but rather a portion of a rainbow or iris, as we call it. The presence of three different colors proves this, as also the ancient custom of days gone by of painting many images of Mary surrounded with a celestial rainbow. Signor Luigi testifies that he made a particular study of this subject.''

A Continuous and Patent Miracle Lasting Centuries

The seventh item of that document of 1747 refers to the "continuous and patent miracle" that the venerable effigy has been performing uninterruptedly since 1467 for all those who observe her:

"Seventh and finally, on this occasion, it was observed and concluded, with greater convenience and with new visual and most subtle consideration and inspection, that it is a continuous and most patent miracle how this holy image, measuring two spans high by a span and a half wide, impressed upon a simple plaster crust, has been preserved for about three centuries, from 1467 until now, and is yet intact, undamaged, and perfect, without the countenance of the Mother or the Son having suffered any damage whatsoever. This is all the more remarkable in that the thin crust of plaster upon which the holy image is seen so well impressed and colored has not behind it any support or anything whatsoever upon which it could rest or by which it could be sustained.''[9]

"Her Appearance Is Sometimes Joyful, Sometimes Sad, Sometimes Illuminated with Rose-Colored Tints, According to the Dispositions of the Visitor"

In a 1754 letter addressed to the Prior of Santa Maria of Genazzano marking the approval of the Pious Union of Our Lady of Good Counsel, Friar Francisco Xavier Vasquez, General of the Augustinians, affirms:

"We saw the very beautiful image that was carried over from Albania in 1467 by the hands of angels and whose beauty captivates everyone's heart. Her appearance is sometimes joyful, sometimes sad, sometimes illuminated with rose-colored tints, according to the dispositions of the visitor who approaches her. Her most beautiful appearance makes her comparable to Paradise, and for this reason she was called, in olden days, Holy Mary of Paradise.''[10]

The Facial Changes of the Image: A Sure Sign That Supplications Will Be Heard

Monsignor Dillon, who customarily refers to himself in the third person, narrates the following episode.

Below. Façade of the shrine of the Virgin Mother of Good Counsel, designed by the architect Fr. Giustino Fanucchi (1840). The mosaics were added in 1956. The main portal was made of white marble in the fifteenth century at about the time of the miraculous arrival of the holy image. The brass doors are contemporary.

Above. Chapel of the Mother of Good Counsel (fifteenth century). The iron grating was built in 1630.

Above right. Detail of the ceiling. Gilded stucco by G. Corsini (1843

Below right. The interior of the Basilica (1621-1629).

"Like all else who come to the feet of Our Lady of Good Counsel, he had favours to ask for others and for himself. He had many times seen the sacred Image, and had learned to love it for the consolation it imparts to all. On one occasion, however, while offering up the Holy Sacrifice of the Mass for some in suffering in whom he took much interest, and for other reasons, he was astonished to find that the sweetly pale features of the figure of Our Lady became joyous, illuminated, and suffused all over with a deep crimson, or rather, vermilion hue. The eyes became more open and brilliant; and this continued during the remainder of the Holy Sacrifice. He felt a great consolation, but, not having heard at the time of the well-known changes in the aspect of the countenance of the figure of Our Lady, he believed what he noticed to be the effect of his own imagination or of some light thrown upon the Image in some unknown way. He therefore kept the matter to himself. However, in reading over, for the purposes of this book, the old and modern Italian histories of the Sanctuary, he was struck with the unanimity with which they all testified to these changes, and with which they all agreed that such as he had noticed were a sure presage of petitions being granted. Some months after, news arrived from Australia[11] that certain favors asked for friends had been in a most extraordinary manner received; and that too, within a few days after the changes had been perceived in the miraculous Image at Genazzano.

"When the writer, afterwards, witnessed the miraculous cure of blindness and epilepsy combined, in the case of Lydia Vernini of Zagarolo, . . . he had no further hesitation in believing that his own unworthy petitions for extraordinary favours had not only been heard, but had been shown to have been heard, by the sweet clemency of the all-powerful Virgin Mother of Good Counsel.

"Then, at other times, the sacred figure of Our Lady seems to speak to the heart of the supplicant; and then his soul receives a strong, irresistible impression or inspiration to act in a manner that never had been thought of before. He rises from his prayer strengthened and illuminated and generally finds afterwards that the course of action, holy and wise, which he felt impelled to adopt at the feet of the sacred Image, was the best possible that he could adopt and blessed alike with temporal and spiritual success.

"Nearly all who visit the Shrine of the Virgin Mother of Good Counsel experience the one assistance, or the other, and often both. That Sanctuary is a hallowed land of miracles, wrought by the power of Mary with Her Son in favour of those sincerely devoted to Him and to Her. No one, of course, is bound to believe this. But the faithful who try the efficacy of a devout pilgrimage to Genazzano, in their spiritual and temporal necessities, invariably tell of wonders worked in their own cases."[12]

"She Yielded to the Slightest Pressure of the Hands"

In 1867, on the occasion of the fourth centennial of the apparition of the image, those in charge of cleaning it marveled that it "yielded to the slightest pressure of the hands, like something isolated and detached from the wall."[13] For the second crowning, carried out in that same year by the Cardinal Bishop of Palestrina, it was necessary to make a support from which the crowns hung, suspended by golden threads.

Canonical Examination of the Image in 1936

Following is the text of the official document of the diocesan authority regarding the latest canonical examination of the image:

"In the name of God, Amen. On Sunday, May 17, 1936, at twelve o'clock, the faithful were made to leave the Basilica of Our Lady of Good Counsel of Genazzano and the doors were closed. The following people gathered in the chapel named for Our Lady of Good Counsel:

"1. His Excellency Bernardo Bertoglio, apostolic administrator of the suburbicarian diocese of Palestrina; 2. The Very Reverend Friar Gabriele Monti, Procurator General of the Augustinians and delegate of the Very Reverend Vicar-general of the Order of Saint Augustine; 3. Friar Giuseppe Rotondi, prior of the convent of Santa Maria, representing also the Very Reverend Father Provincial of the Augustinian province of Rome; 4. Monsignor Serafino de Bellis, vicar forane and pastor of Saint Paul in Genazzano; 5. Colonel Giuseppe Vanutelli, mayor of Genazzano; 6. Friar Giovanni Eramo, O.S.A., pastor of Santa Maria; 7. Dom Andrea Marge, pastor of Saint Nicholas; 8. Friar Benedetto Zunnino, O.F.M., Cap., pastor of Saint John; 9. Fr. Filippo of the Holy Family, C.P., of the monastery of Santa Maria de Pugliano; 10. the Augustinian Fathers Hilary Apelhans (Germany), Rafael Almanza (Mexico), Berchmans Power (Ireland), Alessandro Malfatti and Egidio Giuliani of the Roman Province; 11. Mr. Amedeo Rossigno, jeweler. These remained to make a close inspection of the image that had miraculously appeared on April 25, 1467.

"After invoking divine help through the intercession of the Blessed Virgin, the crystal screen mounted in a metal frame enclosing the fresco was removed.

After a thorough examination of the plaster on which the image is painted, all the aforementioned agreed that the fresco:

"1) bears numerous and noticeable cracks;

"2) from the neck up on both images

(a) is covered with blisters;

(b) leans toward the front;

(c) if slightly struck, gives a clear sensation of hollowness;

(d) if delicately pressed, visibly oscillates;

"3) on the lower edge, rests on a small base on one of the sides, i.e., from the center to the extreme right;

"4) on the right vertical side has no support at all for three-fourths of its height;

"5) as a whole, has a sinusoidal development and,

"6) is in precarious conditions of stability.

"This declaration was drawn up immediately after the aforementioned verifications in the presence of the said persons while all were still in the chapel. The undersigned, after hearing the document read and having confirmed its contents, thanked the Blessed Virgin for the great heavenly favors she has deigned to grant the Christian people. Immediately afterwards, they were present for the replacing of the crystal screen and, filled with touching piety, left the Basilica."[15]

Testimony of a Famous Archaeologist

Many others also attest that the image is painted on a simple plaster crust, is not attached to the wall, and is no thicker than a piece of cardboard.

Among them is the famous historian and archaeologist Giovanni Batista de Rossi, who visited the Shrine several times. During one of his visits, in 1946, he carefully examined the holy fresco and made the following statements that his friend the attorney Galileo Vannutelli, nephew of Cardinals Serafino and Vincenzo Vannutelli, made to the Most Reverend Alfonso C. De Romanis, bishop of Porfirio and sacristan to the Pope:

"I speak as a historian, leaving aside any pious or apologetic considerations. The fresco is on plaster detached from the wall. It has been in Genazzano for centuries, well before the technique of detaching frescoes was known and practiced. Today this is easy, indeed, very easy. However, it was not so in past centuries. In those times, paintings were removed from walls only with the greatest difficulty by cutting out a large, thick piece. So, here we have for the image of Genazzano an unexplainable fact of an occurrence not technically possible at the time—a time, I repeat, in which the image was, like today, already venerated in Genazzano."[16]

Despite all that has been related, some questions still remain unanswered. What was the origin of the holy fresco? Who could have painted it? Was it purely the result of some excellent artist's imagination or did he witness an apparition of Our Lady that he used as a model? What paints were used? Perhaps in the near future—but certainly at the Last Judgment—we will understand the deep and detailed realities of such an extraordinary painting.

As it stands now, the miraculous fresco venerated in Genazzano has a prehistory hidden from our eyes by the veils of mystery. Its most ancient details come to us from a place in the Balkans, Scutari, a city where a prince called Scanderbeg lived. His life as recorded in historical documents often reads like a novel, according to Ludwig von Pastor, the great and distinguished "Historian of the Popes."[17]

CHAPTER 4

Scanderbeg,
"Sword and Shield
of Christendom"

SCUTARI is a small city set on a steep hill in Albania. At the foot of the hill, two murmuring rivers meet: the Drin, rising in the mountains, and the Bojana, born of a lake of the same name as the city.

From this city came the first news about the image that later would be venerated throughout the entire Catholic world under the invocation *Mater Boni Consilii*.

The country was evangelized by Saints Paul and Andrew. The faith flourished in Albania in those early days, albeit confronting numerous hardships: coastal attacks by the Goths, Bulgars, and Normans, and land attacks by Slavs from the East. Later, in 1204, Albania was invaded and divided up by Naples, Greece, and Serbia. Power was distributed among the most important noble families. A century later, the Turks, who had already spread their empire over nearly the whole of the Balkan Peninsula, carried the miasma of Islam to the borders of Albania. In 1361, they invaded the important city of Kroia. It was the first blow in the long agony of the nation.

The Turks began to make successive incursions into the country. In 1423, the followers of Mohammed demanded the four sons of Prince John Castriota, head of one of the noble families of Albania, as hostages.

The Mohammedan generals knew from bitter experience that their religion and depraved customs were incapable of producing fighters as courageous as the Christian warriors. So, they formed an elite corps, the janizaries, comprised of Christians perverted to Mohammedanism in their childhood or youth, educated to hate their parents and the true Religion, and kept under an iron discipline far from the corrupted life of the Turkish court.

The Turkish chiefs now wanted the young Albanian princes as members of this praetorian guard since they were convinced that they could extirpate the true Faith from their souls by cajolery and threats. So, the four sons of the prince of Kroia, Repos, Stanitza, Constantine, and George, were taken to Adrianapolis, whence Sultan Amurath II governed the Ottoman Empire.

The Shrine of Scutari

Like all Albanians, the young princes knew that in Scutari, one of the most important cities in the states ruled by their father, an image of Our Lady with soft, attractive, and maternal features was venerated. It had appeared two hundred years previously, during the same period in which several Albanian provinces were converted to the Faith of Our Lord Jesus Christ. The author of the painting was unknown. Tradition held that the image was brought from the East, by angelic hands, on the same occasion that the house of the Holy Family was miraculously translated from Nazareth to Loreto, Italy.

The beautiful image, whose shrine became the main center of pilgrimages in the small country, poured out abundant graces over the population.

Certainly the four princes had already prayed at the foot of the image which depicted the Patroness of their lands.[18] However, the few records of the time that were saved from the Moslem rampage are silent about this. One thing is certain: devotion to the Patroness of Albania gave the four princes perseverance in the true Faith and made of George, the youngest of the four brothers, a true Catholic warrior, invincible in the fight against the followers of the Crescent.

A Prisoner in the Court at Adrianople

As soon as they appeared before the sultan, the three older brothers were put in chains. Their moral uprightness and the contempt they showed for serving Islam broke any illusions their tormenters had about them.

George was but nine years old. His captors, considering him to be still without personality, circumcised him with the intention of integrating him into the Mohammedan sect. George's natural qualities soon standing out among the intended janizaries, the sultan decided to provide him the best education possible, along with that of his own sons. Meanwhile, his brothers were languishing in prison, being slowly poisoned to death.

The young prince learned to speak Italian, Arabic, Turkish, and Slavic. He was educated in the art of war and won the trust of Amurath II both for his courage and governmental talents. For this and for his princely birth, they gave him the name Alexander the Prince, or *"Iskender Bey"* in Turkish. Thus he came to be known among the Albanians as Scanderbeg.

As a general of the Ottoman armies, Scanderbeg more than once devastated enemy troops that attacked the Turkish empire. Thus, the sultan dreamed of

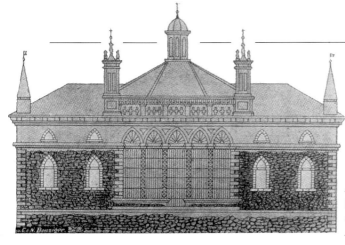

Probable original design of the church of Our Lady of Services, near Scutari, Albania.

View of the ruins of the ancient church. The white circle indicates the niche occupied by the holy image prior to its departure.

***Below.** The citadel of Scutari.*

making Scanderbeg a frightful renegade who would extinguish the remorse of his apostasy by shedding the blood of Christians.

By 1443, the Albanian prince had been held captive for twenty years. In that year, the sultan, having decided to invade Hungary, and after having already given Scanderbeg significant signs of confidence, appointed him to the high military office of *bey generalissimo*. This made it necessary for Scanderbeg to face the courageous Catholic Magyar Janos Hunyadi (c.1387-1456).

Freedom at the Battle of Nish

The Moslem army was comprised of Greek and Slavic soldiers and as many other peoples as the sultan could enslave, all under forced regimentation. Many were Catholics who but awaited the right moment to free themselves from the Ottoman claws. These latter found themselves disheartened with fear in the painful exigency of having to fight against their brothers in the Faith.

Scanderbeg hated the infidels' yoke more than anyone else. In the proposed invasion of Hungary, he saw the providential moment to free himself and all those who wished to follow him. Thus, with some three hundred Catholic Albanians who were to be thrown into the fight against the troops of Hunyadi, he set about making a plan that would free them all.

Eighty thousand soldiers under the command of Schahim Pasha advanced against the Magyars. Schahim Pasha was a bully who boasted with the arrogance and haughtiness proper to infidels: "My sword is a cloud that pours blood instead of water." Hunyadi's Catholic troops numbered just twenty thousand.

On a cold November night, near Nish, the Hungarian vanguard caught sight of the heterogeneous Turkish horde. The warriors of the Cross silently eyed their enemy until the moment Constable Hunyadi joined them and gave the order to attack. Great shouts of enthusiasm resounded on the battlefield as the crusaders' cavalry hurtled forward in a furious charge. Clouds of arrows filled the sky. Taking advantage of the confusion of the first clash, Scanderbeg and his followers passed over to the side of the followers of the Cross of Christ.

The first outcries of the Turks wounded by the Hungarians were joined by furious curses of hatred when they saw, to their amazement, that their own *bey generalissimo* was fighting side by side with Hunyadi.

A tremendous confusion ensued. The Hungarians, fighting with increased strength, won the battle. Thirty thousand Moslems lay dead on the field and four thousand were taken prisoner.

Among the captives was Amurath's secretary of state with his retinue. When he was discovered among the prisoners, Scanderbeg forced him to write and sign a firman. This document ordered, in the sultan's name, the Turkish governor of Albania to hand over the government to the person presenting the document. With the document in hand, Scanderbeg had the secretary and his attendants put to the sword, thus rewarding them with the same fate that had befallen his brothers and servants some twenty years before.

Scanderbeg Enters Kroia

Invoking the protection of the Blessed Virgin, Scanderbeg and his Albanians rode seven days and nights to reach Kroia. The seventh night was already extending its mantle of stars over the sky when they entered the city.

Once in the city, Scanderbeg secretly met with the most important Albanian residents, who promised to help him. As dawn broke, he entered the castle of the Turkish governor. Upon reading the document signed by the sultan's secretary, the governor surrendered the stronghold without suspecting anything amiss. The following evening, Scanderbeg and his Albanians entered the fortress and killed all the Mohammedans.

Scanderbeg thus regained control of the territories that were his legitimate inheritance. He was ready to avenge the anti-Catholic despotism of the Islamics: their deceits, assassinations, abduction of Albanian women to serve in Turkish harems and of Catholic youth to pervert and force into service as janizaries, unbearable taxes, and forcible impression of troops for the sultan's armies.

On November 13, 1443, after two decades of silence, church bells rang out. Catholic Albania, freed from the infidel's yoke through the protection of Our Lady of Scutari, today known as the Mother of Good Counsel, rejoiced.

Revenge of the Sultan for the Audacity of Scanderbeg

The news of Scanderbeg's successful strategy reached the court in Adrianople, inciting Amurath's anger and offending the pride of his people. It was deemed necessary to conquer the Albanians again and enchain George Castriota, that insolent man who had dared to "outrage" the previously undefeated Turkish armies.

Indeed, since 1300, when the first hordes commanded by the sinister Ortogrul started to attack the Byzantine empire, the Turks had never suffered any important defeat. Like dense sulfurous lava, they poured into Asia Minor, crossed the Dardenelles, besieged Gallipoli and Koiridicastron, established their capital at Adrianople on the European continent, and proceeded to invade the Balkan Peninsula, spreading across Albania, Serbia, and Wallachia.

The Ottomans had not demolished Constantinople only because for some fifty years they had fended off the armies of Tamerlane, founder of the second Mongolian empire, in the Asian regions of Turkey. Now, Scanderbeg, heir to small Albania, had the audacity to rise up against the Crescent empire.

The irritated sultan, full of self-love, sent 40,000 of his best cavalry under the command of a skilled general to recapture Scanderbeg. Scanderbeg, however, enjoyed the protection of Our Lady of Scutari, the Mother of Good Counsel.

Albania had not had an army for over twenty years. Even though the return of George Castriota was a cause for rejoicing among the rough mountaineers and an inspiration for them to dedicate themselves to their lord, this was not enough to so quickly prepare an army. Scanderbeg gathered only 15,000 warriors.

On the Borders of Dibra, Our Lady Protects Scanderbeg

The clash that ensued in the Dibra was violent. The battle lasted the whole day. The brave Albanian mountaineers demonstrated exceptional courage fighting under Scanderbeg's command. Such is the capacity of good example, especially when permeated with true devotion to the Virgin Mary.

The setting sun bathed the final skirmishes with its dying reddish rays. Innumerable flags of the Crescent, torn and muddied, and smashed and scattered weapons lay among wounded knights and the bodies of foot soldiers. The moans of the dying hung in the twilight air. The Christians found abundant cause for thanking their Lady of Scutari.

It was indeed a memorable victory. There was, however, no time for resting or feasting. The exhausted cavalry of the defeated Turks had barely returned to Adrianople when two new armies of similar might were en route to Albania. One was commanded by Firuz Pasha and the other by Mustafa Pasha. That they had suffered such a humiliation was indeed unbearable for the Turks.

History does not tell of the sultan's threats to his soldiers should they return defeated; nor does it describe the countless graces poured out upon the few combative Albanians. It records only that after the last attack, when all the spears were broken and the quivers of the archers were empty, the soldiers of Scanderbeg engaged in hand-to-hand combat with all that remained of the numerous Ottoman army, a mere seventy-two Islamics, who subsequently surrendered before the Cross of Christ.

A Providential Man

According to his contemporaries, Scanderbeg was tall and slender with a prominent chest, wide shoulders, long neck, and high forehead. He had black hair, fiery eyes, and a powerful voice. So warlike was his nature that he truly needed to wage battle from time to time. He killed more than two thousand Turks with his own hands. He was a master of all weapons, swift and ingenious, a general with a quick and certain gaze, audacious and resolute. Naturally possessed of a fiery temper, anger would go to his head quickly and set his eyes ablaze. But he would dominate his anger, biting his lips until they bled. His courage in battle stemmed from this struggle over his evil passions. All in all, his customs were pure, his manner noble and elevated. Mary was his strength and inspiration. Under her protection he immediately began rebuilding Albania and preparing it for the new wars that were sure to come.

For one who has Faith, his life is a glorious epic of a devotee of Mary.[19]

In Prince Scanderbeg the people had found courage in battle with certainty of victory; he was the man of Providence, the defender of the country, the protégé of Our Lady. Monsignor Dillon writes: "He loved the sanctuary of Mary with a devoted, enthusiastic love; and Mary in return, not only made him a model of Christian perfection, but also gave him an invincible power, which preserved not only Albania but also Christendom during his reign."[20]

All Christendom Rejoices in Scanderbeg's Victories

All Christendom was encouraged and filled with joy by Scanderbeg's victories. Previous defeats had induced the frightened Serbians and Hungarians to consider a ten-year armistice with the Turks. Now, a new flame of enthusiasm was enkindled. When Julian Cardinal Cesarini, the Papal Legate, preached a new crusade, Janos Hunyadi gathered 15,000 Hungarians. Venice, Genoa, Aragon, and Burgundy sent galleys. Christian troops, eager to defeat the sultan again, flocked from all corners. Scanderbeg intended to join them with his Albanians.[21]

Unfortunately, however, it seems that among the majority of the new crusaders the fervor that had inflamed the hearts in Clermont when Blessed Urban II convoked the First Crusade was lacking.

Amurath, fearing another defeat at the hands of the Christian army, led 100,000 men to the battle. The Catholics numbered only 25,000 troops, because Scanderbeg was unable to arrive in time, detained by a treacherous ruse set up by the king of Serbia with the purpose of gaining the sultan's favor.

The battle took place on a cold December morning close to the city of Varna in Bulgaria. The crusaders suffered an astonishing defeat. Neither the courage of the Polish cavalry in successive charges against the janizaries, nor the swiftness of the Hungarians who attacked the very tents of the sultan, could obtain victory from heaven. King Ladislas of Hungary was beheaded by a janizary. Cardinal Cesarini was killed in the confusion. All the survivors were stabbed to death by order of Amurath. Discouragement once again swept over a mollified Europe.

"Champion and Shield of Christendom"

In 1449, Turkey resolved its unceasing internal rebellions. With his own borders quiet, the sultan assembled an army 200,000 strong that he personally wanted to lead against the little Albanian nation.

The followers of Mohammed blanketed and devastated Albania like clouds of locusts. One fortress after another, even the best defended, fell before him. The few survivors retreated to Kroia to fight the enemy to the end under the protection of Scanderbeg.

The siege lasted a whole year. The heroic Catholic resistance of the Virgin's devotees is described by a historian of the Shrine of Genazzano:

"With matchless strategy he [Scanderbeg] contrived to keep the myriads of his opponents from the walls. With energy almost superhuman, he swept unexpectedly, now here and now there, by night and by day, into the midst of the foe; every swordsman of his band hewed down scores, and his own blade flashed as the lightning and caused Moslem heads to fall like snowflakes where he passed. Thousands of the bravest warriors of Amurath were thus swept away continuously. His hosts were diminishing to the point of danger to his very person. And so, the fierce conqueror of so many nations had to withdraw the remnant of his armies in sorrow and shame from the walls of Croja, pursued with terrific slaughter by the Christians."[22]

The proud Ottoman sultan was terrified at this defeat. His spirit broken, he died of sadness, rancor, and humiliation shortly after returning to Adrianople. All of Albania desired to kneel at the feet of Our Lady in Scutari to thank her for such a victory. Scanderbeg was first in acts of praise and thankfulness to his Patroness. He was a hero formed in the same school as all those who derive their strength from their devotion to the Blessed Virgin. Like a new Saint Ferdinand, King of Castile, Scanderbeg was, under the guidance of Mary, "as gentle in peace, as he was terrible in war."[23] "The good Christian prince was often seen at her feet to beg the protection of his Lady in his greatest afflictions."[24]

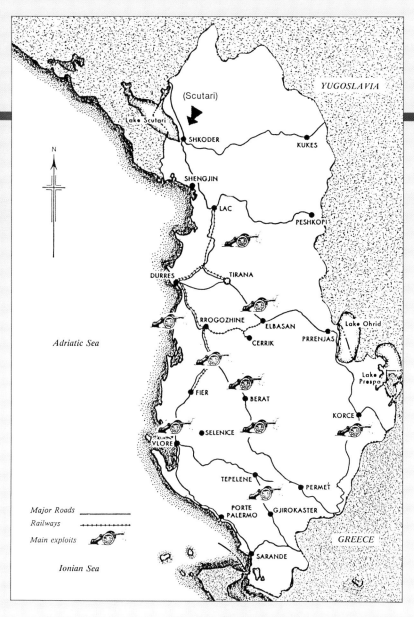

YUGOSLAVIA

(Scutari)

Lake Scutari

SHKODER

KUKES

SHENGJIN

LAC

PESHKOPI

Adriatic Sea

DURRES

TIRANA

RROGOZHINE

ELBASAN

Lake Ohrid

CERRIK

PRRENJAS

Lake Prespa

FIER

BERAT

KORCE

SELENCE

VLORE

TEPELENE

PERMET

PORTE PALERMO

GJIROKASTER

Major Roads

Railways

Main exploits

GREECE

Ionian Sea

SARANDE

Contemporary map of Albania showing the locations of Scanderbeg's main exploits.

When the Holy Father, Nicholas V, heard of this warrior's courage and victories, he sent him a special blessing, calling him the "champion and shield of Christendom." Since time was of the essence, the Pope sent him, in addition to the promises of divine protection, what material resources he could gather so that Scanderbeg could continue his fight against the Mohammedans.

All the Christian princes rejoiced at Scanderbeg's feats and sent him congratulations and aid. Hunyadi, in Hungary, still regretted the absence of the Albanian prince in the battle of Varna. Together under the protection of Mary Most Holy they would have defeated the infidel Turks. From her shrine in Scutari, she protected Scanderbeg, granted him innumerable victories, but gave him no respite from the struggles of this life.

Envy and Betrayal in Scanderbeg's Ranks

The new Turkish sultan, Mohammed II, sent several contingents against Scanderbeg. In 1452, twelve thousand men entered the country through the Albanian mountains. Seven thousand of them were killed in the first battle.

The following year, another general, Ibrahimbeg, leading even more soldiers, tried to avenge the Turkish defeats. Not one, not even Ibrahimbeg, was left alive to relate what happened.

Defeated by the heroism of the Catholic armies, the sultan then attempted to bribe the commanders and their relatives, promising them riches and honors to betray the Prince of Kroia. If there was a Judas even among the Apostles, surely these could be found close to Scanderbeg.

One so inclined was Moses Gobatos. Bowing before Mohammed II in Constantinople, he offered him Scanderbeg's head if the sultan, in turn, would promise him the crown of Albania. The Ottoman potentate agreed to the shameful offer and placed twenty thousand men at the disposal of the traitor. However, Our Lady of Scutari guarded her faithful devotee and the treachery failed. More than ten thousand Mohammedans died on the battlefield. The traitor fled, receiving as payment only the sultan's disdain. Later, tormented by remorse, Moses returned to Albania to implore his lord's pardon, which was generously granted. As we shall see, he subsequently died bravely fighting against the Turks.

Another traitor who allowed himself to be seduced by thirty pieces of silver was Scanderbeg's nephew Hamsa. Going to Constantinople, he renounced the Catholic religion and was appointed vizier. In the summer of 1457, he entered Albania at the head of 50,000 Islamic troops under the Crescent flag. Scanderbeg had only twelve to fifteen thousand mountaineers to face this new attack.

The traitor planned to incite the populace against the legitimate prince. The would-be usurper, well-versed in his country's topography, avoided any dangerous valleys or unsafe areas as he gained ground. Occupation of the whole country seemed inevitable. Then, during one of their final advances, the Turks stopped to rest in the Tomorniza. It was here that Mary Most Holy prepared to defeat them.

With the suddenness of a lightning bolt, Scanderbeg appeared, spreading terror among the enemies of the Cross. Thirty thousand Turks died on the battlefield. Their encampment was seized and fifteen hundred of their comrades-in-arms were taken prisoner, including the renegade Hamsa. Scanderbeg, benevolently sparing his nephew's life, sent Hamsa back in utter defeat to the sultan. The latter, not so magnanimous, repaid the renegade with poison.

Since not even treason could vanquish Scanderbeg, the sultan, fearing new disasters, temporarily suspended hostilities.

Mohammed II, the Conqueror of Constantinople, Declares Scanderbeg Victorious

Mohammed II was so frightened by the "champion of Christendom" that, despite having recently conquered Constantinople, he sent him a letter in a vain attempt to disarm the devotee of the Virgin Most Powerful.

"When I recall the sweet joys of our youth," writes Mohammed (stirring up memories of Castriota's shameful captivity under Amurath, in which he was even obliged to follow the Moslem rites), "it seems that I have an imperious duty to love you and demonstrate this love. My troops," he cynically continues, "devastated your country without my order. Your victories filled me with joy." Mohammed asked, as proof of his correspondence to this love, that Scanderbeg repeat John Castriota's act of submission, and send him his son as a hostage.[25]

The response to this contemptible proposition was not long in coming. George Castriota rejected the ignoble solicitation of the brazen Mohammed, signing himself "Scanderbeg, Prince of the Epirotes and Albanians and soldier of Jesus Christ."

The sultan, finally seeing that he could expect nothing from Scanderbeg, resolved to cease his attacks on Albania. Thus, the most powerful enemy of Christendom acknowledged his defeat before the soldier of Jesus Christ.

Pilgrimage to Rome

George Castriota's renown spread throughout a Europe then steeped in pagan Renaissance humanism. Pope Callistus III praised this hero, this devotee

Above.
Bust of Pope Pius II

Left.
Vatican—Statues on the
Colonnade of
Saint Peter's Square

of Mary Most Holy, as one who "in an excellent way surpassed in the Faith and in the Christian Religion, all other Catholic princes."[26]

In a letter written in Rome fifteen days after the battle of the Tomorniza (1457), the Holy Father affirmed: "Beloved son, continue to defend the Catholic Faith; God, for whom you fight, will not abandon His cause. He will, I am confident, grant success against the Turks and other unbelievers to you and the rest of the Christians with great glory and honour."[27] Three months later he appointed Scanderbeg Pontifical Captain-General against the Turks.

Pope Pius II, successor to Pope Callistus, had the joy of seeing the invincible warrior in Rome. Scanderbeg had crossed the Adriatic to come to the aid of his ally, the king of Naples, who, some years before, had sent fifteen hundred soldiers to fight in Albania. The Albanian prince did not fail to see Pius II to receive his blessing. The Pontiff offered him not only graces and promises of eternal life, but material resources as well for the struggle against the Ottomans. Pius II, seeing in him the sword raised up by Divine Providence to save Europe, began to make plans against the Islamics.

Pope Pius II Attempts to Organize a Crusade

In 1459, Pope Pius II, encouraged by Scanderbeg's victories, invited the Catholic princes to a meeting in the city of Mantua. The pontiff perhaps hoped that by convoking a crusade the graces of Clermont, when Blessed Urban II preached the first crusade, would be revived.

The response of the Christian princes to the Pope's appeal was pitiful and weak. The great majority of them delighted in the atmosphere of the pagan Renaissance then spreading across Europe in an invasion more devastating than the Islamic one. The voice of Peter did not echo in their hearts. Few even sent ambassadors to hear the words of the Vicar of Christ.

When the meeting at Mantua opened, Pius II could only sadly state: "We came full of hope; but we are forced to consider it in vain. We are ashamed that the lukewarmness of Christendom is so great. Some run after their pleasures, others are enchained by avarice. The Turks are ready to face death for their doctrine, but we tolerate neither the least expense nor the most insignificant discomforts for the Cause of the Holy Gospel."[28]

It was the Pontiff's intention that all the Catholic princes would take up arms against the Islamics. The military command would be given to Scanderbeg and the Pope would personally accompany the crusade until the final defeat of the infidels.

Learning of these plans, Scanderbeg quickly organized an army of his war-like mountain men. Taking the initiative, he invaded Turkish territory, anticipating the assistance of Western troops. Meanwhile, the sultan, infuriated by the attack, ordered his general, Scheremetbeg, to invade Albania. This he did in August, 1464. The Moslems suffered yet another defeat, leaving ten thousand dead on the field.

Despite the dearth of assistance, Pius II left Rome, assembled some ships in Ancona and made ready to embark and join Scanderbeg. He was prepared to die, if necessary, at the side of this brave warrior to bring about the success of the crusade. Before the Pope could set sail, however, God called him to His just and merciful tribunal. The Pope's health had been undermined by a persistent fever and, above all, by the procrastination of Venice, which would not release the ships needed to transport the crusaders across the Adriatic. He expired on August 15, the feast of the Assumption of Our Lady, as the Venetian ships were finally entering Ancona harbor.

Scanderbeg was obliged to recast the feasts for the reception of that warrior Pope into ceremonies of mourning.

Renewed Attacks by the Sultan and a Second Trip to Rome

Once again Albania found itself facing the sultan's wrath unaided. Baladam of Badera, yet another Judas, was chosen by Mohammed II to renew his attacks. Cold and calculating, this Baladam assumed command of the Islamic armies.

Although the renegade's first battle was a disaster, eight of Albania's best warriors fell into his hands. The wretch, in revenge for his defeat, had them skinned alive. They, wavering neither as Catholics nor as indomitable soldiers, boldly proclaimed their Faith, refusing to seek any pardon from the apostate. Moses Gobatos, the repentant former traitor, now washed away his old perfidy with his blood, dying like a hero of the Faith alongside the other martyrs.

Baladam invaded Albania again with two new armies. Both were destroyed in two memorable and spectacular victories of the Catholic prince Scanderbeg. Baladam himself almost perished, saving his life only by fleeing at full gallop from the last combat.

Mohammed II, resolving to definitively crush Albania, incorporated two hundred thousand men into his army of janizaries.

Scanderbeg, seeing the imminent danger, hurried to Rome and threw himself at the feet of Pope Paul II, imploring his help.

Entering the resplendent papal court as a simple soldier, devoid of any pomp or circumstance, Scanderbeg spoke the following succinct but glorious words: "After twenty-three years of unceasing war, I present myself here together with the warriors that remain. Ours is a state exhausted by so many battles; Albania is a body of which no member remains unwounded; only a few drops of its blood remain to be shed for the Christian world. Alas, come to our aid, otherwise the last champion of Jesus Christ will soon disappear from the other side of the Adriatic!"[29]

No one in Rome wanted to be a crusader. The money that the Pope gave Scanderbeg was insufficient for even his necessities. Returning to his land unprotected, his one hope for assistance was the invincible Virgin of Scutari. Kneeling at her feet, he implored her that most assuaging and decisive succor that had comforted him so often throughout his life.

Kroia Besieged Again

In the spring of 1466, Mohammed II besieged Kroia for the second time. The whole region around the city was occupied by some two hundred thousand Islamics. Mohammed pitched his tents on the crest of a hill so as to have a better view of the fall of the city. The siege, lasting for six months, was relentless, but the resistance was heroic. Neither the burning heat, nor the nearly constant breathing of air filled with the smoke of the gunpowder, nor the deafening cries of the combatants could dampen the courage of the Albanians.

Scanderbeg did not limit himself merely to a defense of his capital. He and a handful of brave souls camped outside the city walls to unceasingly harass the Moslems.

With the onset of autumn, the sultan was deeply depressed. So, he decided to return to Constantinople. However, the renegade Baladam remained with eighty thousand men to continue the siege. Scanderbeg, with but 13,400 warriors, attacked him so successfully that the bloody traitor lost his life and the terrified Turks fell into retreat.

Once more, Our Lady of Scutari gave the victory to Scanderbeg, her fervent devotee.

A Strong King Strengthens a Weak People

This prince and unvanquished warrior, whose strength of soul gave his compatriots fortitude to throw off their lethargy, courage to rise up against the oppressive infidels, daring to despise death and thus expel them from their country, moved his subjects not only by example but also by his unbreakable faith, his ardent charity, and his unshakable hope. Paraphrasing Camões, the great chronicler of Portugal, one could say that a strong king strengthens a weak people.

Scanderbeg was God's sword against the enemies of the holy Catholic Faith, the impregnable defensive wall protecting his realm. The eyes of all Albanians turned toward him.

The people saw the virtues of the nation shine with noble splendor in Scanderbeg. Admiring its prince, Albania rose to the glowing heights of its ideal.*

He fully embodied the ideal of the Catholic hero, of the strong and just man who lives by faith: "My just man liveth by faith" (Heb. 10:38).

Last Pilgrimage to Scutari, Last Battle, and Crowning Victory

In January of 1467 Scanderbeg felt his strength waning. He visited his beloved shrine for the last time, kneeling at the feet of the Virgin Most Merciful, his constant protectress in battle. She had reconquered his kingdom; he returned it to her hands.

Scanderbeg saw that his son lacked the necessary energy to continue the struggle and to increase the fruits of his victories. He also knew that his warriors would not be so courageous without his presence. Perhaps understanding that their devotion to Mary Most Holy was not sufficiently deep and enthusiastic, he decided to place the shrine and the city under the protection of Venice in a final hope of saving the holy image from Turkish vandalism.

Exhausted, but trusting in divine mercy, he retired to the city of Lesh. With his

---

* The communion of saints is the sublime and divine communicant vessel that makes grace grow in all souls, without emptying one to fill another. It is, rather, the contrary. In this way, an ardent devotee of Mary Most Holy attracts graces so that others become devoted to her. A tireless soldier of the faith obtains graces from heaven for other Catholics to also be combative.

A great Dominican of this century, Marie Michel Philipon, explains this sublime truth: "By the communion of saints . . . a soul that elevates itself carries the whole world with it. A soul that debases itself lowers the whole universe. Men work together either to elevate or lower the spiritual level of mankind. Who could measure the incalculable repercussions of a single human act? The fiat pronounced by Mary contained the salvation of the whole world in a seed. The redeeming action of Christ on the Cross was the ransom for all mankind. The most insignificant human act echoes, for good or for bad, in the whole Church" (M. M. Philipon, O.P., *Los dones del Espíritu Santo* [Madrid: Ediciones Palabra, 1983], p. 109).

penetrating gaze, he read the faces of his soldiers and painfully foresaw the impending fall of Albania. He urged his son to be a worthy ruler and insisted with his nobles to avoid internal conflicts and to fight only against the Saracens.

His last hour came quickly. On his deathbed, he confessed for the last time and received Holy Viaticum. The sweat of agony bathed the warrior's face.

The glacial air of a January morning was pierced by terrible cries, cries not of mourning from the palace where the prince was agonizing but cries of warning from the walls: "The Turks! The Turks! The Turks are here!"

Mohammed II, informed about the general distress of the entire country and taking advantage of its unpreparedness, had sent his hosts against the city of Lesh. A surprise lay in store for him.

Hearing the shouts, the dying man's eyes opened. Color returned to his cheeks. The perspiration of agony disappeared. Scanderbeg pushed death aside and carried it instead to the enemies of Christendom. He ordered his horse and weapons brought to him. Then, a great battle ensued at the gates of Lesh.

The clash was as bloody as that first battle, which he won under Mary's protection. The Moslems, seeing Scanderbeg's eyes blazing with holy wrath, fled in terror. After the battle, the brave warrior had sufficient strength to return to the palace.

Scanderbeg, as in all victories, again gave thanks to the Blessed Virgin for her protection. On that same day, January 17, 1467, before sunset, he slept the sleep of the just.[30]

One of the Albanian generals went throughout the city in a state of distress, weeping and shouting: "Today the walls of Albania fell and its fortresses were demolished! All our strength has vanished and our power is lying on the ground! All our hope is extinguished with this one man!"[31] Thus this warrior of the Virgin of Scutari died at age 53. The sultan, upon hearing the news, exclaimed: "Woe to Christendom! It has lost its sword and shield!"

Eight years later, when the Mohammedans conquered Lesh, they carried away the hero's bones. Dividing them into small pieces, they covered the bones with gold and silver to use as amulets in battle. Such was the renown of Scanderbeg. His helmet, kept in Vienna, is inscribed in Arabic: "God's hero, Iskander Beg."[32]

In Scutari, the holy image became saddened. There were no longer any devotees in all of Albania equal to so generous a Mother. One spring night she manifested herself to two of Scanderbeg's soldiers who, fearing for the future of Albania, were weeping over the death of their general.

CHAPTER 5

Transfer of the Image:
Over the Sea
from Scutari to Genazzano

Previous page, the departure from Scutari. Fresco by P. Piatti (1885).

U NFORTUNATELY, with Scanderbeg's death, the ardor of the Faith and the spirit of combativeness began to wane in Albania. A black mantle of desolation covered the country, and a premonition of defeat by some future Turkish aggression overcame the people.

There consequently arose a great dilemma: abandon their fatherland and with it the Virgin of Scutari, or submit to slavery under the Islamic yoke. Many, heartbroken, chose to leave. Day after day, many faithful flocked to the feet of the holy image to bid their heavenly Lady farewell forever.

The Virgin of Scutari Hears the Prayers of Two Soldiers

Faced with this cruel dilemma, two friends, both courageous warriors of Scanderbeg, remained undecided. The first, De Sclavis, a Slovene, was already past the prime of life; the other, Georgio, was still a young man.

The consternation of both men was not without cause. On one hand, they knew that the Ottoman danger was imminent. On the other, they fully realized that the Patroness of Albania was the real cause behind all the victories of Scanderbeg, her courageous and faithful devotee.[33] De Sclavis and Georgio thus thought that while the Virgin remained in Albania she would perform any and all miracles to prevent the fall of the country into Turkish dominion.

Certainly those two soldiers were fully aware that if the Moslems were terrible, there was an internal enemy no less devastating, subtle, and profound, that is, despondency in the Faith. Lamentably, that disgrace was already penetrating Albania. "It had to be admitted that devotion to it had grown cold. Schism worked its blighting way in Albania. The morals of the people decayed with the purity of their religion. Devotion to Our Lady languished even in Scutari itself. The Turkish invasion, a clear punishment sent from heaven, could not call the mass of the population to repentance. As a writer on the subject feelingly complains, 'the young men and maidens no longer delighted to place flowers on the altar of Mary of Scutari; and therefore, their punishment could not be far distant.' "[34]

One day, when the warmth of spring had already melted the attendant snows of Scanderbeg's death, the two soldiers were kneeling in the small chapel. They felt a special movement of grace so characteristic in supplicants of the holy image, and they left the shrine radiant with a consolation whose only explanation was that the same grace had touched them both. Both resolved to return to the tender Mother to obtain a final solution to their dilemma of whether to leave the country and their Patroness or to fall under the Mohammedan heel.

In addition to that heavenly and imponderable interior communication, the Virgin of the holy fresco appeared to Georgio while he slept. In his dreams, she ordered that he and his friend prepare everything required for a journey, as it had become necessary for them to leave that unfaithful country forever. She added that she herself, in her holy image, would also leave Scutari in order to escape the sacrilegious hands of the Turks who would seek her out in the next invasion to desecrate her. From that moment, her graces and blessings would be reserved for another place. Our Lady ordered Georgio to follow her on all the paths she would tread.

As soon as he awakened, Georgio hurriedly sought out De Sclavis, wishing to relate the details of his marvelous dream. De Sclavis, however, gave his friend no chance to share the story, telling that he himself had received the same heavenly messages while he slept.

Overjoyed at this revelation, they went to pray for the last time at the shrine of the miraculous painting of Most Holy Mary.

The Miraculous Journey over the Waves of the Adriatic

The two soldiers, kneeling and fixing their gazes on the image that hung from the central wall of the shrine, prayed in silence. Suddenly, the fresco smoothly detached itself from the wall before their amazed eyes and enveloped itself within a luminous white cloud, through which the smiling image of the Virgin with the Divine Infant in her arms could be clearly seen.

The two warriors were flooded with joy when the image, thus wrapped, began to move toward the door. Upon leaving the church, it rose slightly and began to move toward the sea.

Georgio and De Sclavis tirelessly accompanied her on the nineteen mile journey from Scutari to the Adriatic Sea. Then a new problem presented itself. The cloud indicated that the way would no longer be over firm, well-traveled roads but over the immense rolling and breaking waves of the sea. What did the Blessed Virgin desire? Was she testing their faith by seeing if they would follow the new way indicated, only then to return to land? Or was she about to perform another miracle?

The two soldiers saw that in the same spectacular manner that the Jews had been guided by Moses through the Red Sea or that Saint Peter walked over the lake of Genesareth, they, too, were walking over the water. They watched in amazement as the watery surface was transformed into solid diamonds under each footstep, then became liquid once again as their feet left the surface.

Filled with courage, they walked all day without feeling the torments of hunger or thirst, heat or cold. This in itself was no small miracle. Later, on recounting the journey, they could not recall having had any material necessity; their sole concern was the holy image. As God had led the Chosen People in the Old Testament, so also the cloud bearing the miraculous fresco shaded them from the rigors of the sun and illuminated the night so that they would not lose their way but have always before them the consoling vision of the Mother of Good Counsel.[35]

By daybreak, the Albanian shore was far behind and they were nearing the Italian coast. We do not know how many days the journey took. However, during this epic trip in which they were guided by the Star of the Sea, they covered the 190 miles that separate the coast of Albania from the Italian Peninsula.[36] The new shoreline was a sure sign that they were reaching another country. No obstacle they encountered could impede their march. The two Albanians, accustomed to so many surprises, were nevertheless still amazed when they saw the towers and domes of the famous Roman churches of Latium on the horizon.

Yet another surprise, not as consoling as the foregoing, was in store for these poor but happy pilgrims.

Two Strangers Lost in Rome

It is difficult to explain just what happened next. The cloud disappeared over the gates of the Eternal City, carrying with it the sole object of the two men's contemplation, their protection, and their consolation. She, who had ordered them to follow her, had suddenly abandoned them. What scruples and trials must have assaulted their souls. Certainly they blamed themselves, perhaps saying: "In some way we were unfaithful. She would not leave us unless we were at fault. Could it be that our love for her has also grown lukewarm and inconstant? Could it be that we do not believe in her as firmly as we ought and, because of this, just as she left our country so, too, she has left us now?''[37]

The two desolate pilgrims, who until the moment of the image's disappearance had not experienced any weariness or hunger, now, upon entering the Eternal City, felt need for nourishment and rest. But how could they remedy the terrible affliction that wounded their souls?

After restoring their energy, they sought their Queen in all the churches of Rome. The history-filled streets and monuments soon became familiar sights to them. In the beginning they had difficulty in their painful search. Not knowing Italian, how could they communicate in this strange country? But they soon noticed that the city was full of their countrymen, who had left Albania to escape from the sultan's yoke, but these could provide no information to aid them in their search.

In the silence of the sacristies, in the sumptuous palazzi, in the noisy streets and song-filled squares, no one really understood what the two anguished strangers were talking about. Georgio and De Sclavis finally concluded that the only way to find the Lady of Consolation was to fold their hands in prayer and storm heaven. Hail Mary after Hail Mary they prayed, sighing, ''Where can our Mother be?''

Genazzano, an Ancient Village of Latium

During this time, there lived in the small town of Genazzano, a short distance from Rome, a very pious widow ardently zealous for the universal interests of the Church and especially for those in the East.

The history of the village of Genazzano mirrored events in Rome. Earliest documents indicate that the inhabitants were neither pastoral nor warlike but lived a life of lustful disorder. Roman civilization was immersed in the darkness of ancient paganism. Sunk, like the modern world, in practical atheism and withdrawn from divine grace, it had degenerated into terrible moral corruption that, eventually, was its ruin. For example, the idolatrous Romans considered the practice of depraved customs as necessary acts of worship in honor of the gods who, thereby placated, preserved the Empire. Saint Augustine masterfully and skillfully documents, explains, and confutes these aberrations in *The City of God*.[38]

Latium was the scene of shameless cults in honor of the stone or metal idols, one of which represented Venus, the goddess of sensual love. Consequently, there were certain days of the year when inhabitants of the region surrounding Genazzano flocked there to engage in all sorts of abominations.

Arrival of the miraculous image in Genazzano.

The *Civitas Romanas* knew moments of splendor, but lacking moral support, it collapsed. Over the ruins of the proud Roman Empire—destroyed by its own internal rottenness—the austere Cross of Our Lord was raised up, bathed in the blood of legions of martyrs. Like the morning light rending the darkness of a somber night, the true Faith illuminated souls. When Constantine granted freedom to the Church, he could already verify a well-known fact: Christianity had long since conquered the souls and become the Religion of the Empire.

One of the gifts that Constantine made to the Church in the time of Pope Saint Sylvester was the *Fundum Caesareanum, situm Via Prenestina distans ab urbe millia XXX* (one of Caesar's estates, thirty miles from Rome). Historians mark it as the present-day Genazzano. After the idols were demolished and no longer honored with immoral rites, Pope Saint Mark, Saint Sylvester's successor, built the first known church dedicated to Our Lady of Good Counsel on the site. A marble bas-relief in honor of the Virgin of Virgins, the Mother of God, was set up for the veneration of the faithful.[39]

The barbarian invaders who a short time later demolished the remnants of the Empire were in turn conquered by the Cross of Christ. Whole races received the regenerating waters of baptism. Their descendants throughout the centuries populated the villages and cities on the peninsula. Genazzano was one such village.

Parishes were established and enlightened religious came to preach fiery sermons. Liturgical worship was embellished with splendid ceremonies. However, the church of the Mother of Good Counsel, the town's smallest, with its primitive marble bas-relief representing Mary Most Holy and her Divine Son, did not seem appropriate for the splendorous tone the liturgy was assuming. First neglected, it was eventually abandoned. Time marked it with signs of age impossible to disguise.

Genazzano in time became a fiefdom of the Colonna family, a representative of the Roman patriciate, who built an imposing castle and fortified the city. The family was entrusted with protecting and maintaining the Church of Good Counsel. In 1356, in order to prevent its further deterioration and to stimulate the piety of the faithful, Prince Pietro Giordan entrusted it to the care of the Hermits of Saint Augustine who had long been a part of the village life and were noted for their apostolic zeal.

The holy edifice once again came to be a site of spiritual renewal. Under the mantle of Our Lady, the Third Order of Saint Augustine was founded and came to include a large number of the inhabitants of Genazzano.

The Prayers of the Widow Petruccia Are Heeded

The widow Petruccia de Nocera, whom we have already mentioned, was extremely active as a member of the Third Order of Saint Augustine and outstanding in her devotion to the Mother of Good Counsel.

Her husband, a caretaker for the Augustinians for many years, died in 1426, leaving a small inheritance sufficient only for her to lead a modest life. So, at age 39, finding herself a childless widow, she decided to dedicate herself to prayer close to the marble bas-relief that represented Our Lady of Good Counsel.

Petruccia's soul burned with zeal for the expansion of Christianity. The convulsions of the fifteenth century opened to Petruccia's eyes a somber panorama that became the object of her long meditations and fervent prayers. Europe, drained of its stamina by Renaissance humanism, devastated by internal wars, and frightened by the constant threat of an overwhelming Mohammedan invasion; Catholic princes, in whose souls the idealistic flame of the Crusades had been extinguished and supplanted by sensuality and softness; general and increasing corruption of customs; vanishing of the Faith; and the distant howls of the Protestant pseudo-Reformation questioning the authority of the Papacy: Such a distressing scene so greatly afflicted Petruccia as to increase her desire for a great and decisive divine intervention.

She hoped for heavenly intervention for many years ("who against hope believed in hope" [Rom. 4:18]) against all hope, until one day the unbelievable happened. The Holy Ghost enlightened her with a magnificent revelation: "Mary Most Holy, in her holy image of Scutari, wishes to leave Albania."

One can imagine Petruccia's shock upon learning of this serious and sublime mission. Her surprise was even greater when she heard that Genazzano had been chosen to be the new seat of the miraculous image. Surprise turned into profound perplexity when the Blessed Virgin herself ordered her to build the temple that would shelter the fresco. Petruccia was already well advanced in years and did not have the necessary means to accomplish such a holy task. However, the Blessed Virgin promised that she would help at the opportune moment.

Why did the Blessed Virgin choose Genazzano for the new seat of her miraculous picture?

Building the Church Amidst the Mockery of Unbelievers—Just Like Noah Building the Ark

Faithful to the heavenly apparition, Petruccia began the necessary steps for the reconstruction of the chapel of Our Lady of Good Counsel so that it might adequately and decently shelter the holy image that would come from Scutari.

Petruccia had never visited Scutari but she kept in her memory the fine features of the vision she had seen: a Virgin with tapered eyes of a clear color like oil, wearing a white veil over her light brown hair, and carrying on her left side the Infant-God Who embraced her with infinite tenderness.

Petruccia used every cent of her meager resources on the work of rebuilding the church, donating even the house where she lived in order to increase the overall size of the new church.

The stone masons began by demolishing one of the side chapels, dedicated to Saint Blaise, which was in total ruin. However, when the walls of the new chapel had risen only one yard, the enthusiastic eighty-year-old widow's money ran out. No one came to her aid. Not only had her own house been demolished, but she had no more possessions. The skeptics heaped mockery and scorn upon her.

She was the object of the unbelievers' ridicule: "This is clearly the imprudence of a visionary! Consider her old age, her scarce means . . . wanting to build a church only because Our Lady supposedly appeared to her! . . . The time of churches built through the piety of the faithful is over. The fifteenth century is not for crusades or cathedrals but for sumptuous palaces, artists, and poets. Imagine! In this century of the rebirth of Roman civilization—redeemed from medieval barbarism—wanting to build one more church!"*

Some, even more impudent in referring to the good Petruccia, quoted Sacred Scripture: "This man began to build, and was not able to finish" (Luke 14:30), to which she always very calmly responded: "Don't, my children, take such notice

---

* The battle against one's environment is one of the most terrible in which a man must engage in this life. It is the world that the renowned Dominican theologian Fr. Antonio Royo Marín describes thus: "The world exalts pleasure, comfort, riches, fame, violence and might. It advises its followers to enjoy life while they can, to make the most of what the world has to offer, to find security and the maximum bodily comfort, to forget about tomorrow and give not a thought to a life hereafter." Having given several examples, Fr. Royo Marín goes on to say that "With good reason could Saint John complain that 'the whole world is seated in wickedness' " (1 John 5:19). Then, having expounded the different means to fight the psychological pressure exerted by the world to drag souls to hell, the theologian concludes: "Jesus said explicitly that He would deny before His heavenly Father anyone who denies Him before men (Matt. 10:13). . . . One who desires to reach sanctity must be absolutely indifferent to what the world may think or say. His only concern must be to do the will of God, cost what it may" (*The Theology of Christian Perfection* [Mt. Kisco, N.Y.: The Foundation for a Christian Civilization, Inc., 1987], pp. 214-216, passim).

of this apparent misfortune, for I assure you that before I die, the Blessed Virgin and the Holy Father Saint Augustine will complete the church commenced by me."[40]

Sarcastic comments followed her along the streets. During celebrations or municipal fairs, small groups standing at a distance would watch the poor woman going into or coming out of church and, amidst general laughter, would retell her story.

At that time, the fairs were held right in the piazza of Santa Maria. On one side of the square were the yard-high walls of the chapel of Saint Blaise that seemed to clearly and loudly proclaim Petruccia's defeat.

April 25, 1467—A Glorious Day

One of these fairs was held on April 25, 1467, the feast of Saint Mark, Genazzano's patron, and the anniversary of the baptism of Saint Augustine, to whom Petruccia was very devoted.

The popular markets were picturesque. Peasants from the area brought their spring fruits; peddlers and small merchants offered fabrics from Genoa or Venice, a variety of wares from Rome, and spices from the Orient. The air was filled with the voices of fair-goers, of songsters, of one vendor or another pushing through the crowd and hawking some elixir of youth or some "very powerful" remedy for fever.

It was about two o'clock in the afternoon when Petruccia passed by that throng of people from Genazzano and beyond. The lively fair was drawing to its close. In just an hour the bells for Vespers would ring out from the belfry of the ancient church of Santa Maria, the church that Petruccia longed to complete. Within the decaying walls of the chapel, a few devout souls and curious onlookers stood or knelt by the altar of Good Counsel. Outside, the tents were being dismantled as everyone prepared to turn homeward.

Let us allow the pen of the distinguished historian of Genazzano, Monsignor Dillon, to describe the momentous event:

"About the twenty-first hour of the Italian day, or about four o'clock in the afternoon, according to our computation, the dense multitude assembled in the piazza of Santa Maria was astonished to hear, high in the clear atmosphere of their country, strains of celestial harmony. Never had they heard such sounds before. It seemed as if the portals of paradise were flung open, and that the choirs of angels were permitted to give mortals some knowledge of the joys of the blessed. With eyes upturned, in breathless attention, and ravished by such

*Fresco of the apparition
of the Mother of Good
Counsel,*

by Prospero Piatti (1883).
It fills the back of
the shrine of Genazzano.

exquisite melody, they anxiously sought to find out whence the sounds came. Soon, far above the highest houses, above the church spires and the lofty castle turrets, they beheld a beautiful white cloud, darting forth vivid rays of light in every direction, amidst the music of heaven and a splendour that obscured the sun. It gradually descended, and, to their amazement, finally rested upon the furthest portion of the unfinished wall of the chapel of Saint Biagio.

"Suddenly the bells of the high campanile, which stood before their eyes, began to peal, though they could see and knew that no human hand touched them. And then, in unison, every church bell in the town began to answer in peals as festive. The crowd was spell-bound, ravished, and yet full of holy feeling. With eager haste they filled the enclosure; they pressed around the spot where the cloud remained. Gradually the rays of light ceased to dart, the cloud began to clear gently away, and then, to their astonishment, there remained disclosed a most beautiful object. It was an Image of Our Lady, holding the Divine Child Jesus in her arms, and she seemed to smile upon them and to say: 'Fear not; I am your mother, and you are and shall be my beloved children.'

"It is easier to imagine than to describe the commotion produced by this event on those people who found themselves in such circumstances. The business of the fair was abandoned; the amusements were no longer thought of. With one voice they cried out, as their descendants, on the recurrence of the anniversary of the apparition, may be heard to cry out today, *Evviva Maria! Evviva Maria! Evviva la Madre nostra del Buon Consiglio!* Others exclaimed, a miracle! a miracle! While, with an instinct of perfect confidence arising out of the wonderful occurrence, the sick, the blind, the lame, and the afflicted of every condition flocked from all parts of the town, and from places far beyond its borders, to obtain healing graces from Our Lady: graces which, as we shall see, were granted in an abundance, 'with a measure pressed down, and shaken together, and flowing over,' which has not ceased from that day to this.

"Senni [an eminent historian of the Genazzano region] tells us that the unusual chiming of the church bells was heard by numbers who, having satisfied their devotion and disposed of their temporal affairs, were on their way home, and that, fearing dangers too common from marauding enemies in those days of disturbance, they returned to Genazzano. All these, to their astonishment, saw the beautiful Image of Our Lady still suspended in the air, without any visible support whatever, and heard from those present of the miraculous circumstances that accompanied its coming. The princes of the house of Colonna, the captains of their forces, the magnates of the town, the Augustinian Fathers, and the secular clergy, all flocked to admire the wonder. And throughout that night, on bended knees, an immense multitude remained in the presence of their blessed treasure, filled with most intense feelings of love and gratitude to God's Virgin Mother of Good Counsel, who thus had honoured their land."[41]

Petruccia's Virtue Attracted the Holy Image of Scutari to Genazzano

Each people has its own characteristics. In European countries—and especially in Italy—the peculiarities vary from region to region. Now, it is well known that the people in Latium cannot be called reserved—even less so when it is a matter of keeping a secret about such a prodigy. The news spread swiftly to other cities and a growing number of pilgrims flocked to the feet of Mary Most Holy.

They asked for graces and she granted them. They implored miracles and she performed them. Near the unfinished walls of Petruccia's church, donations to continue the construction began to pile up.

At eighty years of age, Petruccia was seeing her hopes fulfilled. Walls were built not only for the chapel of Saint Blaise, but for a whole new church. The old rectory was demolished and a new convent erected in its place for the Augustinian friars.

For a long time, Petruccia had been, in the eyes of her contemporaries, a person who did not understand the realities of life. Nevertheless, one of the most distinguished historians comments: "If Mary revealed to her [Petruccia] her departure from Scutari; if she received the charge to build a new temple for her image; if she started the great work under the direction of the Augustinians, her spiritual fathers; finally, if she prophesied this great mystery to her fellow citizens before the prodigious arrival of the holy image and frequently, in ecstasy and full of holy joy, exclaimed: 'Oh! What a great Lady will come to this new temple,' who does not see clearly and understand that heroic virtues, lily-white innocence, lively faith, the simplicity of a dove, and the virginal purity of this beautiful soul were the true occasions for such heavenly riches and such a blessed reward for Genazzano? Such was blessed Petruccia: a polar star toward which the marvelous compass turned, a dawn that brought the sun to our horizon. With her heroic virtues, her most inflamed desires, she sweetly attracted the most amiable and beautiful image of Mary to Genazzano."[42]

Georgio and De Sclavis Find the Holy Image of Scutari in Genazzano

The two Albanian soldiers, Georgio and De Sclavis, were still in Rome anxiously seeking the whereabouts of Our Lady of Scutari when they heard about the miraculous apparition. They joined a group of pilgrims and hastened to Genazzano to see if the image that had miraculously appeared there was the same one that had brought them from their country.

They could not contain their joy upon rediscovering the powerful Virgin who had given the victory in a hundred battles against the Turks—her who, with such a powerful hand, had miraculously brought them across the waters of the sea. Overcome with happiness, they told all the inhabitants of Genazzano about the origin of the image. The origin? No! Only the history of the two hundred years the image had spent in Albania. As mentioned before, until today no mortal has known where she was before appearing in Scutari.

The Holy Father Orders an Investigation

Stories of miracles that travelers brought with them to Rome and that were repeated in the squares and the entrances to churches entered into conversations in sacristies and cloisters and even became a subject of conversation among the Pope and cardinals. To investigate these increasingly clamorous rumors, Paul II appointed two trustworthy prelates to investigate the matter: Gaucerio de Folcarquer, bishop of Gap, and Nicholo a Crucibus, bishop of Hvar, a city close to Scutari.[43] Bishop Nicholo a Crucibus lived in Rome at the time and was frequently given important assignments by the successor of Saint Peter.

Opinions Are Divided about the Origin of the Holy Fresco in Genazzano

According to all historians, the judgment of the pontifical investigation was favorable.[44] This is concluded from the fact that a new association for the cult, in addition to the already existing Confraternity of Santa Maria, spread remarkably quickly. Two organizations were formed even in tiny Genazzano.

The Confraternity of Prayer believed that the image, called the Madonna of Paradise, had come from heaven only to remind the people of Genazzano of their Christian duties and to favor her devotees.

The members of the new Society of Holy Mary held a different opinion. They were in charge of collecting money to finish Petruccia's construction and to build the new friary for the Augustinians. The members of this confraternity piously believed, as did Petruccia, that the image had come from Scutari, fleeing from the Turkish invasion of Albania, just as Georgio and De Sclavis had told them. It was clear to them that a military corps of devotees should be formed around the image to defend Our Lady in the future and enable her to leave Italy if need be as she had Albania. That the image remained suspended in the air about an inch from the wall for many years after its arrival, not supported by the masonry of the church, provided the most obvious argument in favor of this view.[45]

Blessed Petruccia Rests near the Mother of Good Counsel

Having seen the church brought to completion, Petruccia passed away in 1470, three years after the apparition, in the peace of the Lord and under the kind gaze of Mary. From that time she was venerated as blessed. Her mortal remains were laid to rest under the altar of the holy image where they remained until 1734. In 1882 they were moved to the back part of the shrine where the Augustinians have placed a marker as a memorial to her pious life.

De Sclavis and Georgio settled in Genazzano where they began their own families and where Georgio's descendants still live today.

* * *

The miraculous fresco appeared in Genazzano, brought from Scutari by the hands of angels. Let us also be like those pilgrims of Latium, in Italy, or in any other place of the world, who, at the feet of the holy image, kneel, pray, and beseech favors from this heavenly Lady and take part in the splendid miracles that she multiplies daily.

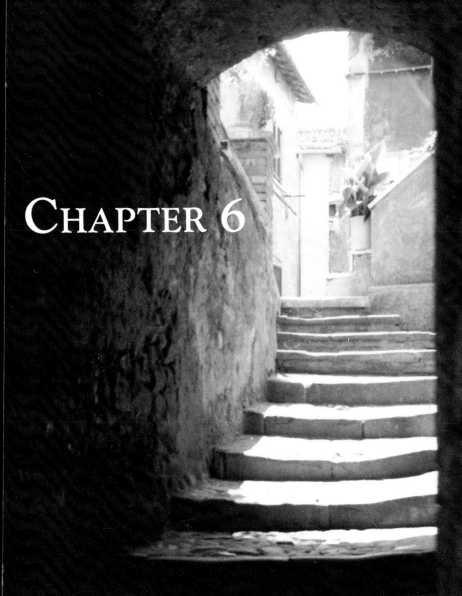

CHAPTER 6

The Blind See, the Lame Walk,
the Possessed Are Delivered:
Miracles and Wonders of the
Madonna of Good Counsel

IN this world where men moan under the weight of original sin, few things are perhaps so coveted as heavenly help that aids in well-being of body and soul.

Whether it be illness, incurable disease, or imminent danger of death; whether it be sufferings of the soul, afflictions of the spirit, desire to overcome a vice, or longing for forgiveness of sin; whether it be the maintaining of good resolutions, the desire for indescribable spiritual goods can only be found through divine intervention.*

God, in His infinite mercy, does not abandon decadent mankind exiled in this valley of tears. Sacred Scripture exuberantly relates innumerable divine interventions in favor of the degraded children of Eve. For example, who, reading the New Testament, is not filled with emotion concerning the miracles performed by Our Divine Redeemer? Here, at the request of His Blessed Mother, He changes a generous amount of water into excellent wine (John 2:3). There, He restores sight to a blind man (John 9:7). Here again, He cures lepers (Luke 17:14).

How much greater, though, are the miracles He performed in the souls that had fallen into the abyss of treason, crime, and unbelief. With an infinitely innocent gaze, He restores Peter's fidelity (Luke 22:61). He promises paradise to the

---

* Fr. Victorino Rodríguez y Rodríguez, O.P., explains this deep feeling of helplessness that every man experiences, especially in regard to graces, with his usual great precision: "Eternal blessedness and the means of attaining it, especially for man weakened by sin, belong to the order of grace; they are not within the reach of the natural resources of man. The arduousness . . . would be called impossibility if the mediation of God's grace did not exist." The illustrious theologian concludes: "If our sufficiency is not born from us or from others because 'cursed be the man who trusteth in man' (Jer. 17:5), it means that help comes to us from God, 'our sufficiency is from God' (2 Cor. 3:5)" (*Temas-claves de Humanismo Cristiano* [Madrid: Speiro, 1984], p. 92).

The following illustration, recorded on May 5, 1467, speaks eloquently to those who are insensible to the apparition of the holy effigy:

"Antonio Cerroni, who was from Pisciano in the diocese of Palestrina approximately five miles from Genazzano, heard, from everywhere, the happy and festive echoes of the people concerning the luminous and admirable circumstances surrounding the glorious apparition of this holy image. Through a diabolical suggestion, he believed that the religious had invented everything about the unexpected, spontaneous, and harmonious ringing of the bells, the confirmed prophecies of the blessed and most fortunate Petruccia, and the splendorous arrival of this venerated image. He foolishly believed [in the suggestion] and, along with others, brazenly expressed himself with laughter and ridicule.

"Some days later he had to travel to Genazzano to attend to some personal and business interests. While there he saw so many people trying to squeeze themselves into the chapel to implore graces from Mary that his curiosity prompted him to attempt to enter. But—miserable unbelieving creature!—he could not enter. When he reached the door of the holy temple, he was seized with such dire and sudden terror that he began to tremble from head to foot. He found himself like a paralytic since birth, unable to walk.

"With his hands and feet paralyzed, he could only utter these tear-filled words to the multitude: 'O good people! Know that truly I was crippled, as can be seen, because of my disbelief. Therefore, in your presence, I recommend myself to the Holy Virgin. If I am speaking the truth, O Virgin Mary, free me, not for my merits but by thy grace.' So, crying, sighing, and confessing publicly the crime of not having believed so many who had confessed and praised the most glorious work of God, he moved and entered the holy chapel in order to obtain from the most clement Mother of Good Counsel pardon of his sin . . . and with that forgiveness, perfect health. An inscription on the chapel wall reads: 'Statim ad ejus, et populi vocem sanum factus est, et sanus recessit' (According to his words and the words of the people, he was immediately cured, and cured, he left).

"Later, the man became a preacher of the glories and prerogatives of the holy image in whose miraculous apparition he did not at first believe."[51]

A Terrible Threat to Those Who Do Not Properly Guard the Holy Fresco: "I Will Leave Genazzano as I Left Scutari"

Another episode, illustrating just how much Divine Providence encourages the faithful to worthily venerate and honor the holy image of the Mother of Good Counsel, is recorded in De Orgio's work. Since it occurred more than two centuries after the holy fresco's arrival in Genazzano, it is not one of the first 161 miracles:

"A lady-in-waiting to Princess Cleria Cesarini Colonna and her sister were traveling from Rome to Genazzano on the day and year previously mentioned [November 5, 1680] since both, having been seriously ill, were miraculously cured when they recommended and consecrated themselves to this holy and very miraculous image.

"As soon as they arrived at the shrine, they went to the holy chapel. It was the hour of Vespers. They asked the priests to kindly uncover the most blessed image since they had come from Rome to visit her.[52] The local superior, having heard the request, called the other priests together to ask their opinion. Together they went to the chapel to begin the sacred function in their usual very devout style.

"First, they drew aside the curtain that hangs in front of the finely carved silver plate to protect the holy and esteemed image. This curtain had been embroidered by one of the two ladies present. Kneeling close to the altar, the women expressed their desire to receive Holy Communion there the next morning and their wish was fully agreed to. So, this having been arranged, all left. Although the priests had decided against leaving the image uncovered because of the exceptional care and veneration due such a great treasure, through an oversight the embroidered curtain was not pulled back over the image.

"At dawn the next morning, after the Ave Maria was rung, the church was opened. It rapidly filled up with people wanting to attend the first Mass which had been celebrated daily for some time. Father Giuseppe Todi, then sacristan and guardian of the holy chapel was climbing a wooden ladder to get the oil for the large silver lamps of the shrine. Suddenly, he heard a continuous noise, sounding as though rings were sliding on a curtain rod, surprising him and all the others present. Because the unusual noise was so clear, the priest became frightened and climbed down the ladder. Together, he and many others present gathered around the holy altar and noticed the oversight of the curtain having been left open on the previous day.

"They were filled with the utmost fear and amazement when, while trying to determine whence came the sound of the sliding rings, they saw the curtain start to close by itself as though pulled by some angelic hand. At the same time, the unseen hand closed the silver tabernacle as well as the silver plate that serves to protect the holy image. O Holy Angels of Paradise who guard this great treasure, how attentive you were on that day in demonstrating with what veneration and respect so venerable an image must be guarded!

"And who can laugh at or describe the chill that each one felt in his blood? Or the great and sudden fear each experienced? What thoughts ran through their minds? Most believed that the holy image would leave Genazzano, just as it formerly left Albania, as a punishment for some serious infidelity committed there. Many others feared that she had already left and that the sudden closing of the curtain was the unhappy sign of such a fatal disgrace, similar to the rending of the veil of the august Temple of Solomon.

"This suspicion grew in their hearts and minds to such a degree that all of them—crying, sighing and raising their voices in clamor and lamentations—beseeched the friars to unveil the image right then and there to see if she really had left or was still present.

"The local superior hurriedly began Mass on the holy altar. After the Gospel, he delivered a brief and tender sermon to the tearful people. Suddenly, frightening screams from possessed persons filled the church. One of these was of a certain Cintia, the daughter of Marco Antonio de Sanctis, who became agitated and exclaimed: 'Ah, she is here! It is certain she is. I must . . . I want to leave!'

"Finally, the holy and unbloody Sacrifice being concluded, the entire holy altar was illuminated. The people in the church pushed and squeezed to enter the holy chapel. A chill ran through the crowd as the noble curtain was opened. The priests themselves trembled as they lifted the great silver plate that—like a half door—partially blocked the view of the holy treasure.

"The screen was slowly lifted. With contrite hearts and reddened eyes all saw the image of Mary shining and glittering before them. The crowd surged forward right next to the silver plate. Behold! Their Lady and Empress appeared serene, smiling, and ruddy colored. She seemed to be gazing at them as the most loving Mother of Good Counsel.

"All lifted up their voices in a joyful and festive cry: 'Long live Mary! Long live our Holy Mother of Good Counsel!' They sang a solemn *Te Deum*.

"At the first bright rays of the holy image, the possessed Cintia fell to the ground perfectly freed from the infernal spirits.

"When the holy image was covered again, all humbly greeted and venerated her and concluded that the incident showed God's desire that the most blessed image be cared for with utmost and exceptional zeal and dignity.

"A public document describing what had happened was drawn up in the church and witnessed by (among many others) the Knight Severa and Captain Alexandre Pupi. The two very devout ladies mentioned above spread the story of the stupendous miracle by word of mouth upon their return to Rome. Others sent letters about it to various places of the Roman Campagna."[53]

The Unusual Flight of the Arrow of the Hungarian Archer

To have some idea of the esteem with which God Himself wants this holy image venerated, honored and respected, it is enough to note the following incident:

"On July 4th of the fortunate and happy year of the apparition of our blessed image, one Mark, a Hungarian, was on his way to Genazzano to venerate and honor the most blessed image. When some idle youths saw him arrive at the gates of the town, dressed in Hungarian fashion and carrying a bow on his back and arrows at his side, they began to mock and make fun of him. One of them was so bold that he took the hat from a nearby beggar and said to Mark: 'Listen, if you have any courage, let us see you send an arrow through this hat that I am placing before this wall.'

"The brave Hungarian, offended by the words and the mockery of these youths, swiftly took his bow in hand, readied it, and shot an arrow right through the hat. The arrow hit the mark but, like that other arrow shot at the bull in Mount Gargano, *'recidit in sagitarium'*—it suddenly ricocheted and seriously wounded the side of the Hungarian who had shot it so daringly.

"Faced with such an unexpected turn of events and hearing the cries of the wounded Hungarian, all began to tremble. In their attempts to find how such a thing could have happened, they discovered that there was a small image of Mary Most Holy of Good Counsel sewn into the hat—as is the custom among the poor.

"They immediately urged the seriously bleeding and afflicted Hungarian to enter the town and have recourse to Mary Most Holy, whom he had unknowingly offended. So, that is what the bewildered Mark did. Prostrating himself in the holy chapel, he confessed his involuntary error and was cured shortly thereafter. With such an example, everyone realized how much zeal God has for this image of Paradise, seeing that even offenses against a simple replica of the original are punished with frightening and prodigious penalties."[54]

Even the Dead Come Back to Life Through the Intercession of Our Lady of Good Counsel

The highly regarded De Orgio recounts this miraculous resurrection: "Constantino de Carolis de Castelfollie, a very faithful servant of Lord Antonietto de Castelnuovo, became seriously ill and was not expected to live. The physicians abandoned all hope, and Constantino received the Sacraments of the Church and expired in the presence of several persons who were attending him. After having had him wrapped in a shroud and laid on the ground, his aggrieved lord went to seek the clergy to arrange for the funeral and accustomed rites. Upon returning home, he spent a long time gazing at the body of the faithful servant whom he had loved so tenderly. Suddenly, he started to shed abundant tears.

"Prostrate on the ground and with these exact words (as he later related in a public document under solemn oath), he exclaimed: 'O Blessed Virgin of Genazzano, I implore thee, if it be for the better, intercede for me with God so that He may return my servant to me, and I promise to take him to Genazzano before thy holy image!'

"Mary, the Blessed Mother of Good Counsel, the Sovereign Empress of the Heavens, having been invoked with such lively faith, heeded those ardent and sorrowful supplications with pleasure. To everyone's astonishment, the dead servant lifted his head and, at the same instant, opened his eyes and sat upright. He, too, was filled with amazement. He saw his afflicted master and, loosening his tongue, said, 'be so kind as to give me a bit of food.' Then, standing up and turning to those around him, he declared that he was cured and free from any discomfort or suffering.

"After hearing the details of his resurrection, he immediately set out with his lord for Genazzano. There they presented themselves in the church and the chapel of the holy image, singing praises and gratitude with joyful voices to the great Mother of Good Counsel."[55]

A Man Condemned to Death Has Recourse to Her and Is Miraculously Saved

Another very touching miracle taken from the first annals of the Shrine is also related by De Orgio. This concerns the release on the evening before his execution of a condemned man named Giovanni di Andrea Foreste from Sarzana: "He was in the public prison of Siena, condemned to death with two of his criminal and villainous companions. A zealous Franciscan friar, despite his utmost efforts, was unsuccessful in preparing the man to die well. Rather, the man repeatedly cried out: 'O Father, give me some way to avoid that deadly blow!'

"After showing the man the impossibility of his being set free or avoiding the execution facing him the next morning, the good priest, exasperated, or perhaps inspired by God, said to him: 'If the miraculous Madonna who recently appeared in Genazzano does not deliver you from death, then without a doubt, tomorrow you will be in eternity.' With this, the priest left in disgust.

Seventeenth-century engraving showing the ex-voto offered by Supreme Commander Filipo Colonna, duke of Paliano, to the chapel of the Madonna, asking for the cure of his wife, Lucrecia Tomacelli. The piece —an engraved silver plaque— was made before 1622.

Below. *The massive Colonna castle, built in Genazzano by order of Pope Martin V (Oddo Colonna, 1368-1431). The castle was heavily damaged during World War II, and the restoration work is still under way.*

"When the good priest had departed, Giovanni threw himself face down on the ground and, crying unceasingly, exclaimed: 'O Blessed Virgin, if thou wouldst grant me such an immense grace, I shall go immediately to thy feet to thank thee for such a great miracle!' Having said this, the fetters on his feet suddenly broke apart. Full of amazement and the desire to flee, he saw a small window in the prison which was beyond his reach. Nevertheless, he approached and easily climbed toward it as if on an invisible ladder.

"Upon reaching the window he became frightened because the drop was so steep that it was impossible to jump without breaking every bone in his body. His companions shouted to him: 'You madman! Come down, come down and prepare for death, otherwise it will be your ruin.' Filled with a lively faith and encouraged by the miraculously opening of his chains and his having reached that window without knowing how, he made the Sign of the Cross, fervently recommended himself to Mary Most Holy of Genazzano, and unhesitatingly jumped, all the while repeating, 'O Holy Mary of Genazzano, help me!'

"What a miracle, worthy of the Empress of Heaven! As though carried by a heavenly little cloud, the man landed on the ground unscathed: *'Invenit se illesum et intactum, tamquam si non cecidisset.'* (He found himself unharmed and intact, as if he had not fallen at all.) Thus it is written in the declaration written right after the event.

"In consideration of this great miracle, human justice decided to set the man free, seeing that the Mercy of God wished him freed for the greater glory of Mary and her miraculous image that had appeared in Genazzano two months before.

"After the other two had been beheaded the next morning, he joyfully set out on the road to Genazzano, arriving on July 11, 1467, to thank his divine liberator and to tell about the great and miraculous event that had happened to him in Siena. He attested to it under oath on the sacred Gospels in the presence of priests, of Benedetto Marroco Altobello of Genazzano, of Melchiorre di Ranciluni, as well as of others."[56]

A Heavenly Trick of Our Lady

At times, the Madonna of Paradise attends petitions promptly, as she did with the prisoner of Siena. At other times, to use words of De Orgio, it pleases her to play loving tricks on her pious devotees.

"On August 7 of the same year [1467], Niccolo Di Giovani of Manfredonia, whose leg was paralyzed due to a painful sciatica and a subsequent stroke, had spent many days in the chapel, which he had reached only with great difficulty, beseeching a grace. Seeing that his prayers were not answered and experiencing more pain and discomfitures, he set out for Rome in order to find some cure for his illness there. Behold, then [there occurred] a loving and gracious trick of Mary Most Holy of Paradise, or of Good Counsel.

"As he slept under a tree along the way, she appeared to him in a dream. It was the hottest time of the summer day and he was exhausted and sad. 'Niccolo, do you know who I am? I am that Virgin to whom you had recourse in your illness' (*Ego sum Virgo illa*).

"Niccolo replied, 'Why, then, most benign and clement Lady, didst thou not hear me?' Mary answered: 'But, my son, you are already cured. Return to Genazzano with joy and proclaim the grace you have received.' Blessing him with the Sign of the Cross, she disappeared.

"The elated man rose up and saw that he was indeed healed. He returned quickly on foot to Genazzano and told everyone he met along the road and at the great shrine of Mary about the miraculous event. Finally, he testified under oath before witnesses."[57]

The Blind See

Paging through the narration of the first 161 miracles, one sees that the cases of the blind who obtained cures through the intercession of the Virgin of Good Counsel are outstanding.

For example, cured were Phillippe de Bartholome of the Province of Burgundy who had not seen the light of day for three years; Filippa di Paliano, eight years old and blind since birth; Guglielmo de Orlandis who had been blind for twenty-five years.

One extraordinary case of restored sight deserves a detailed description.

"In August of 1467, Antonio di Giacomo of Mataloni, working with his donkeys, was transporting lime for construction of the Royal Church of Saint Mark in Rome. On August 7, while unloading some lime in the vestibule of the church, part of the scaffolding suddenly fell from the highest point of the construction and struck him on his head with such violence that he fell to the ground seriously and almost fatally injured. One of his eyes was thrust out of the ocular cavity, causing serious hemorrhaging. He was not expected to live.

"The citizens hurriedly ran to his help and carried him away as he writhed in terrible pain. They noticed fearfully that the eye was outside its cavity and hanging only by a fiber over the cheek. (*'Totalier exiverat, atque inferiius per faciem pendebat,'* as it is noted in the authentic statement made later.) Some-one wiped the blood away and with difficulty placed the hanging eye back into the socket.

"While all this was going on, the poor patient repeated—more with his heart than with his lips—'O Most Holy Mary of Genazzano, help me!' Indeed, what he really desired was nothing less than a great miracle of complete restoration from Most Holy Mary. For, what would it avail him to have his eye restored to its socket if so many arteries were broken or torn and if the arteries, nerves, and ligaments that protect, sustain, nourish, and so admirably enhance it were in the same ruined state?

"Despite all this, Most Holy Mary of Good Counsel, having been invoked at the propitious moment, immediately, with her powerful and invisible hand, set the eye securely and perfectly back in its socket and with such speed that the public registry noted: *'integere et sanus, et liber de dicto oculo ita remansit, ut nihil mali, nihil sinistri appareret.'* (His eye was so perfect, sound, and cured that it had nothing ill nor anything defective apparent.) What a magnificent expression! *'Ut nihil mali, nihil sinistri appareret.'*

"Thus, the good Antonio di Giacomo, filled with tenderness and gratitude, came to the feet of this most holy image and, there, after having shed copious and affectionate tears, and thanking his most benign protectress for so great a favor and miracle, narrated under solemn oath and in the presence of many witnesses in the holy chapel, the whole miraculous event that had taken place in Rome. This account was immediately registered with admiration for eternal remembrance.

"Thus, filled with emotion and admiration, we can also exclaim with Blessed Amadeo: *'O quam pia diligentia humanorum corporum sanitati Maria providet, et medetur'*—Oh! With what loving care Mary protects the health of human bodies and heals them."[58]

The Possessed Are Freed from the Chains of Hell

The motherly solicitude of the Queen of Good Counsel is not limited to the care of bodily necessities. Her care is devoted, above all, to spiritual sicknesses. One of the worst disgraces is certainly to be fettered by the chains of infernal spirits. A young man named Niccolo Greco was in such a situation.[59]

It all began when Niccolo fell in love with a maiden named Orsolina. At first, it seemed that she felt the same as the young man. Later on, though, she decided to rid herself of him, whether for having found someone better suited to her or for having become disenchanted with the relationship. In any case, she thought that the best way to be rid of him would be to give him a bewitched liquor.

After he had taken the diabolical drink, young Niccolo became delirious and then crazy. Soon he was transformed into a complete madman, running from one place to another brandishing an unsheathed sword and frightening everyone. In addition, being oppressed day and night by an infernal fury, he lost considerable weight and at last became gravely ill with tuberculosis. No cure existed for his problems and, even though he had been reduced to such a state, virtually no one dared help him for fear of his violent demeanor.

Now, the fame of the great miracles worked by the Mother of Good Counsel of Genazzano, who had liberated several persons possessed for years by the devil, was spreading. So, Niccolo's hopeful parents decided to take him to the holy chapel. As soon as he was presented to the most august image, the infernal enemy left him, leaving him free and perfectly sound. In this way, the young man, once insane, was made sane (*"de insano sanus factus est"*), regaining the peace, health, and serenity that had been taken from him. The miracle was registered on July 12, 1467, in a public act under solemn oath. As a token of gratitude, Niccolo left that sword he had brandished against the people when he was crazy.

The glorious intercession of Mary Most Holy of Good Counsel also freed Bernardo de Domenico, of Rocca, from the claws of the infernal spirits. His possession caused him to lacerate his own flesh with his teeth. Other cases include that of Maria de Orlandis, from Marano in the diocese of Subiaco, who had been possessed for twenty-two years, and Martina Chiarelli, of Rome, who was tormented by demons for twelve years. A public act was made, attested to under oath, of these miraculous exorcisms.

The Bleeding Crucifix and God's Vengeance Against Sacrilege

There is in the shrine of Genazzano, across the nave from the holy fresco of the Mother of Good Counsel, a Chapel of the Crucifix where a painting of Our Lord Jesus Christ crucified is venerated. During the pontificate of Paul III (1534-1549), that painting was the object of a stupendous miracle. A soldier, infuriated at having lost all his money gambling, entered the shrine blaspheming horribly against God and Our Lady. In his fury, he unsheathed his sword and struck the forehead, chest, and legs of the crucified One. Blood in abundance immediately issued forth from the parts that had been struck. The sword used in this infamous attack assumed so twisted a shape that a talented blacksmith would need quite some time to produce such an effect. Seeing the miracle, the

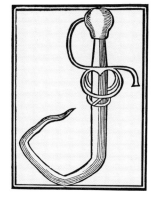

Left page. *General view of the right nave.*

Left. *Engraving taken from the book of Friar De Orgio (p. 230) representing the twisted sword of the infamous, sacrilegious and blasphemous soldier.*

Below. *The altar of the Most Holy Crucifix, in the right nave of the Basilica. The fresco is from the Roman school (fifteenth century) and was the object of an astonishing miracle during the pontificate of Paul III.*

perpetrator of the sacrilege tried to escape, carrying the bloody and twisted sword in his hand. His companions, filled with just indignation, struck him with their weapons, killing him in the square in front of the church.

As a sign of those sacrilegious blows to our Divine Redeemer, some discolored spots can still be seen today on the painting of the body of the Crucified in the places where it was struck.

In 1680, more than a hundred years later, the patriarch of Colonna requested that the sword be straightened. The master blacksmith Andrea Barberano was able to accomplish this using fire and repeated blows of his hammer. However, in the presence of all, the sword immediately returned to its former twisted shape—bending in three places since three was the number of blows suffered by the holy crucifix at the hands of the infamous soldier. The sword, kept until today in the shrine, is an impressive witness to the miracle performed to avenge the glory of the offended God.[60]

Genazzano Specially Protected from Plagues That Devastated Italy

The impressive immunity of the town of Genazzano cannot be omitted from this concise account of miracles. From the moment that it received the honor and happiness of housing the holy image within its walls, it was free from the various plagues that raged throughout the country. "All attribute this wonderful immunity to the protection of Our Lady, and to the possession of Her miraculous Image," writes Monsignor Dillon, who adds: ". . . in the seventeenth century, the house of Colonna with many others experienced the benefit of this immunity, during a plague which elsewhere, scarcely left the living the power of burying the dead. One reads to this day with horror the account of this pestilence in the lives of St. Charles Borromeo and of other remarkable personages of the time."[61]

"In the eighteenth century, the protection extended over Genazzano was so well known that when Pope Urban VIII made his famous pilgrimage to the shrine of Our Lady, his principal purpose was to obtain from the Virgin Mother of Good Counsel an end to the plague that was then threatening Rome.[62]

"But, the most surprising exhibition of this miraculous exception was witnessed in this nineteenth century, the era emphatically of infidelity and materialism, of atheism, and its brood of irreligious systems. With all the improvements science has effected in the arts subserving human comfort and convenience, men in this century have had to die just as in times more barbarous. . . . The terrible Asiatic cholera has swept again and again over all the nations of Europe and over all the islands of its seas. No land has escaped its ravages. It has levelled rulers and subjects with impartial severity. Italy was, of all the countries it devastated, the most severely visited. In 1832, in 1857, in 1867, its population was more than decimated by the fearful scourge. Strange to say, no city or town in all its extent completely escaped the ravages but one, and that one was Genazzano. Stranger still, no part of Italy was more desolated than Latium,'' precisely the region where Genazzano is located. In Albano, about nineteen miles from Genazzano, ''both the Cardinal Bishop and the Dowager Queen of Naples fell victims, the former through zeal for his people. The streets were covered with corpses, which the living for fear of contagion were afraid to bury. The gallant Zouaves, at the call of their commander, performed for many corrupting bodies that last Christian office. So it was with Palestrina, but seven miles distant from Genazzano. So it was with Olevano, Paliano, and San Vito, the latter but three miles away.

''So it was with Capranica, a small town on the mountain at the foot of which Genazzano is built, and which in a direct line is not a mile away. There, several were dying each day. And this continued until nearly the whole population came in solemn pilgrimage to the Shrine of the Virgin Mother of Good Counsel. They advanced on their knees from a considerable distance outside the town, and through the streets until they came into the presence of the miraculous Image. There, suppliantly they besought Our Lady to have compassion on their unfortunate and desolate township. They made, as people in their condition might be naturally supposed to make, many vows and prayers. Mary in Heaven heard them, and from that day the dreadful scourge completely ceased its ravages in Capranica.''[63]

Garibaldi Found Few Recruits in Genazzano

One of the noticeable characteristics commented on by all historians of the town and shrine, especially by Senni and Vannutelli, both natives of Genazzano, just as by Monsignor Dillon, is that, as the last writes: ''even the political visitations which have made such frightful ravages in other parts of Italy, have visited Genazzano with singularly partial effect. Garibaldi obtained few or no recruits from it, and a band of his defeated followers passed through the town without offering molestation.''[64]

The authoritative Vannutelli affirms: ''It stands in the history of human events that this Queen of Heaven holds Genazzano exempt from all the ills of Italy, it having never, or but little, felt the overturning of states; inundations of foreign armies; rapine, the burning of cities, secret societies, cruel conspiracies, immoderate ambition, robbing avarice, the unbridled license of the population, earthquake, drought, penury, desolating malady, public horror, and death from sudden causes.''[65]

*   *   *

Many other supernatural prodigies that occurred during the half millennium since the apparition of the holy image in Genazzano could be added to those already cited. However, it seemed to us that the reader would have a more complete idea of the avalanche of miracles Our Lady lavishly performed by focusing on those that took place during the first months of her arrival. These are seen in the next chapter.

CHAPTER 7

Marvelous Prodigies Light Up the Skies of Genazzano: 110 Days, 161 Miracles

TWO days after the apparition of the fresco, a triumphant procession passed through the town of Genazzano, leaving in its wake cures of the most diverse illnesses of body and soul: a possessed soul freed from the claws of demons; a blind woman restored to sight; a crippled man enabled to walk. In 110 days, Our Lady of Good Counsel performed 161 miracles for her devout faithful! Multitudes converged on Genazzano from all parts of Italy.

The *Codex Miraculorum*

As noted in the previous chapter, the remembrance of these marvelous events was not lost forever. Their echoes resound even in our time because the Augustinians, desirous that future centuries would have trustworthy documents of these abundant and prodigious wonders that occurred daily in the chapel of the holy image, decided that the miracles should be registered by a notary and signed in the presence of eyewitnesses. The register was limited to the first four months; what happened to it later is still unknown.

There was, however, an anonymous pious pilgrim who compiled the acts in a single volume, the *Codex of Miracles*, which was kept for several centuries at the shrine. The devout pilgrim offers the fruits of his labor to Our Lady of Good Counsel in his opening pages:

"Hail, Queen of Heavens! Behold the copies and original records of the miracles performed by thy prayers in favor of the devotees of thy most holy image that appeared on April 25 in the year of Our Lord 1467 in the church of Holy Mary of Genazzano, belonging to the oratory of the Hermits of Saint Augustine. Those miracles narrated and certified in writing were performed throughout the period of three months and seventeen days, in other words, from April 27 to August 14 of that year. As they were registered on many separate sheets, I gathered them into one volume, copying them word by word, not as I should have done, but as well as I could. Confessing my negligence, I ask thy pardon, because when I copied them I could have been more diligent than I actually was.* In spite of my having transcribed them so poorly, please deign to receive them together with my heart so devoted to thee and wishing with thy help to see with my bodily eyes thy miraculous and holy image once more before my death just as I now contemplate it with the eyes of my imagination. Meanwhile, kneeling at thy feet, I plead in a loud voice, pray for me now and at the hour of my death.''[66]

This codex also disappeared in the whirlwind of the Napoleonic invasions and was never found again. However, the historian De Orgio had it in his hands in the middle of the eighteenth century. In his work, frequently cited throughout this book, he published a summary, in Italian, of the miracles narrated in that precious codex.

A reader desiring to experience the incomparable kindness of the holy fresco of Genazzano need only follow the account of the prodigies of her who is ''fair as the moon, bright as the sun, terrible as an army set in array'' (Cant. 6:9).

Miracles of the Sovereign Empress and Blessed Mother of Good Counsel

April 1467

April 27—Today, in the holy chapel, Domenica di Giulani was released from very violent and painful consequences of child bearing; Aquiles, also from Genazzano, was cured of an extended and persistent sciatic pain; and Giovan Cambellotti, of Castel Zangati, of a long and painful illness through which he had lost his speech and was unable to take any food.

April 28—Today, in the same holy chapel, Consolata di Giovan Giordani, who, suffering from a weakness in her limbs, could not move for the last three years, turned with a lively faith to Mary Most Holy of Good Counsel and became sound, free, and full of vigor as though she had never suffered any sickness.

May 1467

May 2—On this day, Mary Most Holy cured Antonio de Benedictis, of Castelo Marfitelli, of the very painful misfortune of having lost the feeling of his whole right side due to a stroke.

---

* For the reader who is little accustomed to a certain style much used in pious writings of times past, these words of the anonymous copyist may seem to detract from his painstaking work. However, profound humility that characterizes the desire for perfection of a truly Catholic soul should be attributed to them.

May 3—Rita de Sanctis, daughter of Giovan Pietro of Castelo di Gerano, who had been possessed for a long time, became free and sound in the holy chapel.

May 5—Today, Our Lady of Paradise cured Antonio Cerroni, of Pisciano, who, as a punishment for his lack of faith before the holy image, had become crippled and paralyzed [this miracle is told in detail in the previous chapter]; also Bernadino, of Piombino, depressed and exhausted by a continuous fever; and Giovanni Francianera, who also suffered from a stubborn quartan fever for six consecutive years; Giacomina de Benedictis, from Olevano, who after having given birth to a baby boy, was flooded with pains night and day for five months; and Bella di Giovan Niccola, of San Vito, who could not stay on her feet because of a very painful woman's sickness she suffered for eight years and that caused her to faint frequently.

May 8—Francesca Ceccarelli, of Palliano, was cured today. She had been blind since childhood and weak her whole life; also, Minna di Giovan Capozzo, of Cave, who had become partially paralyzed in all her limbs and unable to move about for many years.

May 15—Mary Most Holy cured those who had pleaded before her holy image: Philippe Bartholome, from the province of Burgundy, who had been blinded three years earlier; Domenica Tuzi, of Olevano, reduced to a dying state because of terrible convulsive pains; and Antonio Tomassi, of Sclavonia, in Dalmatia, blind for four years.

May 16—Antonio di Pietro, of Trano, an epileptic for fully twenty-eight years, was cured; also, Giacomo Vestri, of Genazzano, set free for the rest of his life from a general torpor and debility that prevented any movement; and Mariano, son of John, an Albanian, whose limbs were so weak he was unable to stand.

May 17—Maria di Notar Onofri, of Civitavella, who suffered for twenty-two years from continuous bleeding, was completely cured today at the feet of this holy image.

May 18—Today, in the holy chapel, Antonio Guastacavalli, of Frascati, paralyzed for twelve years and unable to move about or stand on his feet, and Giacomo de Angelo Antonio Buzi, of Cicigliano, who had become blind six years earlier, were both cured. Tizia Zagarolo, a poor old woman coming on foot to visit this holy image, had fallen into a deep pit filled with thorns and branches while passing near Palestrina. She had called upon Our Lady of Good Counsel and, at that moment, Mary Most Holy appeared to her in visible form and saved her. She arrived in Genazzano eager to thank her and tell about the marvels that she saw and experienced.

May 21—Roscietto, of Genazzano, in his last agony and given up on by the doctors, had already received the Sacraments of the Church. His wife, distressed and anguished over this imminent loss, had recourse to Mary Most Holy. With a lively faith, she promised to go from her home to the holy chapel on her bare knees. She began to fulfill her vow immediately, shedding tears and crying out in pain and prayer. At that moment, her dying husband sat up in bed and, suddenly vomiting, rid himself of seven fetid worms. As soon as he had regained some strength through nourishment, he left his sick bed as though he had never had any ailment.

May 23—On this day, Anastasia Arcite, from Cervara, was on the verge of death. She had been in agony for five days and had not taken any nourishment. Her afflicted mother repeatedly promised to take her to the feet of the holy image. Because of this promise, Anastasia escaped death and immediately showed signs of good health. She asked for nourishment and was enabled to stand; smiling with great joy, she went with her mother to Genazzano to see her Liberatress. Today, also, came Antonio Sollato, of Tivoli, who had become lame because of paralysis on one side of his body. Having made the promise to come on foot to the holy image wearing a cord around his neck, he was instantly cured. Also the holy image cured a woman named Bona di Simone, of Cicigliano. For eight years, she had been so bent over that her face almost touched the ground, and even with the help of a cane she could walk but a few steps.

Also cured were Maria Angela Fucine, also of Cicigliano, who had been blind for six years; Petruccia de Antonio Comparelli, of Tivoli, terribly tormented by the consequence of childbirth; Caterina Cocceti, of Vicovaro, oppressed by the same illness in such a way that she could not find peace or repose night or day for twenty-eight years; Merlino, of Tivoli, blind for many months; twenty-five-year-old Guglielmo de Orlandis, of Terni, born blind, had scarcely entered the holy chapel when he suddenly open two most limpid eyes; Aurelia Palicchi, of Nemi, paralyzed for many years; and Santa, of Trevi, tormented by malignant spirits.

This was a great, happy, and magnificent day marked and made famous by Mary with ten miracles or graces in just a few hours.

May 24—A certain Niccolo Grisanti, of Guadagnola, upon his return to his hometown from Genazzano, was asked if he had seen any miracles of the holy image, to which he replied: "What miracles? What miracles? I did not see anything." The following night, one of his small children, Martino by name, suddenly stricken with violent convulsive pains, was near death. The frightened father, stung by his conscience telling him that this was a punishment for his sins, fell face down on the ground sighing and crying. Then, noticing that his beloved son was beginning to improve, he carried him in his arms to the feet of Mary Most Holy in Genazzano. Here the good little boy was perfectly cured in an instant. The unbelieving father now believed, having seen both punishments and prodigies with his own eyes.

May 25—Today the Sovereign Empress and Blessed Mother of Good Counsel granted Giovanna, daughter of Giovan Niccolo Petrucci of Pereto, of the diocese of Marsi, a longed-for grace. Both she and her sister, Maria, were paralyzed from head to foot. They came to the chapel to be cured and, indeed, they were. Also cured was Stefano Antonelli, of Trappani, who had been bothered many years by terrible pains resulting from an infection of the urinary tract.

May 29—Pietro Niccolo Bucciarelli, of Cerula, went to Genazzano for business and also to visit the holy image. When he returned, he was asked if he had seen any miracles. Unbelieving and resentful like Niccolo Grisanti above, he answered that he had seen nothing and believed nothing. The following night, the great Empress of Heaven, inflamed and filled with indignation, appeared to him. She commanded him to return to Genazzano immediately where he would see many miracles so that he might believe. Filled with tremendous fear, the spiteful man awoke and discovered that his young son, Antonio, had suddenly taken ill and was near death. He grabbed his son in his arms and hastened to the holy chapel in Genazzano. There, moaning and crying, he publicly confessed his guilt. At that instant, his little son became healthy, exceptionally healthy, joyful, and festive. Pietro, repentant at seeing his son cured, amended his life entirely.

Also today, Giovanni, the twelve-year-old son of Giovanni Panenche, of Cantalupo, who had always been paralyzed, acquired complete use of all his limbs. Another still, Pietro, the eight-year-old son of Niccolo Simeone, of Cora, who was crippled and unable to stand, received the same grace as Giovanni. Giacomo Narni Piccinini, blind for four years, regained his sight today in the holy chapel amidst the great joy of all present.

May 30—Perfetta, a dedicated woman of Cora, having heard of the miracle that happened to her fellow countryman Pietro, who returned home cured, was immediately filled with a holy and lively faith. She asked to be taken to Genazzano to obtain the same grace, for she had been blind for six years. Her cure was granted. Basilia, wife of Giorgio of Guadagnolo, became healthy and vigorous as though she had never suffered from paralysis.

May 31—Angela, the daughter of the master Niccolo de Bassiano, had her entire right arm paralyzed by a stroke, so much so that it was like a piece of wood. She had scarcely entered the holy chapel today when she became robust and healthy, moving her arm in a normal way. Francesca Marcellario, of Porcile, who had suffered a woman's illness for fifteen years, on this day became sound and healthy at the foot of the altar of Mary Most Holy of Good Counsel.

June 1467

June 3—Today, Antonia of Castel Sanguigno, wife of Antonio, count of Montefortino, a victim of an epileptic seizure that caused her to lose all feeling in her entire right side, was brought with difficulty to the holy chapel. Suddenly, she became healthy, abundantly so, after having suffered this serious illness for three years and seven months. Antonieta di Antonio Spine, also of Montefortino, who had been deaf in her right ear for eighteen years, was cured at the same hour as Signora Castel Sanguigno. Her deafness vanished as soon as she entered the holy chapel, and she regained perfect hearing.

June 6—Eight miracles of grace mark this happy day. Antonio Catallo, of Sermoneta, was so tongue-tied that it was sometimes impossible to understand him except through his gestures. Today, he was able to talk perfectly. Domenico di Tuziofante, of Olevano, was bitten by a poisonous snake and his body had become swollen and blackened. As soon as he promised to place himself at the feet of the Mother of Good Counsel, he felt fine with no signs of illness.

Santuccia di Bartolomeo, of Subiaco, numbed and shaking with pain as a result of having been bitten by a rabid dog (an incident that caused her to lose sight in one eye and to drag one leg), entered the holy chapel. At the feet of the holy image she was completely cured. Felicita di Bartolomeo, of Subiaco, clearly regained the sight that she had lost through continuous painful spasms in her eyes. Caterina di Giovanni Cocci, of Civitella, was in her last agony, her doctors having given up all hope. But when she invoked Mary Most Holy of Good Counsel, to whom she was devoted, she instantly recovered her senses and became completely cured.

Elisabetta Fantini, of Anticoli, a seven-year-old mute, to the surprise of all, began to talk today in the presence of the holy image. Giovanni di Pietro, of Menecone, today also regained movement and life. For many years, his body from the waist down was like a piece of dead wood that he could not move.

June 10—Francesco di Pietro, of Naples, had been seriously wounded in battle seven years earlier. A lance had struck him in the thigh and severed critical nerves so that he could neither bend his knee nor move his leg. While in Rome, he heard about the miracles of this holy image and asked to be taken to Genazzano without delay. Praying there with lively faith to Mary Most Holy of Good

Counsel, he received the grace he desired in superabundance and became healthy and free of the injury as though he had never been wounded.

June 11—On this day, a Hungarian priest named Janos Martini, who had become blind a year and some months before, instantly received perfect sight again at the feet of Mary Most Holy. On this same day, Pietro di Giovanni, of Marano, whose right arm was crippled, was cured in the holy chapel. Paulo di Giovanni, of Belvedere, who was in such a frenzied state that he would spend the night roaming through the fields, roaring and howling, repented and confessed in the holy chapel. At that instant, he regained his calm and mental health. Also today, Antonuccia di Niccolo of Fumone, a young lady who refused to take any nourishment after having been frightened and terrified by a horrible ghost that appeared to her at her home, was taken by her uncle to the holy chapel. She never trembled or was frightened again. Also on this day at the holy chapel, Bartolomeo di Giovanni, of Sermoneta, blind since birth, received sight in both eyes.

June 12—Behold another day marked by six gracious miracles. Giovanni di Pasquale, of Celle, who had suffered from dropsy for two years, entered the holy chapel and his illness immediately disappeared. Giovanna Petruccia, of Toffia, blind in one eye for twenty-four years, saw the light of day again at the feet of our holy image. Domenico di Antonio, from the Galera region, also blind in both eyes, regained his sight while pleading at the feet of Mary. Stefano di Giulano, from Morlupo, and his sister, Santa, both very young children, had fallen through some broken floorboards in their home onto hard stone and were almost dead when picked up. Their distraught father consecrated them with all his heart to this holy image. Behold! The two children's countenances became serene and joyful and they stood up and turned to their father. He, marveling at such a sudden miracle, brought them immediately to Genazzano to the feet of this most benign Mother.

Lorenzo Cicculi, of Nepi, who suffered spasms and was confined to his bed because of continuous pains in one leg, became healthy today at the feet of Mary. Silvestro Pauletti, of Rocca, tormented for three years and also confined to bed by a very persistent sciatica, turned with ardent faith to this holy image and became healthy right then and there. He ran to Genazzano to thank this most benign and amiable Madonna of Paradise.

June 13—Today, Berardo, the son of master Domenico of Roccantica di Sabina, was overcome with horror and fear upon seeing a diabolical ghost. Bordering on madness, he would tear at his flesh with his own teeth and utter immoral and sacrilegious words. The demon appeared to him again, taking the form of horrible worms. His parents, terrified with the desperate case, finally took him by force to Genazzano. As soon as they had pushed him inside the holy chapel, the son opened his tearful eyes and serenely turned them toward the holy image. At that instant, all his fears and diabolical infestations ceased. Today, also, Vincenza di Domenico, of Castropignano, who was blind in one eye, saw again. Giovanni Niccolo Nardi, of Mont'Acuto, who had been bitten by a poisonous snake and was unable to take any remedy, turned to the holy image. Holding a candle and a lighted torch, he placed himself at her feet, and that heavenly balm was sufficient to cure him. Antonio, the small son of Santo Paladi of Sermoneta, who suffered spasmodic pains due to a urinary tract disorder, was also cured in the holy chapel. Finally, Tomasso Mattei, of the province of Umbria, had been stricken with an epileptic seizure that left his right side paralyzed. Taken to the feet of Mary Most Holy of Good Counsel, he was cured through an obvious miracle.

June 16—Santa di Domenico Rocce, of Collepiccolo, possessed and tormented by diabolical spirits for six years, was set free from them as she saw the holy image.

June 18—Pavolo di Giovanni, of Colle, had such acute leg pains that he could hardly move. He was almost lame. Brought inside the chapel with some difficulty, he became healthy, very healthy, in the presence of Mary and her most blessed image.

June 20—This day is another festive, fortunate, and memorable day, one marked by Mary with thirteen notable graces. Antonio Gianucci, of Mazzola, who had been continuously bleeding from the nose for fifteen days and nights and suffering from constant fainting, was depressed and on the verge of death. As soon as he had recourse to this holy image with lively faith, his health was immediately restored and he came in haste to Genazzano to offer wholehearted thanks at the feet of Mary.

Clement, the totally blind son of a certain David from Hungary, happily recovered his sight today in the holy chapel. Domenico Niccolo di Antonio, of Receto, having spent the night in a hay barn, was bitten all over by poisonous snakes. His whole body was so swollen and blue that the doctors thought he would die that very day, in less than twenty-four hours. In such anguish, Domenico had recourse to this holy and very prodigious image and regained his spirit, vivacity, and courage. He came to prostate himself at the most holy feet of Our Lady and became entirely healthy.

Giacomo Giorgi, of Ferrara, who suffered attacks of epilepsy for seventeen years, was immediately freed of this sickness here in the holy chapel. Maria di

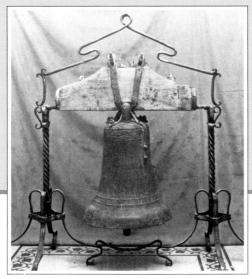

*A*ncient bell of the tower,
cast in 1424, now preserved in
the shrine's museum.
According to a pious tradition,
this is the bell that,
without human intervention,
first began to toll upon
the miraculous arrival of the
holy image on April 25, 1467.

*B*elow is the bell tower.

Stefano, of Colle, paralyzed from the waist down, recovered movement here. Margaret, daughter of Johann, a German resident in Rome who for three years could not move her arms or legs, returned to Rome perfectly healthy after having been taken to the feet of this holy image. Niccolo, son of Giovanni Alici of Rome, had a swollen stomach as hard as a rock and a shaking and unsteady head, but became free of every malady today at this holy chapel. Antonio Niccolo, of Turano, who had suffered from dropsy for three years and whose eyelids were so swollen that he could not open them, was likewise cured. Domenico Castaro, on whom the doctors had given up hope because of his stubborn and profuse bleeding, ran to the feet of Mary and there found the source of balsam and remedy for the illnesses. The same happened to Pietro di Giovan Mattei, who was cured of a year-long passing of blood.

Felice Girolamo de Laurentis, the son of Paolo from Rome, had stopped drinking his mother's milk. His virtuous mother consecrated him to this holy image and he began to breathe and nurse again. The happy parents brought him, now healthy and vigorous, to the shrine of Mary here in Genazzano. Paolo di Giacomo, also from Rome, was cured today of a malignant fever accompanied by sharp pains. Lastly, Fiora, daughter of Signor Magno Rellajo of Padua, had lost all movement on her right side and was so immobilized that she had to drag herself about miserably through life. She resolutely asked to be brought to this holy chapel in Genazzano where she devoutly pleaded before this holy image whose constant miracles resounded throughout Italy and where, today also, she was cured in an instant and shed many, many tender tears of intense joy.

June 25—Francesca di Giovan Tinelli of Olevano, a little girl of one-and-a-half, was dying from not nursing. Her mother consecrated her to this holy image and today she was cured and began nursing again. Because of this, her good mother brought her to the holy chapel. Also today, Rosa di Bartolomeo, of Gojo, whose arms had been crippled for seventeen years, started to move them again at the feet of the most holy image, happily and fully recovered.

June 26—Francesco di Paolo Nardi, of Castelo de Acumino, who had been possessed for almost two years, was brought to the holy chapel today and set free from the diabolical spirit. That same spirit appeared to him the following night and gave him a hard slap in the face, saying: "Traitor, I will blind you." However, the next morning Francesco confessed his sins with bitter tears and obtained from Mary the double grace of being cured in both body and soul. Stefana di Antonio, a resident of Rome from Tivoli, had her foot broken in three places when a large stone fell upon it. Distressed and covered with tears, she had recourse at the same moment to this holy image. Having been cured, she ran in haste to the feet of Mary. Also today, Ruggiero, of Tarante, who was suffering from a desperate puncture and given up on by the doctors, was cured instantly. Pietro Buonomo, of Faenza, obtained two notable graces this day: arriving at the holy chapel deaf and with an intestinal illness, he returned healthy and cured of both afflictions. Finally, Domenico Giuliani, a hopelessly ill four-year-old boy, was brought by his distressed parents to this holy chapel and became well at the same time as did the other sick people already mentioned.

June 27—Elizabeth, a daughter of a Fleming named John, whose whole right side was paralyzed for one year and three months, here received the grace from Mary Most Holy of Good Counsel that she had so long desired and prayed for. Also today, Margherita di Stefano, of Bionza, who limped miserably, walked properly again. And Juana Leone, a Castilian who had been paralyzed for thirty-nine years, was entirely cured and strengthened in this holy chapel. Margaret, daughter of Mark from Ragusa in Slavonia (now Dubrovnik, Yugoslavia), who was paralyzed in her right arm for six years, also received the same grace. Maria di Domenico, from the Canemorto region, whose nerves were rigid, recovered freedom of movement. Four-year-old Gabriele Niccolo Mariani, of Rome, who suffered from an intestinal hernia causing parts of his body to be blackened and swollen, was brought to the holy chapel by his parents today and suddenly cured. Giovanni di Arci, of Marino, who arrived at the feet of Mary totally blind, was favored with two clear pupils. Lorenzo di Pietro Paolo, of Rome, hung the crutches with which he arrived on the wall of the holy chapel as a sign of the grace he had received. *"Bacula dimisit, et sanus et liber factus est"* (He dropped his crutches, being cured and freed), states the public registry.

June 28—Dianora di Giovanni, a young woman from Bologna paralyzed since her sixteenth month, was immediately cured here in the holy chapel. Martina Chiarelli, of Rome, possessed for seven years, was set free today from the infernal spirits. Angeletta Nardi, of Rome, obtained the grace to be cured from her three-year paralysis. The public notice written then reads: *"Ex quo intravit Sacram Capellam, illico sana, et quieta estitit."* (Entering into the holy chapel, she immediately became calm and regained her health.)

June 30—Behold another joyful and fortunate day on which God further glorified the most adorable image of the Blessed Mother of Good Counsel with new and noteworthy graces. Antonella di Niccolo Pipeo, of Vicovaro, was continuously tormented for five years with the painful consequences of childbirth. So painful was her situation that many times she found herself on the brink of death. Today, having been brought here and having entered the holy chapel, she was completely cured and became so healthy that she regained all her lost vigor and strength. Angelo, the son of Giovanni, of Poggio, was cured today of his lame foot. Bona Narducci, of Alatari, paralyzed from the waist down, had her health completely restored. Giovanni Francesco, of Anticoli, a boy with an intestinal hernia, was brought by his mother, Margherita Schiavi, to the holy chapel and so miraculously cured that no sign of the sickness remained. Santo, the son of Bartolomeo Salini, of Morlupo, crippled for many years, was instantaneously set free from his sickness and became healthy and vigorous at the feet of the august image. Santa di Domenico, from Castelnuovo, whose limbs were paralyzed for two years, was brought here today and obtained movement, health, and strength.

Also, Maria di Bartolomeo Stefano de Orlandis, of Marano, who had been possessed for twenty-two years, found herself free of all the bonds of hell in the holy chapel. A certain man of Frascati whose last name was Guastacavalli woke up one night and found his throat inflamed and with three pustules in his mouth the size of hazelnuts from which a putrid, black liquid exuded. He searched in vain for three days for a remedy for this sudden and dangerous illness. As soon as he made a promise to go to the feet of this most holy image, he was immediately cured *"quasi ei nihil evenisset"* (as though nothing had ever happened to him). Finally, Gabriele, of Cremona, was gored by a furious bull so that a pocket of blood formed. He was near death amidst pains and contortions. Distressed and asking for mercy, he immediately turned with lively confidence to Mary Most Holy of Good Counsel. He was cured in an instant and came joyful and satisfied to visit the blessed image in Genazzano. He testified thus under solemn oath in the holy chapel: *"Ita se icolumen, sanum et liberum invenit, tamquam si nihil eidem accidisset."* (He found himself so unhurt, healthy and cured, it was as if nothing had happened to him.)

July 1467

July 1—Today, Nicholaus Ozzigi, a German who was completely weakened by a very stubborn quartan fever he had suffered for many years, came to visit this holy image. He immediately received from her the cure and the sought-for grace.

July 3—Margaret, a daughter of Johann, also from Germany, whose left arm was paralyzed, came today to recommend herself to the holy image. At the very moment that she prayed, her arm was cured.

July 4—Mark, son of a man named Stephen, from Hungary, came to visit this shrine in Genazzano. Having shot an arrow into a beggar's hat that held a small picture of Our Lady of Good Counsel, he was wounded when his arrow ricocheted off the hat in a wondrous manner. Distressed to the point of tears, he immediately entered the holy chapel. Mary Most Holy forgave him of the involuntary guilt and instantaneously cured him of his wound. [The complete story of this miracle is recounted in Chapter 6.]

July 5—Eleven-month-old Mariano di Giovanni Vecchi, of Palestrina, paralyzed since birth so that he could not stand even for an instant, was taken by his mother to the holy chapel and there consecrated to Mary. Immediately the child was perfectly cured to the joy of the whole family. Catherina, a German, had such a painful impediment in her limbs that her hands had been clenched into fists that she had been unable to open for a long time. In the presence of this holy image, her hands opened immediately and her painful paralysis disappeared completely.

July 7—A ten-month-old baby boy, Domenico Saracini of San Vito, had not taken any milk for six days and six nights and was already dying. After his distressed mother consecrated him to this holy image, he immediately recovered his strength and was cured. So, his mother brought him today to the sacred altar of Genazzano to tenderly present the small child as a gift to her.

July 9—Onorato Lecchi, of Piperno, was walking with a scythe on his shoulder. It suddenly fell and cut his foot so deeply that the bone was exposed. Maddened with pain, he extracted the point of the scythe. The foot remained limp and motionless, throbbing with incessant pain. He came today to the feet of this holy image to plead with her and received such a remarkable grace that his foot was entirely cured, leaving no scar.

July 11—Seven beautiful and very noteworthy graces mark this 11th day. Niccolo di Giovanni Muroli, of Agnani, reduced to extremity by a persistent fever, had just made a promise to come barefoot to the feet of the holy image when he was immediately cured. Santo di Pietro, also from Anagni, depressed and weakened by an obstinate fever, came pleadingly before the holy image and was perfectly cured. Angelo Pasquale, of Torre, lay dying for three days and three nights. When he was on the brink of death, his parents vowed to bring him here to visit the miraculous holy image and he immediately began to improve. To fulfill the promise, he came today in haste and full of joy. Giuliano Migri, also of Anagni, was sick with a very stubborn fever. As soon as he made a vow to visit the holy chapel he found himself cured and healthy. Giovanni Andrea Foreste, of Sarzano, rescued from death and prison in Siena came to Genazzano today to render ardent thanks to Mary Most Holy of Good Counsel. [This episode is also described in detail in Chapter 6.] Graziano, of Nepi, suffered from a serious intestinal hernia. Today, as soon as he prostrated himself pleading at the feet of the holy image: Immediately the interior organs were restored to order—*"illico viscera intus redacta sunt,"* as is noted in the public registry. Ambrosio Gasparini, of Stigliano, who fell from opulent riches to poverty, became a furious madman. Today, when brought with difficulty before this most blessed image, he was changed into a serene, calm, peaceful, and completely cured person: *"statim sanus factus est"* (he was cured immediately), as is noted in the public registry.

July 12—Antonietta di Niccolo, of Aquila, was possessed for three years in such a way that she would shake and howl as though possessed by a large pack of infernal wolves. Today, in this holy chapel, she was set completely sane and free. Niccolo Greco, deceived by a young woman named Orsolina, became possessed through a diabolical potion. So terribly possessed was he that day and night he would run through the city roaring and threatening people with his unsheathed sword. Brought with extreme difficulty to the feet of Mary Most Holy of Good Counsel, he was immediately set free of the horrible spell the moment he saw the holy image. [Niccolo's miracle is told in full in Chapter 6.]

July 15—Santo Mattei, of Nepi, was working in the fields during harvest when he suddenly succumbed to the plague then raging in the city. He immediately made a promise to visit the holy image and at once the poisonous condition disappeared. Pietro Giorgi, a Slovene afflicted with a deadly illness for whom the doctors held no hope, heard the following words from a companion who was returning from a visit to the holy image: "Oh, Pietro, why don't you make a promise to that miraculous image of Genazzano?" Turning his supplication toward her, he rose from his bed healthy and sound: *"statim dimisit illum febris, tamquam si nihil mali habuisset: et subito fortis et gaudens iter arripuit, ut Sanctam Imaginem visitaret."* (Immediately, the fever left him as though he had never been ill. Feeling strong and happy, he set out on his way to visit the holy image.) Thus was this miracle inscribed for all time in the register. Also, Giovanni di Angelo, of Paliano, who was infirm, depressed, and weakened by a persistent quartan fever, was completely cured while in the holy chapel. On this same blessed day, Troila, a beautiful young lady of twenty years who had been born with one leg shorter than the other, obtained from Mary the grace of a cure.*

---

* Having spent the entire day in the holy chapel imploring for a miracle, she returned to her town, Scrofano, the next day. Tired from the trip and afflicted because she had not been heard, she went to bed and fell into deep sleep. Suddenly she awoke with the sensation of having been cured, which indeed she had been. She then returned to Genazzano on July 17, 1467, to give thanks to the Mother of Good Counsel (cf. De Orgio, pp. 53-54).

July 18—Giovanni, son of Giovanni di Montefortino, was in Genazzano at the same time that the whole village of Segni had come, a few days before, to plead with the Empress of the Heavens to free that village from the contagion of the plague. With sudden surprise, he discovered a black tumor on his thigh; but he went to the holy chapel where he found himself freed from this danger of imminent death.

July 23—Daniele di Antonio, of Narni, who was horribly possessed and would lacerate his body with his own teeth, was set free from that hard and infernal slavery today in the holy chapel. Sebastiano and Lucia, the small children of Antonio Marciotti, of Genazzano, were near death. As soon as their mother promised to present wax images of them in the holy chapel, they left their beds joyful and jubilant and, along with their faithful mother, went to the holy chapel to give lively thanks to Mary.

July 28—Jean Godfrey of Orleans, who lived in the city of Sutri, was suffering from a painful intestinal hernia due to a severe accident. He was seized with fainting fits and spasms. As soon as he promised to go on foot to prostrate himself before the most holy image, he was cured.

July 31—Angelo Mattopelle, of Scrofano, whose left foot was lame, entered the chapel and was cured instantaneously. Angelo Mione from Montegiovito was a victim of a sudden illness that caused his doctors to abandon all hope. As soon as he promised to visit this holy chapel, he was freed from his sickness. Giacomo di Orazio, of Aquila, taken by a worm fever, was at death's door. When his father promised to take him to the feet of this holy image, he obtained the desired grace immediately. Finally, Francesco di Giovanni, from the Scrofano region, had paralyzed muscles and was unable to move. He turned to this holy image with a lively faith and was suddenly cured, freed of any impediment, and so went joyfully to the feet of Mary Most Holy of Good Counsel to fulfill his promise.

August 1467
August 1—Lucia Spalatri, of Subiaco, whose dropsy caused her whole body to swell, promised to come here with a wax statue of herself. She was miraculously freed from the painful sickness without delay. Giacomo, a Venetian physician in Casel Fajano, was kicked violently by a horse and seriously injured. As soon as he had recourse with lively faith to Mary Most Holy of Good Counsel, he suddenly found himself cured by an invisible hand. Gaspar Ciotti, of Avignon, a resident of the city of Nepi, was surprised by the contagion of a black swelling and, stunned by the unexpected calamity, he had no sooner made a promise

to the blessed image than he became freed and sound. Finally, Paolo, of Morlupo, who lives in Castel Fajano and who had been blind in the right eye for forty years, was happily cured in this holy chapel today.

August 6—Caterina Tome, of Nepi, was near death as a result of a black swelling from an infection that had afflicted the whole town. No sooner had she gazed upon a small tin image of Our Lady and Mother of Good Counsel that was brought to her in bed than the poisonous swelling disappeared. She got up and joyously came today to Genazzano to give due thanks to the holy image.

August 7—Behold, another very jubilant day illuminated by eight admirable graces of Mary Most Holy. Niccolo di Giovani, of Manfredonia, afflicted for a long time by a persistent sciatic pain which had caused lameness in his foot, had prayed for some days at the holy chapel, seemingly without being heard. As he was on his way back to Rome today to seek some relief, Mary Most Holy appeared to him and cured him instantaneously. [See De Orgio's account of this in the previous chapter.] All hope of recovery had been abandoned for Giacomo Petrini of Caprarola, who suffered from a putrid fistula in his leg. He had tried, without result, *"multas et infinitas medelas per diversos medicos"* (several and unending remedies from divers doctors), as is noted in the public registry after later verification of what had happened. Today he arrived to pray in the holy chapel and left totally healthy and free from any illness.

Constantino de Carolis, of Castelfollie, who died duly fortified by all the rites of the Church, rose up three hours later through the intercession and invocation of this Holy Mother of Good Counsel. [The complete account of this miracle is also to be found in Chapter 6.] Angelo Paolo, of Rome, on the verge of death caused by a malignant fever and sharp pains, consecrated himself to this holy image and immediately obtained the grace of leaving his sick bed healthy and sound. Antonio di Giacomo, of Mataloni, who lost an eye while carrying lime for the construction of the Church of Saint Mark in Rome, was miraculously cured by the opportune invocation of Mary Most Holy of Good Counsel. [See the complete description of this miracle in the previous chapter.] Also today, Matteo di Antonis of Nepi, who had been blinded by a blow to his eye, was cured and regained perfect vision in this holy chapel. Santo di Angellis, also from Nepi, suffered from four tumors but was miraculously cured by this holy image. Finally, Pietro Marcelli, also from Nepi, had been bedridden by a fever. He had scarcely entered the chapel when he was cured of his stubborn sickness.

August 9—Matteo di Carmignola, of Alatari, was relaxing at home when suddenly his house collapsed and buried him alive under the rubble. Everyone thought him dead and so set about removing his body from amidst that heap of wood and stone. At the moment of the collapse, he had shouted, "Blessed Madonna of Genazzano, help me!" To everyone's surprise, he was found alive, unhurt, and healthy. Also today, Angelo di Amico, of Rome, turned with ardent faith to this holy image and suddenly found himself free from an infectious fever that had caused him to vomit large worms.

August 14—Antonio Testa, of Campagnano, was a victim for a year and a half of a stubborn hemorrhage that caused him to lose a large amount of blood, as often as eight or ten times an hour on some days. Because of this loss of blood, he was weakened and expected death at any time. Urged to turn to this holy image with confidence, he promised to prostrate himself at her feet in Genazzano. As soon as he followed such good advice, he was instantly and miraculously cured. Similarly, Niccolo di Giovanni, of Civitaducale, a fragile little boy, had fallen from the city walls and was taken to his home almost dead. As soon as his parents turned with copious tears to this very miraculous image, he recovered and became healthy, smiling, and vigorous. Today, they came in haste to the shrine of Mary Most Holy of Good Counsel of Genazzano, gratefully bringing their healthy little boy and testifying to the miraculous event under oath in the holy chapel.

*   *   *

For the reasons mentioned earlier, the register of the first miracles of Mary Most Holy of Paradise or of Good Counsel were recorded up to this point.

During just one hundred days, the sick recover their health; unbelievers are punished, repent, and are forgiven; the dying return to life in a most surprising way; the possessed are freed from the claws of the devil; the Blessed Virgin appears. In other words, there occurred almost every miracle that can be imagined to preserve the bodies and save the souls of the devout faithful.

Now, the Mother of Good Counsel, so solicitous in heeding the petitions of each one in particular, also shows that she is touched by the necessities of Christendom as a whole. The following chapter is devoted to two celebrated interventions of Our Lady in favor of Christendom in which the devotion of its protagonists to the Virgin of Good Counsel is not lacking.

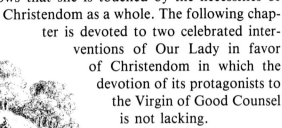

A Present-Day Testimony

FOR many years now, we have been surprised and amazed to frequently see foreign young men recollected in deep prayer in the chapel of the Madonna. We decided one beautiful day to speak with them, asking why they came so assiduously to our shrine. They told us they felt much attraction to the very beautiful image of the Madonna of Good Counsel, who showed special favors to the founder of their association: Plinio Corrêa de Oliveira. We expressed to them our desire to have some testimony about the matter, and Professor Plinio was kind enough to send us from Brazil the *Dichiarazione* that is printed here:

"*I*N December 1967, when I was fifty-nine years old, I had a severe case of diabetes. As a result, my right foot became gangrenous. For this reason, the doctor had to amputate my four small toes.

"This measure was taken without any hesitation, since he seriously feared that the gangrene would spread to the entire foot, which would then require a much larger amputation. In such a circumstance, would it be preferable to perform that larger amputation, once and for all? In view of this, I remained under observation in the hospital.

"Now, it so happened that some time before those events, I coincidentally began reading the book La Vierge Mère du Bon Conseil by Monsignor George F. Dillon (Bruges: Desclée de Brower, 1885). During the reading, I experienced a sensible consolation in my soul.

"Before my illness, my friend, Dr. Vincente Ferreira, had traveled to Italy and had the kindness of bringing me a picture from Genazzano representing the venerated painting of Our Lady of Good Counsel. That picture arrived at the moment of a spiritual trial that made me suffer much more than my physical malady.

"Since 1960, I had been president of the National Council of the Brazilian Society for the Defense of Tradition, Family and Property. Circumstances, not proper to go into here, gave me the certainty that it was in the designs of Divine Providence that this organization might *perform an extensive action on behalf of Christendom in Brazil, in all of South America, and even on the other continents.*

"On the other hand, I was convinced that my death, in this situation, would be ruinous for the effort which was beginning to flourish vigorously . . . an effort that I ardently desired to achieve for the greater glory of Our Lady before dying. So, I was in a state of true anxiety regarding the uncertainties of my clinical and surgical situation.

"On December 16, another friend, Dr. Martim Afonso Xavier da Silveira Jr., gave me the aforementioned picture on behalf of Dr. Vincente Ferreira. When I fixed my eyes on it, I had the unexpected impression that the figure of Our Lady, without changing at all, expressed for my sake an indescribable and maternal sweetness; that she comforted me and instilled in my soul (I do not know how) the conviction that the Blessed Virgin was promising me that I would not die without accomplishing the desired work. This suffused my soul with tranquility.

"I hold that conviction until today. And, by the grace of Our Lady, that work has prospered admirably, warranting the hope that it will reach its goal. When I was favored with this 'smile-promise' of Our Lady of Genazzano, I did not say anything to those present. Only much later did I speak of this to my friends. Two of them, who were visiting me at the hospital at the time I received the picture, upon hearing my narration, said that they had noticed that the figure of the Mother of Good Counsel looked at me with great pleasure, which fact caught their attention. However, they did not notice the 'smile-promise' that I mentioned. They sign the present declaration with me.

"Thanks be to the Blessed Virgin, my health was then restored in such a way as to amaze the surgeon and render the second operation unnecessary.

"I write the present declaration with my heart overflowing with love and gratitude to the Mother of Good Counsel of Genazzano.

> *"Plinio Corrêa de Oliveira.*
>
> *"São Paulo, May 10, 1985."*

In 1986, the July-August issue of *Madre del Buon Consiglio*, a magazine published by the Augustinian Friars of Genazzano, printed a testimony by Prof. Plinio Corrêa de Oliveira concerning a special grace—which he called a "smile-promise"—that he received from Our Lady of Good Counsel through means of a printed reproduction specially brought to him from Genazzano. The Italian text, as found in the magazine, can be read in Appendix 2, pp. 225-226.

CHAPTER 8

Lepanto and
Vienna:
Victories of
the Queen
"Terrible as
an Army Set in
Battle Array"

The Battle of Lepanto, 1571.

CONTEMPLATING pious pilgrims enraptured before the Mother of Good Counsel, lighting candles, and praying in silence, someone might be misled regarding the general state of Christendom in that second half of the fifteenth century.

Let us leave the small town of Genazzano, with its multitudes of pilgrims hastening to the feet of the holy image. Let us go instead to the city par excellence, Rome, the Seat of Christendom, the magnificent pedestal for that highest of thrones, the Chair of Saint Peter.

The Decline of Civilization: Fruit of the Decadence of Faith and Morals

To properly appraise that century, there is nothing better than hearing him of whom it can be said that he was "set over the nations and over kingdoms" (Jer. 1:10), him who, like the spiritual man of whom Saint Paul speaks, "judges all things and he himself is judged of no man" (1 Cor 2:15).

Four years prior to the translation of the image of Our Lady from Scutari to Genazzano, Pope Pius II addressing the College of Cardinals in the Secret Consistory of September 23, 1463, thus admonished the Pontifical Court:

"They say that we live for pleasure, . . . and there is some truth in their words: many among the Cardinals and other officials of our Court do lead this kind of life. . . . We must enter upon new paths, . . . Temperance, chastity, innocence, zeal for the Faith, ardor in the cause of religion, contempt for death and the desire for martyrdom, have exalted the Roman Church, and made her mistress of the world. She cannot maintain her position unless we follow in the footsteps of those who created it. It is not enough to profess the Faith, to preach to the people, to denounce vice, and extol virtue. We must make ourselves like those who offered their lives for the heritage of the Lord!"[67]

A terrible acknowledgement: "the fish stinks from the head downwards," says a well-known adage. If the Pope saw stigmas of decadence in his own Court, what is to be said of temporal society?

"The appetite for earthly pleasures is transformed into a burning desire. Diversions become more frequent and sumptuous . . . the growing yearning for a life full of delights of fancy and the senses produces progressive manifestations of sensuality and softness."[68] Thus does Prof. Plinio Corrêa de Oliveira describe the collapse of medieval society—austere, hierarchical, and sacred—before the first of the great revolutions that devastated Christendom: the Renaissance, soon followed by Protestantism.

The psychological and moral atmosphere at the end of the fifteenth and the beginning of the sixteenth century is likewise described by another author in these words: "The Renaissance threw Europe into the enjoyment of all kinds of abuses, sensations, and experiences with the wildest speed, as if it were a late revenge on the upright Christian vision implanted by asceticism and medieval practice. These latter constantly taught the painful way of life toward death as a preparation for a better eternity, proving the emptiness of pleasures, the merits of discipline and renunciation, the joys of Faith and the stable pleasures of the future Paradise. The great carnival of the Renaissance splashed everything with its shining foam, and the life of piety, in general, demonstrated a disturbing decadence of Christian fervor."[69]

The Painful Situation of the Church

The generation that witnessed the prodigious apparition was yet living when the abominable Lutheran heresy broke out, snatching away from the bosom of the Church a substantial part of the German empire and the Nordic countries and spreading foul emanations throughout Catholic Europe. The situation was such that Pope Adrian VI wrote at the end of 1522:

"We frankly acknowledge that God permits this persecution of His Church on account of the sins of men, and especially of prelates and clergy; . . . our sins separate us from Him, so that He does not hear. Holy Scripture declares aloud that the sins of the people are the outcome of the sins of the priesthood. . . . We know well that for many years things deserving of abhorrence have gathered round the Holy See; sacred things have been misused, ordinances transgressed, so that in everything there has been a change for the worse. Thus it is not surprising that the malady has crept down from the head to the members, from the Popes to the hierarchy.

"We all, prelates and clergy, have gone astray from the right way, and for

Falling into a Situation of Collective Sin Is Worse Than the Scourge of Wars or Natural Cataclysms

Regarding the manner in which the sin of a whole society comes to pass, Fr. Victorino Rodríguez y Rodríguez, O.P., writes: "There are specific collective sins of an enormous seriousness . . .: the democratic laws of abortion, of euthanasia, of antireligious teaching, of collective aggression, of generalized apostasy." He quotes Saint Paul: "And as they liked not to have God in their knowledge, God delivered them up to a reprobate sense, to do those things which are not convenient; being filled with all iniquity, malice, fornication, avarice, wickedness, full of envy, murder, contention, deceit, malignity, whispers, detractors, hateful to God, contumelious, proud, haughty, inventors of evil things, disobedient to parents, foolish, dissolute, without affection, without fidelity, without mercy. Who, having known the justice of God, did not understand that they who do such things, are worthy of death; and not only they that do them, but they also that consent to them that do them" (Romans 1:28-32). Father Rodríguez then comments brilliantly on the words of the Apostle: "With this text in view, it is easy to notice that the worst chastisement or punishment for sin is for God to permit a situation of collective sin. It is more painful than a scourge of epidemics, floods, accidents, war and all other physical evils with which God may punish sinful mankind in this world" (pp. 188-189).

long there is none that has done good; no, not one. To God, therefore, we must give all the glory and humble ourselves before Him; each one of us must consider how he has fallen and be more ready to judge himself than to be judged by God in the day of His wrath.''[70]

Consequently, the historical situation was disastrous. Nothing was more indicative of this than the European indifference in face of the brutal advance of the Ottomans. Few were the princes who resisted, few who followed the example of Hunyadi and Scanderbeg, devotees of the Blessed Virgin Mary. The majority let themselves be lulled by humanistic ideas, delighting in the atmosphere of the Renaissance and forgetting about the enemies of Christendom. Little by little, the Cross of Christ was set aside, supplanted by pleasures. The ''rebirth'' of the arts was nothing more than an excuse of the humanists for unearthing the old pagan world, buried a thousand years earlier under the ruins of the Roman Empire. Statues of beardless saints with the face of Apollo, Susannas with the face of the indecent Venus, bearded hermits reminiscent of the short-tempered Hercules, began to appear everywhere. Decadence was not the failing of just some souls; rather, decadence became the sin of a whole society.

In the book *Revolution and Counterrevolution* cited earlier, Prof. Plinio Corrêa de Oliveira describes in a masterful way the causes that led Christendom to this process of decadence that has continually worsened until our time.[71]

The Solution for the Crisis of Christian Civilization Can Come Only from Confidence in Divine Mercy and the Rejection of Vices

Whenever a crisis looms on the horizon, trying, like a black cloud, to darken the Church beneath its shadow, God sends His punishment, tempered with mercy. That mercy, without limits, has, like the sea, a name: *Mary.**

---

* God ''has wished that Mary should be so intimately associated with the divine plan of redemption and sanctification that they cannot be attained without her. . . . She is immaculate, full of grace, co-redemptrix and mediatrix because she is the Mother of God. Her divine maternity places her on such an exalted level that St. Thomas did not hesitate to say that it bestowed upon her a certain infinite dignity (cf. *Summa*, I, q. 25, a. 6, ad 4). And Cajetan says that Mary touches the boundaries of divinity (cf. *In* II-II, q. 103, a. 4 ad 2).'' These brilliant words of Fr. Antonio Royo Marín, O.P., in the aforementioned *The Theology of Christian Perfection* (p. 168), summarize the doctrine of the Church about this important point with much clarity and unction.

As we have seen, Albania, having succumbed to Mohammedan slavery for twenty-five years as a consequence of its sins, was at last able to free itself thanks to the devotion of its people to the image of Scutari. This deliverance was above all due to the devotion shown to her by one providential man, Scanderbeg. Since, however, the devotion of the people was not as it should have been, there appeared no one to follow in the footsteps of that great prince after his death. This being so, Our Lady left that nation.*

She established herself, then, in Renaissance Italy, in a Europe gone soft, and gave proofs of her amazing affection and mercy by performing innumerable miracles, as has been related in the preceding chapters. That devotion to the Mother of Good Counsel was not confined to Genazzano but, like a gentle wave running over the sands of a beach, spread throughout Christendom, perhaps searching for a new Scanderbeg. From the Pontifical States it passed to Naples, to Sicily, and thence to Spain. Crossing northern Italy, it reached Austria, Bavaria, Flanders, and Hungary.

First Effects on Christendom of the Devotion to Our Lady of Good Counsel

The warriors who defended Catholic Europe from the Mohammedan advance came from the regions where devotion to the Mother of Good Counsel had been spread. Despite the braveness of some, in several places they no longer fought against the Ottoman threat. Meanwhile, another more tremendous invasion was felt throughout Europe: that of Luther and Calvin. For the heresiarch of Wittenberg, "to fight against the Turks is to go against the will of God who uses them to punish our iniquity."[72] Yet, while attempting to stop the struggle against the

---

* Let us quote some words by which a great Mariologist of our times, Friar Antonio Bandera, O.P., briefly demonstrates the principle of the necessity of devotion to the Blessed Virgin: "Is it necessary to count on the help of the Virgin? Yes, because that is the way designated by God, from Whom all good comes. It is not sufficient, then, to be saved with Christ alone? Christ has enough power and more than enough to save. But it was He Who decided to exercise His unlimited powers uniting the Virgin to Him. In virtue of this will of Christ, there is no grace of salvation that is not related to Mary as His Mother." He adds: "If anyone would consciously depart from the idea that it was God Who assigned to Mary the place she has, he would be hopelessly separating from God Himself because whoever consciously rejects God's ways cannot walk in His direction" (in Ildefonso Rodriguez Villar, *Conoce a tu Madre: Mariología en diálogo*, adaptation and complement of Fr. Antonio Bandera, O.P., and Fr. Constantino Martinez, O.P., 7th ed. [Madrid: Editorial Fernando III El Santo, 1987], pp. 44-46).

followers of Mohammed, Luther, as well as Calvin, took up arms in a relentless fight against the Papacy and the Holy Church. In so doing, they dragged more than a third of Europe—until then solidly Catholic—into the dark abyss of their errors. It is significant that in the regions leavened with the blessings and graces of the devotion to the Queen of Good Counsel, the putrid emanations of Protestantism were curtailed in their advance.[73]

In spite of the ominous consequences of the Renaissance, this general decadence did not occur in Italy. There, devotion to the Madonna of Good Counsel produced an outstanding increase in fervor in all social classes. Concerning this, Monsignor Dillon writes:

"It may be here again remarked that one of the effects of the renewed devotion to Our Lady in Italy, consequent upon the coming of the miraculous image, was a vast improvement in the morals and religious fervour of the masses. This ascended from the populace and made its beneficial effects be felt in time amongst every class, until, at length, a saint of the truest type was elevated to the Chair of Saint Peter. This was Saint Pius V, who . . . was very devoted to the Virgin Mother of Good Counsel. It is incredible how much good this extraordinary Pontiff contrived to effect in the few years he reigned over the fold of Christ. He thought of everything. He forgot nothing. He cared for no man's praise or censure. He looked to God alone. Mary gave him, in a measure vouchsafed to few, that gift most needed for a ruler—the gift of Good Counsel. He reformed the Church truly and so effectively that no abuse escaped correction. While then the great Pontiff spread beautiful order in all the house of God within, he curbed at the same time the progress of the poison of Luther, and then prepared with all his powers to face the formidable, and more than ever threatening audacity of the Crescent.

"In this undertaking he looked, as he ever did in all his actions, to the Virgin Mother of Good Counsel for her powerful aid. He obtained it in wonderful measure."[74]

Winds of a New Crusade

Saint Pius V clearly perceived the urgency of unleashing a unified attack by the forces of the Catholic nations against Islam as an indispensable measure for the salvation of Christendom. Threatening Christendom by sea through the Adriatic and by land through the Balkans, the followers of Mohammed had created an enormous pincers by which they were trying to break Catholic Europe in two and reach its heart, the See of Peter. Indeed, the arrogance of the

Moslems had reached such a point that one of the sultans bragged of his intention to enter Saint Peter's Basilica on horseback.

Faced with this threat, Saint Pius V assumed the difficult task of bringing the Catholic powers together. Unfortunately, the princes were divided by their distrust of one another and variance of opinion as to the opportuneness of a new crusade and were moved first and foremost by their particular and selfish interests.

Just as it was with the Chosen People whose success in battle depended much more on their spiritual condition than on the numbers of their adversaries, as narrated in the Old Testament,[75] so, too, the victory of Christendom over the Crescent could be obtained only if the nations of Christian Europe, heeding the desires of the Holy Father, united and fought against the enemies of the Cross of Christ. But these spiritual prerequisites were lacking in Europe.

From Rome, Saint Pius V saw the intensification of the Ottoman danger and put all his energy into creating a military alliance among the Catholic kingdoms. The holy Pontiff wrote letters of concern—albeit in vain—to the emperor of the Holy Roman Empire; to the kings of France, Spain, and Portugal; and to the doges of the republics of Venice and Genoa, exhorting them to join together for the defense of the Church and of their own states, so threatened by the cruelty of the infidels.

The Pope relied, ultimately and above all, on one powerful ally who would help solve the difficulties. Saint Pius V was very devoted to the Mother of Good Counsel, to whom "he had recourse in all his necessities, more than a loving son, putting all his confidence in her in the most difficult trials. And he always besought from her, as his counselor, light and wisdom."[76]

With this assistance, the insistent papal diplomacy finally succeeded, after years of disappointment. Difficulties were resolved and a Holy League was formed consisting of Spain, Venice, Genoa, and the Papal States. Saint Pius V appointed Don John of Austria, son of Emperor Charles V, as supreme commander of the League. Marc Antonio Colonna, an Italian prince of thirty-five years who had lived in the shadow of the shrine at Genazzano, was selected to command the pontifical navy. He was intelligent, courageous, and, above all, devoted to the Mother of Good Counsel. Marc Antonio embarked with his troops and rendezvoused with John of Austria in Messina. The two men warmly embraced amidst the splashing of the sea, the shouts of sailors, and the salutes of cannons.

Good Counsel Determines the Future of Christendom

On September 10, 1571, the commanders met aboard Don John's flagship, *Reale*, to decide the armada's course. The Papal Nuncio spoke first, encouraging them to depart quickly. However, when news reached them that the Ottoman navy consisted of 286 ships—over one third more than the 208 in the Catholic fleet—Andrea Doria, the commander of the Genoese fleet, suggested that it would be imprudent to engage such a disproportionate force in combat. He added that the weather would be unfavorable because of the approach of winter. So, in the name of "good sense" and "prudence" all those who wished to avoid the fight fell in behind the Genoese admiral.

At that decisive moment, Marc Antonio Colonna intervened, vigorously defending the need to act immediately, it being the wish of the Holy Father, and his as well. He wanted to act "even at the cost of his own life." His resoluteness had its effect on the wavering "prudent" souls. The Christian commanders then unanimously decided to seek out the fanatic followers of the Crescent and engage them in battle.

This episode illustrates how a "yes," a "no," or a "maybe" uttered by a single person can alter the course of serious events, as has often happened in history, and thus determine the future of a people, a nation or even, according to circumstances, all of Christendom. It also serves as a precious lesson in marking the spirit with the constant necessity of good counsel—so abundantly dispensed by the Mother of God to those who ask for it with faith and perseverance.

As the final preparations for battle were underway, confessors made themselves available throughout the galleys. The Papal Nuncio proclaimed a plenary indulgence for those who, having confessed their sins and having received Holy Communion, prayed for the victory of the armada. The entire fleet fasted for three days. A Jesuit, repeating Saint Pius V's message to his appointed commander, said to Don John, "Hesitate not to engage in battle, for, in God's name, I assure you of victory."

Lepanto

On October 7, 1571, under a brilliant sun and cloudless sky, the fleets of the Cross and the Crescent faced off in the Gulf of Lepanto. Although a light breeze favored the Turkish galleys, a warm gust of divine grace filled the sails of the Cross of Christ.

The Ottomans, commanded by Ali Pasha, fired the first shot. This was immediately answered by a Christian cannonade that sank an enemy ship. The terrible battle of Lepanto had begun. Shots crossed in the air. The shouts of the boatswains could be heard above the thunder of the gunpowder. Whips cracked down on the bare backs of the galley slaves in the Turkish ships, urging them ever closer to the Christian vessels. The sea, red with the blood of Christian and Turk, was filled with the dead and wounded floating amidst debris of every kind.

At 11:45, Ali Pasha's galley took a shot that knocked down one of its enormous lamps. Still, it raced across the waters and, with the grinding noise of wood against wood and the cries of the sailors, rammed its prow into Don John's galley. Stuck fast together, the two ships formed an enormous fighting platform on the rolling seas, and a ferocious and relentless hand-to-hand combat ensued.

Twice the Turks invaded the admiral's ship, and twice the Christians drove them back, each time advancing as far as the mainmast of the Islamic vessel. In the third Ottoman onslaught, the janizaries surrounded Don John, who fought them off as the bodies of fallen comrades mounted up beside him. At this critical moment, Prince Colonna came to his aid. Driving his galley into the Turkish galley, the commander of the pontifical armada broke off the enemy's prow and quickly turned the tide of the battle. The followers of the Crescent were hurled into the already reddened waters. Ali Pasha was killed and his head, cut off by a soldier, was impaled on the point of a lance. The Catholic warriors shouted their victory and unfurled the standard of Christ on the Turkish galley mainmast.

The victors were later to learn that at the peak of this decisive battle, a radiant Lady had appeared in the sky, terrifying the Mohammedans with her majestic and threatening countenance.

Our Lady granted the victory to the Catholics, having inspired them with the "good counsel" of attacking. As the moment of the triumph approached, she revealed to her devotee, Saint Pius V, that victory was at hand. The Holy Father, then sitting in a splendid room of the Vatican palace listening to a report of his treasurer, at a certain moment stopped him with a gesture, approached the window, and entered into ecstasy. After a few minutes, he turned to the treasurer and said: "Go with God. This is not the time for business but for thanking God for the great victory attained over the Turks." The Pontiff went at once to his private chapel. As when Moses descended from Mount Sinai, rays of light emanated from his face. All of this occurred just as Don John was engaged in hand-to-hand combat with the Turks, and as Prince Colonna, inspired by the Holy Ghost, attacked the Ottoman galley, thereby snatching victory from defeat.

Two weeks later, the news confirming the victory reached Rome. The simultaneousness of the victory of the fleet and the vision of the Holy Pope was

Left. Standard of Lepanto (Museum of Santa Cruz, Toledo).

Below. Don John of Austria, Supreme Commander of the Catholic fleet (painting at the Palace of El Escorial, a replica of the original by Sánchez Coello, 1580)

Right. *Saint Pius V.*

Below. *This painting by Prospero Piatti (1885) of the holy image's solemn coronation shows some of the trophies taken from the infidels at the Battle of Lepanto adorning the chapel of the Mother of Good Counsel of Genazzano, where they were kept until the end of the eighteenth century.*

confirmed beyond doubt by calculations of the days and meridian. As a perpetual reminder of the power of the Mother of God, Saint Pius V added the invocation *Auxilium Christianorum* (Help of Christians) to the Litany of Loreto. Today, the Church celebrates the victory of Most Holy Mary at Lepanto in her Liturgy with the feast of Our Lady of the Holy Rosary—that powerful weapon used to vanquish the infidels.

No historian has ever dared to deny that the victory of the Catholic armada at Lepanto forever ruined Moslem power in the Mediterranean Sea. The faith and courage of Marc Antonio Colonna contributed greatly toward such a victory. John of Austria justly praised him in a letter to Saint Pius V. Recognizing the zeal of his captain, the Pope rewarded Marc Antonio with the great and ancient honor of a triumphal entry into Rome. He thus acknowledged that the glory of the victory was placed, in great part, on the prince of Genazzano. Flags captured from the Moslems and even pieces of their ships adorned the shrine of the Madonna of Good Counsel for a long time.

"That the Holy Pontiff," concludes Monsignor Dillon, "attributed the victory to the Virgin Mother, who gave him both the counsel to plan and the strength to effect his vast designs against Islam, is evidenced by the fact of his having enriched her sanctuaries."[77]

Trophies of Lepanto at Genazzano

Several young men from Genazzano fought alongside Marc Antonio Colonna in that historic naval battle. They, like their prince, brought back with them numerous trophies taken from the infidels to adorn the chapel of the Mother of Good Counsel. Those trophies were displayed there to celebrate the faith and courage of the valiant men of Lepanto and to stimulate the lofty admiration of successive generations.

However, at the end of the eighteenth century, the French Revolution erupted, and its effects overflowed the borders of France. In 1798, the revolutionary wave reached Rome where a Jacobin-style republic was proclaimed. During that emergency, Philip III Colonna, prince of Genazzano, gave his full support to Pope Pius VI who, in turn, appointed him general of the pontifical army.

In revenge, the republican troops retaliated against the Colonna possessions. "The shrine of Genazzano was despoiled of every ornament and, in particular, of the precious treasures and trophies of the war against the Turks who had been conquered with the help of Marc Antonio and his captains from Genazzano."[78]

Mohammed's Followers, Defeated on the High Seas, Continue to Harass Christendom on Land

The following century was also witness to a most powerful intervention of the Queen of All Hearts in the destiny of Christendom at the supplications of her pious and courageous sons.

Since its outbreak in the sixteenth century, Protestantism had continued its infiltration of the Christian nations all through the seventeenth century. An impassive England witnessed the beheading of Charles I, a victim of the extreme Protestant sects. In perpetual disputes, kings and princes in Europe, forgetting their concordat with Jesus Christ, did not hesitate to ally themselves even to the sultan of Istanbul in order to favor their own self-love.

In Rome, Blessed Innocent XI was at the helm of the Barque of Saint Peter, trying to open the eyes of a sinful Europe to the constant Moslem advances. Following their overwhelming defeat at Lepanto, the Turks never again assembled such a powerful fleet. However, their numerous infantry continued to make frequent and bloody raids into Hungary, Austria, and Poland, transforming churches into mosques but leaving the Protestants their temples. The Islamic generals used appropriate names, such as, "Ibrahim the Devil."[79]

Catholics Forgetful of the Interests of Christendom Consider Only Their Personal Advantages

The stories of the atrocities perpetrated by the Ottomans neither moved Christendom nor caused indignation. At the same time, Catholic blood was being shed in torrents in fratricidal wars, such as the mutual decimations of the French soldiers of Louis XIV and the Spanish *tercios* of Charles II. Indeed, given this lack of harmony among Christian princes yearning for small worldly glories rather than the glory of God, Christendom was on the verge of perishing. "Every kingdom divided against itself shall be made desolate" (Matt. 12:25).

The decisive factor for the future of Europe was the unity of the princes and their respective peoples against the common foe. They, unfortunately, no longer understood the necessity of living, fighting, and dying according to the august Cross of Christ that justly rested atop the royal crowns. So, the critical struggle would take place, not on the battlefields, but in the royal palaces.

As with Lepanto, history was repeating itself. The victor of this battle of souls rather than of swords would be the one who could unite the Catholic princes and make them turn their armies against the enemies of Christendom.

This glorious victory would fall to the Mother of Good Counsel of Genazzano!

The Holy Father, Innocent XI, in the Chapter of Saint Peter in Rome, decided to crown the image of Good Counsel of Genazzano with gold and precious stones and to implore heaven to bring about an agreement among the Christian princes so they would fight against the Turks.[80] So it was that, on November 17, 1682, the holy image was crowned by a canon of the Chapter of Saint Peter before a great multitude of the faithful.[81] In so doing, Blessed Innocent XI expected to procure special blessings that would effect a quick and favorable answer from the Catholic princes to his call for a crusade, a crusade for which he could already call on the services of the brave general John Sobieski.

John Sobieski—A Tireless Fighter

John Sobieski was born in Poland in 1624 to a family of crusaders. His contemporaries used to say of him that he was a man "whom you could not please unless you would please God."[82]

Chosen as king by the Polish magnates in 1674, he was from that time an untiring fighter against the Turks, sparing no effort to gather his turbulent nobles against the infidels. As early as 1679, Sobieski had called the Christian princes to a crusade against the Ottomans. He found but one echo, but a joyful echo, in Innocent XI, who called him the "bulwark of Christendom, the wall of bronze!"

In 1683, a few months after the crowning of the image of Good Counsel, many of the difficulties disappeared. On March 31, Leopold I, Emperor of Austria, and King John Sobieski promised to unite their respective forces against the enormous army that Mohammed IV was preparing for the invasion of Vienna.

Vienna Surrounded by Islamic Forces

The Moslems left Constantinople like infuriated animals, plundering, burning, profaning, and killing on their way to Vienna. The Christian troops had yet to reach the Austrian capital when, on July 7, the fires set by the Turkish hordes became visible from the imperial city. The emperor, lacking the means to defend the city, had to abandon it. More than 100,000 inhabitants fled with him. Seven days later, the Ottomans surrounded the capital of the Holy Empire.

Seeking divine help for the defenders, the Pope ordered the Blessed Sacrament to be exposed in all the churches in Europe. The Islamics bombarded the city for a month and a half convinced of conquering it before the arrival of the Catholic armies. Finally, Sobieski and his troops joined with troops of

Charles of Lorraine on the hills overlooking the capital. On Sunday, September 12, thirty-two princes of the blood, accompanied by thousands of nobles, attended Mass before the battle on Sunday, September 12. The celebrant, sent by Innocent XI, was an eloquent and fiery Capuchin friar who had an aura of holiness about him. The king of Poland served as acolyte. All the nobles received Holy Communion and the Capuchin blessed them saying: "In the name of the Holy Father, I tell you that, if you confide in God, the victory is yours!"

With the cry "God is our help" filling the air, 84,000 Catholic warriors advanced over the last hills toward the 300,000 Turks. The Moslems fought ferociously, the Christians, audaciously.

Owing to the Turks' overwhelming numerical superiority, the battle still hung in the balance at six o'clock in the evening. Finally, despite the imbalance in numbers, Our Lady granted victory to those who fought with faith. The Moslem camp, with its immense riches, fell into the hands of the Catholics. Vienna was saved.

King John Sobieski entered the city and went to the Augustinian church of Saints Sebastian and Roch. There, a *Te Deum* was sung in thanksgiving. This church was very near another Augustinian church in which a copy of the fresco of the Mother of Good Counsel, which had been touched to the original, had been venerated for more than a century. Thousands of ex-votos, many of them of pure silver, had been left there attesting to the shower of miraculous graces Vienna had received since the arrival of the image. Now another miracle, and no small one, could be laid at the feet of Our Lady: the salvation of the city from the Turks.

The multitude of people surrounded John Sobieski as he left the church. They kissed his hands, boots, and mantle, shouting *"fuit homo missus a Deo, cui nomen erat Joannes"* (John 1:6), repeating the words of the Gospel that Saint Pius V had applied to John of Austria on the victory of Lepanto: "There was a man sent by God, whose name was John."[83]

From that time, the Ottoman military power began to decline in Europe. Blessed Innocent XI, in thanksgiving for the victory, extended to the Universal Church the feast of the Holy Name of Mary, celebrated on September 12, and he ordered the crusade to continue under the dual command of John Sobieski and Charles of Lorraine. Again, Sobieski's courage stood out at the siege of Belgrade. In 1686, Budapest was reconquered after a century and a half of Turkish control.

The Queen of Good Counsel—Protectress of Christendom

The future of Christendom was at stake both at Lepanto and Vienna. At each battle, the heavenly protection of Our Lady of Good Counsel was felt. This is

Above. King John Sobieski, who was known as the terror of the Turks. This Polish king (1674-96) is considered the greatest of all of Poland's warrior-kings. In his early youth he showed great promise in the military by distinguishing himself against the invasions of the cossacks, Tartars, and Russians. He defeated the Turks under Mahomet IV and took their fortress of Kotzim in 1671, and was elected king of Poland in 1674. He went to the relief of Vienna when it was besieged by the Turks in 1683, was successful and expelled the Turks from the country. In this action he became the first Supreme Commander of combined military forces, all of the Austrian, Bavarian, and Saxon armies.

Top of next page. The armor worn by King John Sobieski at the Battle of Vienna.

Right. The relief of Vienna, 1683, by Frank Geffels. *Canvas*. Historisches Museum Der Stadt Wien.

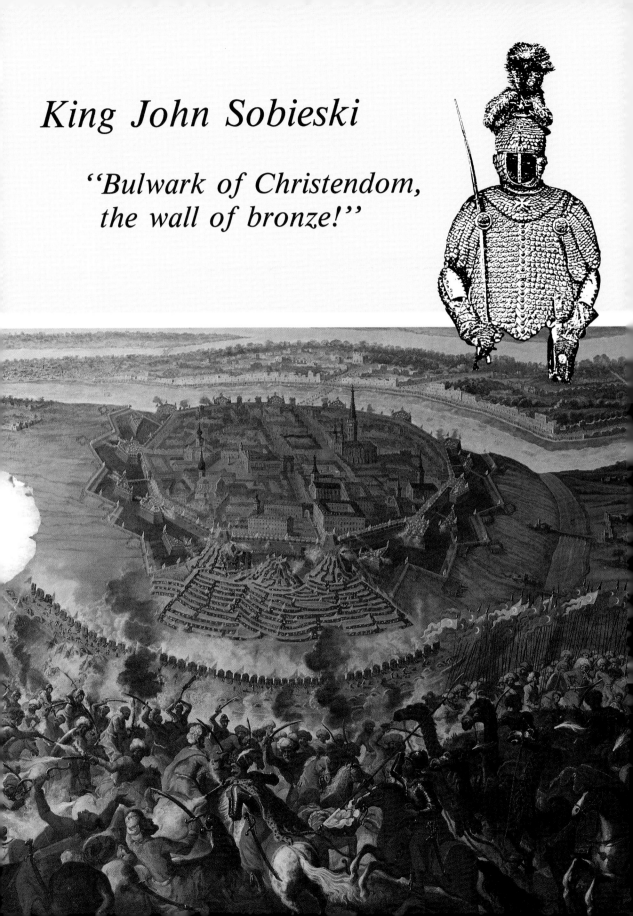

King John Sobieski

"Bulwark of Christendom, the wall of bronze!"

certainly one of the characteristics of the miracles of the holy image of Genazzano: She not only dissipates anguish and removes the difficulties that afflict all men individually, but she also protects them as a whole when they are threatened with destruction.

There is a verse of a Marian hymn that certainly applies to these two historical examples: "He who fights in the shadow of the Immaculate does not fear a thousand soldiers!"

*　　*　　*

We have already presented in the two previous chapters a summary of the first 161 miracles that the Madonna of Good Counsel deigned to work through her holy image of Genazzano. But there is more to this story of Our Lady's generosity, as historians are unanimous in recognizing: Copies of the image have also been miraculous and instruments of miracles in the same way as the original, even regarding changes in the color and physiognomy. This is especially true when the features and colors of the copy are close to those of the original. We will now go on to see some proofs of this.

CHAPTER 9

Not Only the Original, but Even Copies Work Wonders

CONCOMITANT to the growing renown of the prodigies performed through the holy fresco of the Mother of Good Counsel in Genazzano, Rome saw a flourishing of oratories under this invocation. In addition, reproductions in bas-relief, paintings, engravings, terra-cottas, and pen and ink drawings multiplied—all inspired by the original fresco in Genazzano.

From the Eternal City, copies quickly spread throughout Italy, launched out over the shores of the peninsula, and crossed the oceans—reaching as far as Patagonia and Indochina. Indeed, during the first few months after the apparition, holy cards had already begun to circulate in abundance. Beggars even had them inside their hats. It is not known how faithfully these reproductions imitated the original but, at any rate, the Mother of Good Counsel made good use of them to work her prodigies.

In Modena, One of the First Copies of the Holy Fresco

The oldest known copy, painted in the days immediately following the original apparition, is venerated in the city of Modena, in the parish church of Saint Francis. The considerable number of ex-votos in the chapel of the Madonna of Genazzano is undeniable proof of the motherly interventions of Our Lady in making use of this copy.

A short distance from Aquino, birthplace of the great Saint Thomas, there stands a high hill, Monte Cassino, the veritable eagle's nest chosen by Saint Benedict, patriarch and founder of Christian Europe, for the construction of one of his most famous monasteries. In that ancient abbey a copy of the image of the Mother of Good Counsel works its miracles. Since 1765, she has been the Patroness of the place, a title bestowed on her because of the constant protection she has always dispensed to its devoted inhabitants.

An Impressive Miracle: The End of the Siege of Genoa

In the eighteenth century, Genoa still maintained the remnants of its ancient splendor. Although the great admirals no longer lived there, it was still an independent aristocratic republic having among its glories sons spread throughout the peninsula and many cities of the world. Genoa, "The Superb," calmly hugging the shores of the Mediterranean, always knew how to gallantly resist the attempted sieges and invasions by its enemies.

But suddenly the unexpected happened: In 1773 the walls were breached and the city was seized. For three months, it was occupied by Austrian troops who forced the doge and several other nobles to pay homage to an alien sovereign. This so infuriated the Genoese that they rose up heroically and cast the enemy armies outside the damaged walls.

Winter imposed a truce on the hostilities. However, with the advent of spring, the thundering of cannons and the shouts of soldiers resounded once again over the reconstructed battlements. The cannonade continued night and day, irreparably damaging the hastily patched walls. Genoa was about to fall again into foreign hands, to the great indifference of its neighbors but not to that of its scattered sons.

An Augustinian Genoese living in Rome who had great devotion to the Virgin of Genazzano, besought that Intercessor on behalf of his native city. He ordered Luigi Tosi, one of the finest artists in the Eternal City and also a native of Genoa, to paint a copy of the image and display it in Genoa. He was confident that the Mother of Good Counsel would not permit a city placed under her motherly protection to be destroyed.

So, on a warm June day, the two of them, together with several religious from the Augustinian house, went to the shrine of Genazzano to pray before the holy image. Tosi, who had never been to Genazzano, marveled at seeing the delicate features, kindness, and grace of the Mother and the Infant. "Of all the copies, . . . none properly resembles it," he said enthusiastically, further affirming that "the features and lines . . . are so fine, delicate, graceful, amiable, and singular that the whole seems rather an angelic than a human work." [Tosi's complete declaration is transcribed in Chapter 3.]

Considering Genoa's urgent need of help from heaven, Tosi set up his easel and prepared his paints to begin the work. However, the more he looked at the holy image, the more perplexed he became. The images, seemingly alive, changed from one moment to the next, so that he knew not how to begin. The variations in color and expression were at once a cause of difficulty and of great joy.

Therefore, he humbly knelt before the image, reverently and respectfully beseeching the Blessed Virgin to enlighten him. Everything immediately became clear to him. He felt as if the features of the original had been engraved in his mind. Taking his materials in hand, he was thus able to begin. The artist spent a full two days on the work, doing almost all of the painting while on his knees and enraptured by the wondrous changes in the countenances of the fresco. The features and colors of his completed painting are so similar to the original that it is considered one of the best likenesses in existence.

The work finished, the artist returned to Rome to present it to the Augustinian, who had returned there to pray for his city. With the painting in hand, that pious religious immediately set out to cross the enemy lines and enter Genoa.

Fortunately, he was able to penetrate the siege and accomplish his objective. The Genoese received the painting with great demonstrations of joy, and they immediately organized a procession, which passed by the breaches the enemy had made in the walls, as if saying in their affliction, "Mother, behold our plight." Following the procession, the image was solemnly enshrined in the Augustinian church where multitudes flocked to her to plead on their knees for succor.

That same night, the Genoese were astonished by an unusual calm. The deafening roar of the cannons had ceased. The sentries, on duty atop the half-demolished walls, observed the fires in the enemy's encampment being extinguished one by one. With the light of dawn they verified, to their surprise, that the tents of the besieging troops had been struck and carted away. In the Mediterranean, the enemy fleet was unfurling its sails to catch the outgoing tide and reach the high seas. The siege of Genoa had been lifted.

Since that time, the Genoese have celebrated a solemn feast of praise and thanksgiving to the Mother of Good Counsel, who had saved the noble republic of Genoa.

The Eyes of a Painting in Frosinone Moved

Many of the prodigies worked by our Mother of Good Counsel are carried out deep in the silence of souls: inexplicable conversions, notable increases in fervor, flourishing of lofty vocations. These are beautiful realities, but invisible for eyes without faith. Sometimes, however, even unbelievers are obliged to recognize the intervention of Most Holy Mary.

An example of this is found in Frosinone, where a beautiful copy of the image is venerated in the church of Saint Benedict. This beautiful copy had previously been venerated, long time, in the private oratory of the Ciceroni family villa in that town.

In 1796, there was among Our Lady's devotees an honest and hardworking servant, happy in her modest condition—for that time was far removed from the false myth of the revolted humble classes—and even happier for being able to pray in her leisure time at the feet of the picture of Good Counsel.

In the calm of the evening of July 10 of that year, this young servant of the Ciceroni household and her fifteen-year-old sister were entertaining themselves after completing their chores. They decided to go to the oratory to pray before the copy of the Mother of Good Counsel. To the surprise of both, as they knelt in prayer, they saw the image open and close her eyelids and clearly move her eyes in various directions. The astounding phenomenon repeated itself to the great joy of both sisters who ran to call all the household—ladies, gentlemen, and servants—so that they, too, might witness the miracle. All of them crowded into the oratory to catch a glimpse of the prodigy. They were not disappointed, for the eyes moved once again. It was not possible! A painting whose eyes moved? The news spread quickly.

The next day, neighbors, relatives, friends, and acquaintances flocked in great number to see the painting and pray. The Virgin continued to open and close her eyes. In a short time, all Frosinone knew of the events. The population hastened en masse to see the prodigy, for, despite the uninterrupted repetition of the miracle since its beginning, no one knew for sure that it would continue on the next day. Nothing like this had ever been seen before—and in front of so many people.

The street was thronged. Even though the house was large, it could in no way satisfy the desire of all the devotees to see the painting. All the town's residents simply could not fit into one house. So, the Ciceronis, the owners of the painting, presented the problem to the priests of the church of Saint Benedict. They, in turn, quickly prepared an altar in the sacred place. So the image with the eyes that moved was taken there. The miracle persisted at least six months and was viewed by thousands of people. So great were the conversions and graces that there is not sufficient space here to describe all of them.

Even today, almost two centuries after the supernatural event ceased, that reproduction of the Madonna of Genazzano is still a source of gifts from the Immaculate Virgin.

In Madrid, Another Copy Spoke

An even more impressive miracle occurred on another occasion. A copy of the painting in Madrid moved its lips and spoke with a human voice.

A young son of a marquis wanted to especially preserve, among all the virtues, perfect chastity, virginity of body and soul. In his attempts to follow such a high ideal, however, he was besieged by temptations and occasions of sin everywhere. Social life offered him endless pleasures and all the easy paths to sin. His resistance took perhaps more courage than that of Scanderbeg against the Turks. The Albanian hero overcame fear in face of physical violence; the young marquis fought moral violence in face of human respect, mockery, ridicule, malicious insinuation, and general scorn. The shrewd enemy, the devil, constantly preparing traps for the young man, could count on powerful allies: the passions that raged inside him. In a word, the coalition of the world, the flesh, and the devil engaged in one assault against the young man.

This young noble frequently knelt to pray before a copy of the fresco of Genazzano, seeking counsel and strength. One day, while so praying at her feet, Our Lady, who never forsakes anyone who seeks her help, moved her lips and spoke to him. She advised him to leave the world and join the Society of Jesus, and gave him all the strength needed to face the obstacles presented by his relatives regarding this new and solemn decision. The image spoke several times to the young man, who eventually became a great saint and was proclaimed a patron of youth: Saint Aloysius Gonzaga.

"In the Jesuit Church at Madrid a picture has been placed to commemorate this event. Aloysius is represented kneeling before Our Lady, who holds the Divine Child in her arms. Above her head the Holy Ghost hovers, and she is surrounded by angels. The picture bears the inscription: '*S. Maria boni consilii, quae in Collegio imperiali Matritensi B. Aloysio voce clara et manifesta suasit, ut Societatem Jesu ingrederetur*' (Holy Mary of Good Counsel, who in the Imperial College of Madrid advised the Blessed Aloysius, with a clear and obvious voice, to join the Society of Jesus)."[84]

This painting was burned by the communists in the 1930s. It had been venerated since time immemorial in the church of the Imperial College of the Society of Jesus, today the Cathedral of Madrid, and was one of the favorite images of Madrid's faithful. On another occasion, the image spoke to Diego de San Victor, a martyr of the Marianas Islands.

A Copy Unscathed in a Flaming Oven

The Beloved Disciple, Saint John, says at the end of his Gospel that Our Lord performed so many miracles that "if they were written every one, the world itself would not be able to contain the books that should be written" (John 21:25).

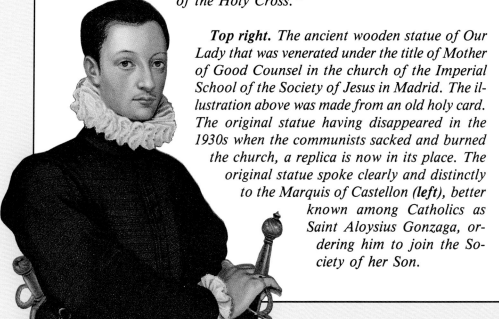

Painting of the Mother of Good Counsel taken to Brazil by Fr. José de Campos Lara in 1785 and venerated for years in the chapel of the Saint Louis Jesuit High School, first located in the town of Itu but later in São Paulo. The origin of this at once admirable and mysterious painting seems to conceal the secret designs of the Mother of God toward Brazil, the "Land of the Holy Cross."

Top right. *The ancient wooden statue of Our Lady that was venerated under the title of Mother of Good Counsel in the church of the Imperial School of the Society of Jesus in Madrid. The illustration above was made from an old holy card. The original statue having disappeared in the 1930s when the communists sacked and burned the church, a replica is now in its place. The original statue spoke clearly and distinctly to the Marquis of Castellon (left), better known among Catholics as Saint Aloysius Gonzaga, ordering him to join the Society of her Son.*

Mutatis mutandis, if it were possible to tell about all of the miracles of the Mother of Good Counsel, where would we find the space and the time to do so? How many decades the editing of so many graces granted by Mary would demand! For example, how interesting it would be to present an account of the reconversion of Calabria to the practice of religion by virtue of a likeness of the painting taken there by an Albanian of tireless zeal, Father Stephan Andrea Rodota.

Let us pause here only to admire with pious devotion the events that took place in the city of the Popes when a copy of the image, inadvertently thrown into the fire, was miraculously saved from the flames. Monsignor Dillon recounts the event:

"On that day [September 4, 1796] it happened that the Master of the bakery of Monte Compatri, belonging to the Prince Borghese, had occasion to white-wash his premises. While preparing to do so, a picture of Our Lady of Good Counsel printed on common paper got accidentally detached from the wall and, inadvertently of course, became mixed with firewood. With the same inadvertence, the paper was thrown with the wood into the oven. As usual, the whole mass was ignited and, in a little while, when the wood was supposed to be sufficiently consumed for the heating purposes, the baker looked within and, to his astonishment, saw a piece of paper unburnt amidst the red hot embers. His first impulse was to mix it anew with the burning matter, and he actually did so. To his still greater astonishment, however, his efforts were useless. He therefore withdrew the paper from the oven, and found it to be the picture of the Madonna of Good Counsel inadvertently mixed with the firewood. His surprise and that of all who heard of the miracle may be more easily imagined than described."

Monsignor Dillon says further on that "there is yet a slight sign of burning at the extreme edges, and a few sparks have apparently alighted upon the figures of Jesus and Mary. The devout Romans continue to visit this picture, now enshrined under a tabernacle, and to pray there for the dead. They call it "the Liberatrix of souls from the pains of Purgatory."[85]

Much could also be said about the miracles brought about by reproductions of Our Lady of Good Counsel in the Imperial Court of Austria and in Bavaria. No less impressive is the protection she dispensed in the Low Countries to those who venerated copies during the terrible cholera epidemic of 1859. Many of her devotees were miraculously cured, and not one of them died. The supernatural prodigies she performed in Prague, by means of another copy, would also furnish material for a long narration.

The Liberatrix of the Souls in Purgatory

IN the chapel of the Teutonic cemetery in the Vatican, a reproduction of the image of Our Lady of Good Counsel of Genazzano is venerated as the "Liberatrix of the Souls in Purgatory." The picture, slightly burnt at the edges, is set on a small easel. On the back, on an attached sheet, the following declaration is found:

"On September 4th in the year of Our Lord 1796 // Ad perpetuam rei memoriam. *We make known to everyone that the image of Most Holy Mary of Good Counsel that is seen on the front of this small picture on slightly burnt paper, was previously hanging on a wall in the room of the Master of the bakery of Monte Compatri. Since he wished to paint his room, he took this image down and inadvertently placed it among the bundles of wood used for heating the oven. After those bundles were burnt, the baker, Pietro Settele, approached the oven opening it in order to remove the coals. In doing so, he saw a piece of*

paper and, not knowing what it was, pushed it in so it would burn. Some time later, seeing the same paper, he removed it from the fire to look at it, and saw that it was a picture of the miraculous image of Most Holy Mary of Genazzano. It was marvelously preserved from the oven flames, being burnt only on the bottom edge and on one side. Mary and her Most Holy Son, as can be seen, were only touched by some small sparks of the fire. That portentous miracle happened in the oven of Monte Compatri, feudal property of His Excellency, Prince Borghese. It was recorded here on the back of the aforementioned most holy image so that its memory may pass from father to son and from son to grandson and so on perpetually in order that the devotion to such a great Mother be kept forever and increasingly alive; Pietro Settele, to this purpose, had this small tabernacle built so as to perpetually preserve it, as well as for his own private devotion.''

Short Prayer to Mary Most Holy of Good Counsel to Implore Her Protection

O Mary of Good Counsel, inflame the hearts of all thy devotees, so that all of them have recourse to thee, O great Mother of God. Deign, O most worthy Lady, that everyone choose thee as teacher and wise counselor of their souls, since thou art, as Saint Augustine says, *et consilium Apostolorum, et consilium omnium gentium*—the counsel of the Apostles and counsel of all peoples. Amen.

A transcription of the original Italian is found in Appendix 2, on p. 227.

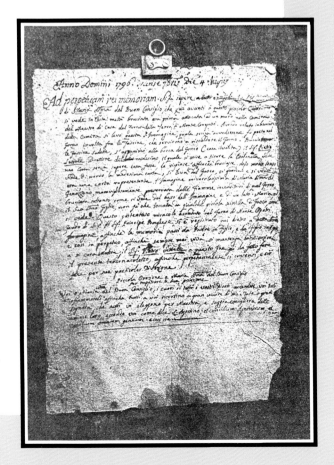

The Mother of Good Counsel in Brazil

Brazil: Who would have had that country in mind when Petruccia prayed by the unfinished walls of her church waiting for the holy image? Who could have even suspected the existence of such a land when Scanderbeg, under the protection of Our Lady of Scutari, defeated the traitor Hamsa or the renegade Baladam? The Catholic Faith was carried there by Portuguese ships. With this Faith came devotion to Most Holy Mary, our very loving and kind Mother, revered, among other titles, precisely as Mother of Good Counsel.

Images of Good Counsel are venerated today in many places in that continent-size country. *Bom Conselho*, or Good Counsel, is, in fact, the glorious name designating a city in the state of Pernambuco in the interior of the country. A painting of Our Lady is honored under the invocation *Mater Boni Consilii a Genazzano* in a convent founded in that city.[100]

Among the many reproductions of the holy fresco in Brazil, there is one in particular which proves that the country was the object of special protection, for it was the Mother of Good Counsel herself who deigned to send it there.

A Brazilian in Italy

In 1760, King Joseph I of Portugal, whose sovereignty spanned the Atlantic Ocean and encompassed Brazil as well, expelled the Society of Jesus from all his lands. Two brothers, scions of the Campos Lara family, one of the most distinguished in the city of Itu in the state of São Paulo, were then novices in the ranks of the sons of Saint Ignatius of Loyola serving in that country. The two, Miguel and José, wanted to accompany their brothers-in-vocation into exile. Their relatives, friends, and acquaintances, however, deeming exile too radical a step for such young men, argued that the brothers could still become priests in another religious order.

A difficult and painful discussion ensued. Finally, however, God's call prevailed and Miguel and José de Campos Lara left for Rome along with the Jesuits. Upon completing their priestly studies in Italy, they were ordained. A short time later, Miguel died, and José was sent by his superiors to various locations.

The Masonic governments at that time were strongly pressuring the Pope to suppress the Society of Jesus. The defamations and demands reached such a point that in 1773 Clement XIV abolished the Society. This act posed an unexpected dilemma for Father José de Campos Lara. It seemed that the Vicar of

Christ himself, to whose very service he had been consecrated in the ranks of Saint Ignatius, was now sending him away.

From then on, his life was not easy. Perseverance demanded both sublime faith and a high degree of heroism. Years passed under these trying conditions, ten long years without family or friends, distant from his native land, an orphan in his own religious order. Ten years, living amidst a softening and fawning world that at every instant whispered: "Forget vain idealism. Leave the prejudices of the past, this is the century of the Enlightenment and of liberty! Look for a wife—or a companion; work feigning honesty; take advantage of this short life. You are still young and intelligent!" Europe, in the constant pursuit of the enjoyment of life, was sliding heedlessly toward the horrors of the French Revolution and the bloody Napoleonic wars.

An Unexpected Encounter at the Seashore

Then came the year 1785. Twenty-five years had elapsed since José de Campos Lara had left Brazil. It had been twelve years since he had worn a cassock, or, better, the uniform of the Society of Jesus, that militia of Saint Ignatius formed under the banner of Christ the King. One day, Father de Campos Lara went for a walk along a deserted beach in order to spend some solitary time in thought. The pleasant murmur of the waves breaking upon the shore provided a soothing balsam for his sorrows and worries.

Suddenly, he saw a young man approaching him. They exchanged greetings and, then, the young man offered him an oil painting of the Mother of Good Counsel, asking him to take it to Brazil. The stranger told him that in the place she would be venerated a large Jesuit school would one day be built. The surprised priest objected that he had not the resources for such a trip, but the unknown young man replied that the captain of a certain ship which had just arrived in port would provide him free passage. Consoled with such news, Father Campos wanted to bid farewell to his interlocutor, but, behold, the young man disappeared before his eyes. Convinced that he had seen a heavenly spirit under the guise of a young man, the priest rushed to the quay and found the indicated ship. The ship's captain agreed with exceptional compliance to take him on as a non-paying passenger, thus fulfilling the mysterious stranger's first promise.

Travel by ship in those days took a long time. So, Father Lara was able to pray at leisure before the beautiful copy of the Mother of Good Counsel, beseeching her to grant him much counsel about his future course.

A Long-Suffering Man with Holy Desires

After disembarking at the Brazilian port of Santos, he travelled thence to his native city of Itu. The second part of the angelic message had been accomplished: He had arrived safely and soundly in his native land with the painting. Now, the only remaining step—*only*—was the restoration of the Society of Jesus and the opening of a school in Itu. He had only to confide, to pray, and to wait. His parents, who had died some years before, had left him a country house as an inheritance. There he built a chapel to venerate the image.

Obviously, Father Campos had been called by Our Lady to be the classic "man of desires" (Dan. 9:23), a long-suffering man with holy desires, like the old Simeon. He, however, had not the opportunity on earth like this prophet to sing *"nunc dimittis servum tuum, Domine"* (now thou dost dismiss thy servant, O Lord, Luke 2:29).

He had already spent twenty-five years waiting in Italy. In Brazil, the time before the accomplishment of his mission on earth was to be even longer. "Here, on this farm and in this house," he used to tell his acquaintances, "the Jesuits will come to establish a large house of education."[86] Among his listeners, there were, possibly, some who were skeptical: "Poor man, so many sufferings must have affected him." But, there were also men of faith who noted a prophetic resonance to his words.

In 1814, twenty-nine years after his arrival in Itu, news arrived from Rome that Pope Pius VII had restored the Society of Jesus! Full of emotion, Father Campos thanked the Mother of Good Counsel. Another part of the prophecy had been fulfilled. His wait, however, was not yet at an end.

Thirty-five years after his return to Brazil, Father José de Campos Lara closed his eyes forever. "Blessed are the dead, who die in the Lord" (Apoc. 14:13). He died in the peace of the Lord, in which peace he had always hoped, as against human hope.

After Eighty-Seven Years, the Jesuit School Becomes a Reality

Father Lara left both the farm, with its large house and a church already under construction, to Father José Galvão de Barrosas Franca, his nephew. This exemplary priest gave the property to the Society of Jesus when the Jesuits resumed their activities in Brazil. In 1868, the sons of Saint Ignatius laid the foundations for a large school, which was completed four years later.

In 1872, the painting of the Mother of Good Counsel that had been venerated until then in the old chapel of Father Lara (transformed into a council room of the Confraternity of a Good Death and the Assumption) was enthroned above the high altar of the new church of the school. Eighty-seven years had passed since it had been miraculously delivered to the Brazilian Jesuit on the sands of an Italian beach.

In 1918, when the Jesuit school was relocated to the city of São Paulo, the copy of the image of Genazzano was transferred as well. For a time, the school at Itu was converted into a barracks and the chapel was used as a dormitory for troops. In the 1980s, the chapel was reconsecrated and the Jesuits have placed a reproduction of the famous painting there.

*   *   *

It is impossible to write about Our Lady of Genazzano at any length without having one's thoughts occasionally return to Albania, that country so afflicted by infidelities but so definitively linked to the holy fresco. In this, one turns one's eyes to the city of Scutari where another impressive miracle took place. That reproductions of the painting are means of extraordinary graces, as we have just seen, is no small thing. Such considerations move one to greater piety and Faith. In the next chapter we will see yet another miraculous manifestation of Our Lady's munificence, a strong action of presence in an empty niche.

The old Saint Louis High School in Itu (São Paulo State, Brazil).

CHAPTER 10

A Light Illuminates
an Empty Niche

AS we have seen, the same fresco of the Mother of Good Counsel that
is found today in Genazzano was venerated in Scutari for more than
two centuries, and devotion to the holy image was the impetus behind Scanderbeg's heroic resistance against the Mohammedans for two decades. After the
death of this warrior, the Albanians still held out against the Turks for twelve
additional years. Scutari, besieged several times, faced its worst onslaught in 1474.

Eight thousand battle-tested Ottoman troops surrounded the city. Despite the
fact that they had destroyed all the walls, the city still resisted. The Catholics
faced extreme deprivation and more than two thousand inhabitants died of thirst
and hunger. Still they fought on.

The entire population knew that the holy image of the little chapel of the Annunciation, also called Our Lady of Good Offices and now known as *Mater
Boni Consilii*, was no longer in her shrine to dispense her motherly protection
against the enemy. The soft- and faint-hearted wanted to surrender, succumb-
ing to and arguing with the false boast of the Turks that, after the death of Scanderbeg, Albania "was given them by God because of the sins and unworthiness
of the Christians."[87]

Nevertheless, the flame of Faith still lived in many souls. The Catholic lead-
ers preached the need of penance as the way to attract the protection of heaven
and the holy fresco. Expiation rose to heaven like a perfumed incense. Providence did, indeed, intervene. The Turkish cannon shots hurled against the church
of Saint Nicholas of Bari ricocheted and, returning to the Moslem ranks, decimated the infidels. This time the city was saved.

The defeat aroused such hatred in Mohammed II that, as a symbolic reminder,
he ordered a herald to remain at the door of his palace to proclaim at his entering or leaving that Scutari was not yet Turkish. His wishes were soon to be rewarded.[88]

In 1478, the number of those besieging the city reached 300,000. During the siege, 100,000 Islamics had died, but the inhabitants of Scutari could resist no longer. By the end of the year, a surrender was prepared. The gates were opened and the city was delivered to the followers of the Crescent on January 26, 1479, twelve years and nine days after the death of Scanderbeg.

Despite this defeat, the nation and city which sheltered the holy image were not forgotten by her in this hour of misfortune. Miracles performed on behalf of the faithful Albanians continued to take place with special brilliance in the ruins of the ancient shrine at Scutari.

The Little Chapel Was Not Destroyed

The vicar-general of Scutari, Monsignor Angelo Radoja, wrote in 1878: "The Turks, then, exasperated for the loss of innumerable soldiers, were scarcely masters of Scutari when, worse than Vandals, they destroyed all inscriptions and marks of the Christian Religion, and burned books and other scientific and religious objects. . . .

"It is an incontestable fact that they themselves in their fury left intact to the Christians the two churches, namely the little church dedicated to Our Lady of Scutari, and the other to Saint Mary Magdalen of Tebuena, four minutes walk from the market, which yet subsists in our power. They turned into mosques the other churches, but nevertheless, they could not succeed in obliterating from the memory of the Christians that, in the little church at the foot of the fortress, in the suburb of the Turks called Ali-Begh-Mahalasi, there did exist the miraculous image of which we speak."[89]

The Catholics exiled from Scutari received permission to live in the nearby localities of Susa, Tebuena, Berdizza, Cucci, and Remanagi. From time to time they would secretly come to visit the church that had sheltered the miraculous image. Why were they so moved? It was the certainty that the holy image had been there, affirms Monsignor Radoja.[90]

"The conditions imposed by Mohomet upon the vanquished," states Monsignor Dillon, "were conversion, tribute, or extermination. Conversion secured the goods and civil rights of the apostates. Consequently, the rank and file of the invaders generally preferred that the conquered should hold fast to their religion. That course secured the largest amount of spoils to the victors. Christians worsted in war and unable to fight further had, therefore, either to expatriate themselves, or to descend into a condition not far removed from slavery. As a rule, those who could do so, fled as soon as it became certain that resistance was useless; and so, it often happened that the Turks, on becoming masters of a city, found it deserted by its Christian inhabitants. Sometimes, policy caused Christian traders and artificers to be kept, but generally, jealousy led to their exclusion altogether, more especially when their presence might prove dangerous.

"This was to a great extent and for a long time, the case with Scutari, one of the strongest fortresses in Albania. Every stranger was regarded with suspicion. Inquiries about religious matters always met with instant repression. Therefore, after the Turkish occupation of the city, it was clearly impossible for the Fathers of Genazzano to learn anything regarding the condition of the little church out of which the miraculous image had departed.

"About the middle of the last century, however, this surveillance, though still strict, relaxed somewhat, and enabled the agent of the Catholic missions of Albania in Rome to give most interesting information regarding the Madonna of Genazzano.

"From this source it was gathered that not only had the people of Albania known of the existence of the sacred Image, but they had never lost their devotion to it. They all knew that it had departed from its original temple. . . . The remembrance of their last king, and of his deep devotion to it, still subsisted. Even the very walls of the sanctuary in which it once stood were deemed sacred, and whenever the Turks permitted, were most piously visited in pilgrimage by the surrounding country people. Furthermore it appeared that no power of the Turks was able to convert its temple into a mosque—a fate which befell all the other Catholic churches of Scutari—because of supernatural prevention. Neither could they, though they often tried, convert its materials to profane uses. Lastly, it was believed that many miracles and supernatural occurrences took place in its ruins. The first account furnished comes from the Albanian nobleman Count and Captain Stephen Medin, and was written as early as 1745, to Signor, Count John Baptist Medin."[91]

Miracles of Our Lady around an Empty Niche

Count Stephen Medin visited Scutari to undertake a detailed investigation of the miracles that had taken place in the church of the Annunciation, the ancient shrine where the holy fresco of the Mother of Good Counsel was venerated for two hundred years. In a letter of July 25, 1745, to a relative, Count Medin narrates some extraordinary miracles.

"As regards the commission Your Excellency gave me to examine whether there still be a church in Scutari dedicated to the Blessed Virgin and if there be in its interior a niche, or another place, known to have had at a certain time

A short distance from Scutari stood the church of Our Lady of Good Counsel, destroyed by the communists in 1967. It had been built over the ruins of an ancient church, where the holy image of Genazzano was venerated centuries ago.

340 Catholic Albanians in Genazzano during a pilgrimage lead by the Right Reverend Lazaro Mjedja, metropolitan archbishop of Scutari, in 1932.

A marble plaque they affixed on a wall of the shrine pleads, in both Albanian and Italian, "Return, O Lady of Good Counsel."

an image of Our Lady, all that I could ascertain from the oldest inhabitants of the region—persons worthy of credibility—is that there is a church, almost in ruins, dedicated to the Blessed Virgin of the Annunciation, in the suburbs of that city and that there she does not cease to perform constant and frequent miracles. Among the most important of these are the following.

"No attempt of the Turks to transform that church into a mosque could be carried to term, for whatever they built up during the day collapsed during the night. Every time the *hosa* (a kind of Turkish priest) tried to walk on the walls and cry out, according to [Mohammedan] custom, to call the people, a sudden wind would come like lightning and the *hosa* or priest would be thrown into the Boja River and there submerged. Some years ago, a mufti, or high priest, came to the aforementioned church and mistreated a sacred painting on the wall, piercing its eyes and damaging it with certain other degradations. Upon returning home, he found his seven children dead, and he himself went crazy.

"Such miracles that have happened and that still occur have caused the doors to remain open day and night; and no Turk has dared to make the least irreverence toward that temple, which is nearly in ruins. Two beams, as though suspended in the air, support part of the roof. This itself is also an obvious miracle. And more: every year on the night of the most holy Annunciation, a votive candle is seen burning in front of the abandoned altar. The place that the image of the Blessed Virgin occupied can also be seen. The holy image is no longer there as we know from tradition. According to some, it was taken away; others affirm that it left by itself."[92]

Our Lady Miraculously Protects Even the Stones of the Little Chapel

On February 9, 1748, Niccola di Antonio Cambsi, a nobleman of Scutari, declared under oath in Rome that the church, although in ruins and without a roof, still has the wall where the holy image used to be, and that on that wall there is an empty niche surrounded by effigies of the saints. He adds that the aforementioned niche was the same size as the image in Genazzano.

Cambsi further declares that, "the Catholics of the same city hold as true tradition that a very important Turk among the infidels, with the title of *effendi* in their language, wished to transform the church into a mosque because it was close to his house. He climbed a ladder to its roof to call the Turkish people to practice their prayers therein according to their sect. At that very moment, his head was twisted around and he started to bleat like a goat. Abandoning his plans he climbed down from the roof.

"Another very important Turk named Vegliada Zerode," he goes on to say, "began to build a bridge near the church over the Bojana River. Having dared to pull stones out of the church walls, he placed them on the backs of donkeys to be carried down to the river. As soon as the stones were taken off the donkeys, they fell dead instantly. Despite this, the man persisted in his designs and the bridge was built. When finished, however, the bridge collapsed in utter ruin. This having occurred, the Turks returned the stones to the church, and the one giving witness [Nicholas Cambsi] saw them on the ground close to the wall of the church when he left there three years ago. These events instilled such fear in the infidels that they dare not touch even some of the trees close to another church not far from the one mentioned."

A Light Illuminates the Empty Niche

Cambsi further testifies that, "he frequently heard other Catholics living near that church say that on some occasions they have seen with their own eyes a light descend at night over it and burn miraculously."

He affirms also that, "the church had been reduced to walls only, without a roof; . . . the concavity of the arched roof that serves for the portion of the wall . . . where the [image] of the Blessed Virgin detached itself, is still in the air. The vassals of the Most Serene Republic of Venice and other merchants hasten there to venerate those walls where such a miraculous image had been. They wholeheartedly call happy those inhabitants of the city who are so fortunate to have [that temple] in their neighborhood."[93]

Terrible Interventions of Our Lady Certified by the Bishop of Scutari

In the same century, in 1754, the Most Reverend Paulo Cambsi, bishop of Scutari, registered the following declaration:

"We, the undersigned, declare as pure truth that, in our city of Scutari, in Albania, there exists a church, which has been there from ancient times until today, about which a tradition is known and still persists that from it emigrated a miraculous image of Our Lady that was miraculously transported to other regions. In said church, the faithful of Scutari frequently receive graces from the Blessed Virgin despite [the fact that] the image venerated so long ago is no longer there.

"We also declare that almost every year, on the night following July 21, an unusual brilliance is seen over the aforementioned church and sometimes a likeness of a white cloud. This is also seen with admiration by the Turks themselves.

"Besides this, we declare that in the year 1741, precisely on the night after July 21, a venerable Lady appeared to His Excellency, the Governor of Scutari, Mutfar Bassa, in his dreams. At the urging of his counselors, he had taken, in the same month of the previous year, much money from the devout Christian faithful of that church in order to cover the roof of his house. The praised and venerated Lady spoke to him thus: 'You have despoiled the faithful of my house of their money; consequently, you shall leave your house tomorrow, never to return to it. Moreover, your house will be consumed by fire, especially the tiles bought with the toil of my faithful.'"

"This indeed occurred the next day, on July 23, when he was miserably assassinated outside his home, and his enemies set fire to the house, in accordance with the divine Lady's warning. As a result, a great fear took hold of his wife and many other inhabitants of Scutari. Because we know these things and others worthy of consideration with certainty, we sign in our own hand with full faith in these admirable things. The wicked one who had prompted the governor [to charge the Christians] was suddenly punished with a great chastisement: A serious fire was set in his house by an invisible hand, and he thus justly suffered the loss of all his belongings. The instigator's name was Hagi Muharreni."

A Lady Clothed in Light Descends from Heaven

The bishop continues: "We declare for the greater glory of Holy Mary, our Mother of Good Counsel, that approximately seventy years ago, around midnight of a certain day, a distinguished Turkish man of Scutari, Haidar Aga by name, saw from his palace, in the direction of the aforementioned church, a very eminent lady clothed in light who was descending from heaven and who remained about one hour over the church. Pondering on this with admiration, he advised other magnates who were friends of his so that they, too, could see and admire the sight. Finally, he saw that noble and saintly lady surrounded with light rise up heavenward. The following day he called the bishop of Scutari, told him everything he had seen and said: 'We can see indeed that your Faith is true and great.' "[94]

Ruins Venerated Like Relics by the Faithful

Of two very interesting documents known to us regarding acts of piety and miracles performed around the empty niche of Scutari, one deserves to be transcribed in its entirety because it demonstrates remarkable devotion to the Mother of Good Counsel. It is the report prepared in 1878, more than 100 years after the documents we have just quoted, by Father Mariano de Palmanova, Superior of the Albanian missions. This study was prepared at the request of Friar Pietro Belgrano, Prior of the Augustinian convent of Genazzano and himself an author of a book about devotion to this marvelous image of Our Lady.[95]

"Praised be the Lord and Most Holy Mary, because finally it is possible for me to transmit to you the result of the investigations made at your request in your very esteemed letter of the 29th of May. Since my office as superior of the Albanian mission did not permit me to stay long in Scutari—so necessary for attaining the desired objective—I judged it better to address the Very Reverend Friar Giampiero de Bergamo, Apostolic Prefect of the Castrati Missions and superior of the Franciscan convent in that city. Several times, I informed him about the memorandum and your Excellency's questions, asking him to consult the traditions and historical facts concerning the church of Our Lady of Scutari; and also to have recourse to the vicar-general of the archdiocese, the Very Reverend Monsignor Angelo Radoja, and other competent persons with the view of making careful investigations of that matter and later to visit the place where tradition and historical documents indicate the aforementioned church was located. Following, Very Reverend Father, is the letter of Friar Giampiero concerning the matter entrusted to him. 'My dear Father Mariano,

" 'I have the pleasure and honor of telling you that the Very Reverend Monsignor Angelo Radoja and the Most Reverend Pascoal Lunchi accepted with great interest the responsibility of making investigations concerning the church that a long time ago sheltered the venerated and amiable image of Our Lady which is presently honored in Genazzano. They also agreed, with real pleasure, to accept the assignment of going to the place where the venerable little church is believed to have been located in order to make a more careful and detailed examination there.

" 'Because of that, on the 8th of this month, I left with the aforementioned Monsignor and Father Pascoal in search of the fortress on whose perimeters are found the ruins that the faithful venerate as relics of the church of their Lady with pilgrimages and promises. I brought along with me our brother Anselmo de Gorle, a Franciscan, since he, as a capable architect, would be useful to us in the difficult examination of those ruins. Monsignor Radoja and Father Pascoal took with them a native of Scutari, well-versed in the traditions and history of his country.

Confirmation of the Site of the Little Church of Our Lady of Scutari

" 'The result of our inquiries and observations made in that place, especially around the walls that still exist on the slopes of the hill where the fortress of Scutari is found, correspond perfectly to our liveliest hopes.

" 'In the most perfect agreement, it was unanimously admitted that:

" '1) The place where the ruins are found is really the same and unique place where tradition and the historical memoirs of Friar Angelo Maria De Orgio say that this fortunate little church of Our Lady of Scutari existed.

" '2) The ruins there, which every day receive manifestations of the piety of the faithful, are precisely the remains of the little church so much esteemed.

" 'The description of the aforementioned historian [De Orgio] leads us to this sweet and consoling conclusion. First, it is noted that the place chosen to be examined, that is to say, where the collapsed walls of a building are found, approximately one half an Italian mile from the ancient city of Scutari, is located close to the banks of the Bojana River where the ruins of a demolished bridge can be seen (perhaps the one that the rich Moslem tried to build with Our Lady's stones). Not far from there, on the opposite side, a small mosque rises, which had been a church dedicated to Saint Lawrence some time ago. In front are two large and majestic trees considered sacred by the Moslems. Evidently, they are the ones referred to by the quoted author as being located in front of a church not far from that of Our Lady and respected by the Turks themselves.

" 'Secondly, the ruins that rise in this place, as they presently appear, seem to be of a secular house. Attentively considering the interior arrangement and the signs of age and purpose, the ruins reveal themselves as being really and undoubtedly the remains of the small church that Scutari historians (alluded to by De Orgio) visited one hundred and thirty years ago and declared to be the ruins where, for a long time, the blessed image of Genazzano was found. Indeed, after a diligent and detailed examination, it was noted:

" '1. The middle room (the building consists of three rooms) is slightly different from the two adjacent ones in regard to the style of the doors and the placement of windows in two side walls. On the main wall of this same room, there are three large niches; the smallest, in the middle, is by the entrance door that can be seen on the still existing part of the central wall.

" '2. Above the central niche, the wall still has the lines of a vault or an arched roof as an ornament for the same niche.

" '3. The windows that opened on each side of the room, as well as the two doors close to the wall through which people passed to the side rooms, have as an architrave an acute Gothic arch.

" '4. The walls of this room still bear, in various places, the marks of inlaid polished red stucco.

" '5. The two side rooms are perfectly alike, in their measurements, in the design where their arches meet, in the lack of niches or other empty spaces in the walls. All of this convinced us that the central room was used as a church, while the two side ones served as galleries where the devotees could remain on feast days or other days of great influx. It is also noted that, according to the evidence given by Niccola Cambsi of Scutari, the small niche in the first wall of the room is precisely located in front of the main entrance door; that above the niche, at a proportionate distance, there was an arch in the form of a vault and that the dimensions of the niche correspond to those of the image venerated in Genazzano. Finally, it is noted that in front of the three rooms mentioned before, there was an atrium as long as the building with entrances on both sides with two wide and spacious doors. By these evident clues and signs, which correspond entirely with the constant information of the authentic historical reports, we deem to declare that these ruins are the remains of the church that, a long time ago, possessed the blessed image of Genazzano.

The Turks Abandon the Idea of Destroying the Ruins

" 'Concerning the antiquity of the ruins, they extend as far back as an epoch before the Turkish occupation. The shape of the building, which has nothing in common with what exists in the rest of Albania, as well as the rusty and bronze-like coloration of the stones with which it was built, prove sufficiently that, since the times in which persons of Scutari made this narration until our time, the Turks never again wanted to build any house or mosque there; but only to destroy, ruin and leave that place completely abandoned.

" 'Yet another fact proves the antiquity. The Turks would certainly not have permitted foreigners to build houses for their own use according to European style. If some had the idea to build houses for themselves, the conquerors would have forced them to adopt the Berber style, which was invariably the style they themselves were adopting for their dwellings. Furthermore, during the hundred and thirty years that elapsed since the time in which certain respectable persons of the place declared that they encountered there the ruins of the church of Our Lady, and during which the Turks, for fear of catastrophe, had put aside the idea of erecting a mosque over these ruins or of raising an arm to destroy them, there was no one, neither Christian nor Mahometan, who was able to remember any construction in this place, whether of houses or any other edifice, whether for religious or secular purpose.

" 'Tradition, in turn, teaches us that the Catholic faithful of Scutari and of all the neighboring regions have always given proofs of their devotion with pilgrimages to these ruins, even in the times when the Moslems have sought to impede these religious manifestations. The conviction that these ruins were formerly the said little church is today current not only among Christians, but even among the Turks themselves, and such a number of others who frequently turn toward them in penitential pilgrimages, to procure relief in spiritual and temporal necessities with extremely lively and ardent devotion.

" 'Women of all conditions and ages, even of the upper class, go there barefoot and prostrate themselves in front of that place where the small niche still exists. After having walked through the building several times, they remain for hours in fervent prayer and do not leave without shedding tears. Frequently, as a result, many not only obtain spiritual and temporal advantages from those pilgrimages, but return from them strengthened by remarkable and miraculous graces. I could relate a great number of such graces that have the characteristics of true miracles, but for brevity's sake, I will limit myself to just two.

A Boy Cured of Rickets

" 'Mr. Tuke Berdiza, whom Your Paternity knows well, had a ten-year-old son named Giovanni who was affected by rickets to such a degree that he was unable to walk. Since all remedies had proved useless, the man followed his pious wife's advice to make a promise to Our Lady of Scutari and to go on a pilgrimage to the aforementioned place, taking the sick child with them. The devout parents carried the boy there in their arms, and as soon as they had fulfilled the promise inspired by their devotion they saw their son, to their amazement and unexpected consolation, stand up on his own feet. His condition was such that he was able to follow shortly behind them on the way back to their home in the city.

A Poor Turk's Blindness Cured by the Lady of the Christians

" 'A poor Turk, blind in both eyes and not having recourse to any medicine, decided to visit the ruins of the church of Our Lady, praying there in his own manner. Three days after that visit he is able to see without any difficulty and boasts of the grace received from the Lady of the Christians.

Oratory dedicated to the Mother of Good Counsel in the Jardim São Bento seat of the Brazilian TFP, São Paulo, where the author resides.

" 'Our Lord, by performing such special miracles, aside from rewarding the faith of those who pray to His Holy Mother with devotion, seems to wish through this means to confirm their pious belief. As such it is noteworthy to point out how He punishes with manifest chastisement those who, out of spite or even inadvertence, try to disrespect that sacred place by using it for profane or improper purposes.

Four Hundred Years after the Departure of the Holy Fresco, Punishments for Those Who Disrespect the Ruins

" 'Thus, on many occasions, Turkish shepherds wanted to take their flocks into those places to spend the night, even when their neighbors tried to dissuade them from it. So it happened that Our Lord made it impossible on the following morning for the shepherds to remove the animals. The animals were unexpectedly struck by a mysterious malady that drained them of their strength so they could not stand up. Only after the shepherds had repented of their fault, having been obliged to declare that place as sacred, and had lit candles at their own expense and prayed to the Supreme Protector of that same place, were they able to remove their animals safe and sound.

" 'Mohemet Cialacu, a well-known Turk in this city, had the audacity to take stones from the walls of the church and carry them away for the purpose of building his house. However, as soon as the carts arrived at his house, to the utmost amazement of all present, the oxen suddenly died.

" 'A Christian, who is still living, tells that when Ham Aga had constructed his inn (*han*), he carried away several stones from the little church, on orders of that powerful Turk. The next day the stones were miraculously found back at their place of origin.

" 'This was, dear Father, what I was able to gather and tell you, either as regards the minute and conscientious investigations taken from history and tradition about the site of the little church of the holy image of Scutari venerated in Genazzano, or as a result of the visit made to the site of the venerable ruins by the Very Reverend Monsignor Angelo Radoja, vicar-general of the archdiocese and pastor of Scutari; the Very Reverend Iunchi Curato; and myself.

October Celebrations in Scutari

" 'Finally, I must relate some details regarding the veneration still given to the blessed image in Scutari today [that is, about the year 1878, when this report was made].

" 'Each year, on the third Monday in October, the feast of Our Lady of Scutari is celebrated with extraordinary pomp, with the attendance of a great number of people from all the surrounding regions and even from afar. A copy of the image venerated in Genazzano, commissioned by the lords of Scutari at some unknown date, is exposed over the main altar. The day's sermon deals with the sad event of the departure of the holy image from this city and the necessity of asking the Madonna to comfort the country once again with her protection. During that sacred event, the people parade in a well-attended and pious procession. The numerous confraternities carry their respective standards, all portraying Our Lady of Scutari on one side of the cloth. The chief confraternity is that of Our Lady of Good Counsel, whose standard portrays the painting of the blessed and venerated image of Genazzano being carried by angels. Under the image are the historic details of her flight from Scutari.

" 'A group of boys and girls sings a little sacred song in the Albanian language. After each stanza, in most touching words, the desire that the Blessed Virgin return to these shores is repeated. They also beseech the holy image not to prolong the abandonment of her repented children.

" 'This feast, publicly celebrated with so much splendor, dates from ancient times when the Catholics in Scutari, oppressed by Moslem fanatics, were not allowed to display their religious sentiments and attest to their devotion. It is also said that, *ab immemorabili* [from time immemorial], images of the Blessed Virgin of Good Counsel, under the current invocation of Our Lady of Scutari, were venerated in chapels, oratories, and even in homes, and the holy image was always exposed wherever the faithful gathered for Holy Communion.

" 'Embracing you wholeheartedly, I remain Friar Giampiero de Bergamo, Pro Pref. Apost. // Copy faithful to the original: I, Friar Giampiero de Bergamo, attest to the authenticity of the above copy. // I, Father Pasquale Iunchi, verify the above. // I, Msgr. Angelo Radoja, vicar-general of the archdiocese, verify the above. // Confirming the authenticity of these signatures, Scutari, July 16, 1878. // + Carlos, archbishop of Antivari and Scutari.

Father Mariano de Palmanova adds: " 'Before publishing the present report, I also visited those fortunate ruins and would prostrate myself in front of that niche where the holy image of Our Lady, venerated today in Genazzano, formerly dwelt. I could also verify many things that tradition keeps ever alive in this people regarding the truth of the events. Having written this report, I had the members of the commission sign it and the signatures recognized by His Excellency, the Archbishop, who was pleased with the matter and congratulated us for the happy result attained for the greater glory of God and His Divine Mother.

" 'I hope that this answer to the questions formulated by Your Very Reverend Paternity is in accordance with your lively desires. May you also grant me your complaisance for my having left you for so long a time in painful expectation.

" 'Please receive, Very Reverend Father, the proofs of my deep esteem, while I have the honor of declaring myself, sincerely, the very humble, devout, and obedient servant of Your Reverend Paternity, Friar Mariano de Palmanova (M.Oss.), Pro Pref. Apost. of the Mission of Epirus [Albania].' "

The Niche, Respected Even by Moslem Fanaticism, Destroyed by Catholic Hands

In the twentieth century, after more than four hundred years of Turkish domination, Albania temporarily regained its independence. On December 17, 1920, it was accepted as a full member of the League of Nations in Geneva. The Catholic Church saw her freedom of action, slowly reemerging during the time of the decadence of the Turkish empire, reinforced.

The majority of the inhabitants of that unfortunate nation had apostatized during the almost five hundred years of Turkish rule and had become Moslems. A lesser part, although still a great number, adhered to the schism of the so-called Orthodox Church. Only thirteen percent remained faithful to the Church of Jesus Christ. Almost all of these Catholics lived in the north of the country around Scutari where the fresco of *Mater Boni Consilii* had remained for two hundred years, another marvel certainly attributable to the Lady of Scutari.

However, the chapel "that Moslem fanaticism had respected" would suffer an unfortunate end, affirms the Most Reverend Leone G. B. Nigris, archbishop of Filippi and Apostolic delegate in Albania.[96]

Writing in Rome on December 28, 1946, after having been expelled from Albania the preceding year when it fell under communist domination, Archbishop Leone stated:

"That chapel has not existed for the last twenty-five years. In its place, there is a modest church, unfinished in its ornamentation. But a great mistake was committed: the wall with the empty niche that held the fresco, which detached itself and now resides in Genazzano, was demolished—without a thought that a first-class document in favor of tradition was being demolished.

"What remains, and indelibly so, is the widespread and lively devotion to Our Lady of Good Counsel, venerated as patroness of Albania, and the desire that the revered image return from Italy to its original place. When? When Albania becomes Catholic again, they say."[97]

. . . and Albania Falls under the Worst of Tyrannies: Communism

"When Albania becomes Catholic again." The words of the Apostolic Delegate resounded in 1946 in a situation incomparably more tragic than that of 1467.

On November 29, 1944, the so-called National Liberation Front seized power and established an iron-fisted communist dictatorship, which unleashed a ruthless religious persecution immediately after World War II.

The Most Reverend Gaspar Thaci, archbishop of Scutari and principal figure of the Catholic Church in Albania, under pressure from the communist authorities to separate from Rome, died under house arrest in his residence on May 25, 1946.

That same year, the Most Reverend Gjergj Volaj, bishop of Sappa, presided over the celebration of the feast of Our Lady of Good Counsel in Scutari. During the homily, the prelate denounced the new regime and its atrocities committed against Catholics. He urged the people to remain firm in their devotion to Our Lady of Scutari no matter what happened. Imprisoned in January of 1947, Bishop Volaj was shot on the morning of February 3, 1948.[98]

The shrine was converted by the communists into a restaurant and dance hall. Two decades later, in 1967, in the year of the five hundredth anniversary of the miraculous transfer of the Mother of Good Counsel from Scutari to Genazzano, the Red Guards, aping the furious style of Mao's Cultural Revolution, destroyed the church completely.[99]

Unfortunate Albania began to slip toward the precipice of the most radical forms of communism. The German magazine *Der Fels* stated that "in 1976, a constitution was promulgated in Albania whose article 37 says: 'The state recognizing no kind of religion, supports and develops atheist propaganda with the purpose of instilling the ideology of scientific materialism in men." Article 55 stipulates: 'Any kind of organization of fascist, antidemocratic and antisocialist activities is forbidden, as are fascist, religious, militarist, antisocialist activities and propaganda, as well as the promotion of hatred among peoples and races." Article 49 reads: 'parents are responsible for the well-being and communist education of their children.' "

"In 1967, Envere Hodsha proudly proclaimed Albania 'the first atheist state in the world.' Between 1949 and 1967, all of the 2,169 churches and mosques were closed. All religions became illegal and relations with the outside world were severed. According to the latest information, sixty-eight percent of Albanians are Mohammedan, nineteen percent are Greek orthodox and thirteen percent are Catholic.

"The Catholic Church, which numbers about 300,000 faithful, saw, since the communists seized power in 1944, 120 priests and religious martyred. . . . The number of laymen who have been imprisoned, denounced for having an underground church, for keeping crucifixes, for having tried to gather religious books or teach religion, is not known. Persons may be sentenced to six months in a concentration camp for making the Sign of the Cross or for participating in an act of worship."[100]

In spite of all this, today under the most tyrannical and atheistic Marxist dictatorship, pilgrims still go to pray at the place where the church of Our Lady of Good Counsel formerly stood.[101] There they most assuredly and ardently implore that communism be banished from their country as well as from all the other lands in which it was installed. From their souls a tender canticle rises up, a prayer to the Patroness of the lands of Scanderbeg, one that the Albanian refugees in Italy have always sung since the time of the Ottoman invasion: *"torna presto, o Madre pia, torna presto in Albania!"* ("Return quickly, O gracious Mother, return quickly to Albania!")

"Pray for Us in This Century of Confusion, O Mother of Good Counsel"

Presently, the red octopus that was spreading its tentacles over the entire Free World a short time ago, assumed a new and unforeseeable aspect. Everywhere people are boasting about the "death of communism" as a hasty invitation to the nations of the West to psychologically and militarily disarm themselves in face of the threat that supposedly has ceased to exist. Thus, the confused and unexpected situation was created, because no serious guarantee is presented regarding the authenticity of the transformations taking place in the countries formerly behind the Iron Curtain. Consequently the sinister shadow of this regime of moral and material misery, very justly labelled the "shame of our time," persists.[102]

Faced with this dark horizon, heavy with uncertainties, let us turn our eyes to the Help of Christians with the same faith, confidence, and love that encouraged the brave Catholics of Lepanto. Let us make our supplication that of Prof. Plinio Corrêa de Oliveira: "Pray for us in this century of confusion, O Mother of Good Counsel."[103]

Chapter 11

THROUGHOUT the centuries, from her shrine in Genazzano, the Madonna of Good Counsel has been attracting saints and sinners; nobles, bourgeois and the common people; simple clergymen and even members of the ecclesiastical hierarchy, including the Sovereign Pontiffs.

Following are some remarkable examples of popes and saints who had devotion to the Mother of Good Counsel.

Saint Pius X Prays to the Mother of Good Counsel for Light

At the beginning of this century, when mankind was submerged beneath the wave of materialism generated by the great technical and scientific inventions, the gale winds of the terrible modernist heresy blew within the Holy Church[104] threatening to destroy her centuries-old stability.

When Leo XIII died in July of 1903, the Conclave met to choose his successor. In view of the serious danger facing the Church, what heavy responsibilities would hover over the head that would wear the pontifical tiara? If the elected Pontiff were to be an innocent and saintly man, would he not tremble interiorly in contemplating the greatness of his vocation upon hearing the liturgy repeat the words of the Savior: *"Tu es Petrus, et super hanc petram aedificabo Ecclesiam meam"* (Thou art Peter and upon this rock I will build my Church, Matt. 16:18). Were he not assisted by the Spirit of Fortitude, how could he face this sublime and august mission?

The Cardinal Patriarch of Venice, Giuseppe Sarto, never imagining himself worthy of the supreme throne coveted by so many, traveled to Rome with a round-trip ticket, the only Cardinal to do so. "He hath exalted the humble " (Luke 1:52). But it was God's will that this heroically humble Cardinal Sarto should occupy the Chair of Peter and should watch with "solicitude for all the churches" (2 Cor. 11:28).

In the Conclave's fourth scrutiny, the majority of the votes began to favor Cardinal Sarto. During the fifth and sixth scrutinies, that majority grew. Still, it was not enough to elect him. He affirmed that he would refuse the tiara if he were chosen by the Conclave, fearing the heavy burden that God would place on his shoulders. Filled with anguish, he went to the altar of the Mother of Good Counsel, erected by Pius IX in the Vatican Palace, to implore her sweet and maternal help.

It is not difficult to imagine him remaining a long time at the feet of Mary, Comforter of the Afflicted, filled with tribulation and hesitation, awaiting her counsel that for him would be almost a command. At this time the Cardinal Dean, Oreglia di Santo Stefano, sent Monsignor Merry del Val to seek out the Patriarch of Venice to ask him if he persisted in refusing his election and if he authorized his decision to be announced to the Conclave. Monsignor Merry del Val, whom Our Lady was about to use to utter a word of encouragement so sought after in the heavens by Cardinal Sarto, approached the altar of Our Lady of Good Counsel.

Cardinal Merry del Val relates how he fulfilled this very delicate mission that was to have so many consequences for the future of the Church: "It must have been about midday when I stepped into the dark and silent chapel. The lamp before the Blessed Sacrament burned brightly and there were candles lighted high above the altar, on either side of the picture of Our Lady of Good Counsel. I noticed a cardinal kneeling on the marble floor in prayer before the tabernacle, at some distance from the communion rail, his head in his hands, with his elbows resting on one of the low wooden benches, and I do not recall the presence of anybody else in the chapel at that moment. It was Cardinal Sarto. I knelt down beside him and addressing him in a whisper I secured his attention and delivered my message.

"His Eminence raised his head and slowly turned his face toward me as he listened to the question I laid before him. Tears were streaming from his eyes and I almost held my breath awaiting his reply. 'Yes, yes, Monsignor, tell the Cardinal to do me this act of charity.' He seemed to be echoing the words of his Divine Master in Gethsemani: *'Transeat a me calix iste'* [That this chalice be taken away from me]. The 'fiat' was still to come. The only words that I found strength to utter in reply and which rose to my lips as if dictated by another, were: *'Eminenza, si faccia coraggio, il Signore l'aiutera.'* (Eminence, take courage, Our Lord will help you.)"[105] Some hours later, Cardinal Sarto changed his mind and agreed.

The people assembled in Saint Peter's Square waited with increasing anxiousness for the famous white smoke that indicates the election of a new Pontiff. Finally, on the fourth day of the Conclave, the longed-for white smoke issued forth from the small chimney of the Palace. The faithful, filled with emotion, immediately began to applaud and shout *"Abbiamo Papa, abbiamo Papa!"* (We have a Pope.) The window of the balcony of Saint Peter's opened and in a strong solemn voice the Cardinal-Deacon Luigi Macchi proclaimed: "We have a Pope and his name is Pius."

The multitude of the faithful crowded the Basilica where, a short time later, Saint Pius X appeared already dressed in his white cassock to impart the first *urbi et orbi* blessing of a pontificate that would be filled with so much struggle and suffering and that would give so much glory to the Holy Church.

Throughout this beneficial pontificate, Pope Pius X kept a small picture of the Queen of Good Counsel on his desk—that same desk where the Pontiff signed his great encyclicals, where he received ambassadors from all the earthly powers, and where he read the humble petitions of innumerable faithful.[106]

Devotion of the Sovereign Pontiffs to the Madonna of Good Counsel

The first Pope to become acquainted with Genazzano was Paul II. In 1467, the year of the miraculous apparition of the image in Genazzano, he sent a commission of bishops to investigate the insistent rumors reaching Rome about miracles. The report prepared by the commission verified that everything was worthy of belief. So, the bishops authorized the conclusion of the construction of the shrine started by Blessed Petruccia and permitted public veneration of the holy painting.[107]

Pope Paul's successor, Sixtus IV, was so touched by the miraculous apparition that he had the church of Santa Maria del Popolo built in Rome and entrusted it to the Augustinians, hoping thereby to attract to the Eternal City graces similar to those that Our Lady had granted to the Augustinian shrine in Genazzano.

Alexander VI, aware that there were those who dared to plunder the shrine, threatened to excommunicate such thieves, calling them "children of iniquity." To each Mass celebrated on the altar of the Mother of Good Counsel in Genazzano he granted the special privilege of freeing a soul from the sufferings of Purgatory.

Saint Pius V, the Pope of the battle of Lepanto, that firm pontiff who brought about the Tridentine reform and the reform of customs and morals, that one who showed himself an open enemy of compromise with Protestantism, had recourse to Most Holy Mary of Genazzano in his necessities.

From the days of Paul II, who occupied the Chair of Saint Peter in 1467 when the holy image appeared in Genazzano, until the present time, a great number of Sovereign Pontiffs has manifested a special devotion to the Madonna of Good Counsel.

In the twentieth century, the tender intercession of the Mother of Good Counsel played a relevant role in the election of the great Pontiff Saint Pius X (left), who kept an image of the Queen of Good Counsel on his office desk throughout his reign.

Blessed Innocent XI, ardently desiring a crusade against the Turks, successfully besought the Virgin of Good Counsel for concord of the Christian princes.[108]

Clement XI granted to the shrine of Genazzano privileges identical to those of the shrine of Loreto where the Holy House of Our Lady of Nazareth was miraculously transferred by angels.

When Benedict XIV approved the Pious Union of Our Lady of Good Counsel, he wanted to be the first to join it.[109] That confraternity has been called the "Pious Union of Popes" because of the great number of Pontiffs who have entered its ranks: Pius VI, Pius VII, Pius VIII, Gregory XVI, Pius IX, Leo XIII, and, more recently, John XXIII.

Pius VI approved a proper Mass and Office for the feast of Our Lady of Good Counsel (April 25) for Genazzano. This feast was later extended to many other dioceses and is celebrated on April 26 so as not to conflict with the feast of Saint Mark, commemorated by the Universal Church on the 25th.

On April 22, 1903, Leo XIII included the invocation *"Mater Boni Consilii"* (Mother of Good Counsel) in the Litany of Loreto. He also instituted the scapular for that devotion and, from his pocket, constructed hospices for confessors and pilgrims at Genazzano.

Pius XII visited the shrine countless times, since his seminary days.

Paul VI publicly announced his intention of visiting Genazzano on the five hundredth anniversary of the miraculous apparition. For health reasons, he was unable to fulfill his wish. However, he sent a hand-written letter and was represented at the commemorations by Cardinal Aloisi-Masella.

On October 25, 1978, in one of his first general audiences, John Paul II, explaining the necessity of prudence for all men, asked himself: "What should the new Pope do so as to act prudently? . . . He should pray and try to have the gift of the Holy Ghost called the gift of counsel. Those who wish that the Pope be a prudent Pastor of the Church should implore for him the gift of counsel and should also pray for that gift for themselves through the special intercession of the Mother of Good Counsel."[110]

In addition, Gregory XIII, Paul V, Innocent XII, Benedict XIII, Clement XII and Pius XI approved devotion to the Mother of Good Counsel and granted special benefits to her shrine.

Papal Visits to the Shrine

Three Pontiffs came to Genazzano to kneel at the feet of the holy fresco. The first to visit the Patroness of Albania after her arrival in Genazzano was

Urban VIII. Distressed by the terrible plague raging throughout Italy, he visited the shrine on October 21, 1630, amidst great pomp and solemnity. The Pope left Castelgandolfo, where he dwelt at that time, followed by a magnificent entourage consisting of three cardinals, his nephew, Prince Thaddeus Barberini and other Roman princes, the baron of Solio, first officers and ministers of the Apostolic palace and numerous prelates and men of his court.

In Cave, they were met by Cardinal Colonna and Prince Philip Colonna, duke of Paliano and lord of Genazzano, grand constable of the kingdom of Naples, who was accompanied by his sons, the Princes Giovanni and Pietro. With them came the Pope's escort of three thousand foot soldiers and eight hundred knights. The entire way was decorated with flowers and triumphal arches. One witness attests that nearby regions became vacated as all the inhabitants hurried to places along the road in order to acclaim the Pope and receive his blessing. At the entrance to his domains, the constable offered the keys of his fortress and palace to the Roman Pontiff, his sovereign and lord. "Cannons roared and trumpets sounded, and then amidst all possible regal and ecclesiastical pomp, the great Pontiff advanced to the beautiful Sanctuary of Mary."[111] Holy Mass was celebrated on the altar of the miraculous fresco, and those present saw him shed tears contemplating the holy painting.

Two centuries later, Pius IX was elevated to the Pontifical Throne. Since his youth, he had great devotion to the Mother of Good Counsel. At his ordination, he insisted on celebrating his first Mass on an altar dedicated to her under this invocation in Rome. It was he who ordered erection of the altar in the Vatican's Cappella Paoline where Saint Pius X was to pray in such great affliction prior to his papal election.

On the feast of the Assumption in 1864, His Holiness Pius IX wished to pray at the shrine in Genazzano to present his concerns to the Virgin about the summoning of the First Vatican Council. The whole town rejoiced at the arrival of the splendid entourage of cardinals, prelates, and monsignors, attired in purple and red, and of nobles of the pontifical guard vested in uniforms and shining armor. The Vicar of Christ was received by Cardinal Amat, bishop of Palestrina, by Prince Colonna and other gentlemen, the municipal authorities, the Augustinian prior, and a great number of representatives of the regular and secular clergy. The multitude of the faithful crowded together in the square in front of the shrine.

Pius IX entered the shrine and went immediately to the chapel of Our Lady. He remained in prayer there for a long time. Afterwards, standing up, he closely observed the holy image "with much devotion, joy, and consolation."[112]

Later, he stayed at the Colonna Palace. Wearing his pontifical vestments, he blessed the crowd from a loggia. In the evening, prior to leaving Genazzano, he wished to pray once again in front of the miraculous fresco, and he did so at length. The memory of that visit was kept in Genazzano for many years.

John XXIII also prayed before the image of Genazzano, on August 25, 1959. It brought to mind Pius IX's visit 95 years before. He asked all those present to pray so that the great Pope of the last century be raised to the honors of the altar as soon as possible.

Saints and Other Venerable Persons among the Pilgrims to Genazzano

Among all the faithful—from Popes to beggars—who have knelt before the image over the centuries, several devotees have been raised to the glory of the altar. Aside from Blessed Petruccia, the old Augustinian annals mention two additional "blesseds," Potentia and Santa, who lived and died under the protection of the shrine.

Saint Alphonsus Mary Liguori, a great Bishop and Doctor of the Church, prized as his greatest treasure a picture of the Mother of Good Counsel that presided over the desk whereon he wrote more than one hundred books dealing with delicate theological and moral matters. Saint Alphonsus, when nearing death, sent that picture to the religious of the Annunciation, who had asked him for some memento, writing, "I leave you my heart."

Saint Gaspar del Bufalo, Saint Paul of the Cross, Saint Clement Mary Hofbauer, and Dom Luigi Orione were among the noteworthy pilgrims to the shrine.

Saint John Bosco also visited there together with Blessed Michael Rua to ask for the good counsel of that most clement Mother in one of his afflictions concerning the founding of the illustrious Salesian congregation. By no means easy were his efforts at establishing this great work that was the fruit of a life filled with struggles and of persecutions of this great founder.

Saint John Bosco was in Rome and had been received by the Holy Father Pius IX with great joy. During Holy Week ceremonies, the Pope himself took the initiative of giving that great apostle and educator of youth a place of honor in the Vatican basilica, in the section reserved for the diplomatic corps. He considered him "an ambassador of the Most High."[113]

Saint John Bosco wanted to reserve the eve of Palm Sunday for a Marian pilgrimage to beseech heavenly help for his enterprise. The Augustinian friars in Rome directed him to the shrine of the Mother of Good Counsel. He went there the same day, celebrated Mass on the altar of the miraculous painting

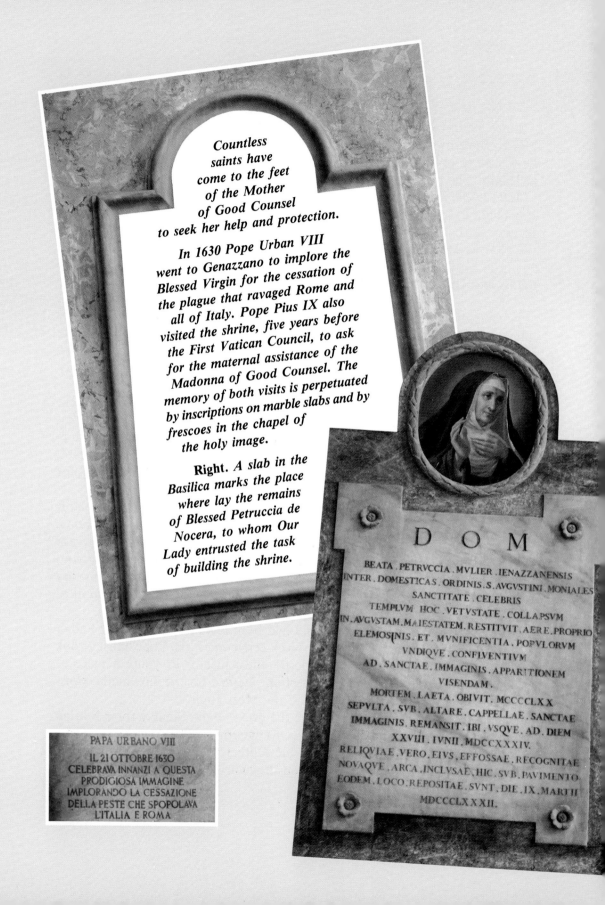

Countless saints have come to the feet of the Mother of Good Counsel to seek her help and protection.

In 1630 Pope Urban VIII went to Genazzano to implore the Blessed Virgin for the cessation of the plague that ravaged Rome and all of Italy. Pope Pius IX also visited the shrine, five years before the First Vatican Council, to ask for the maternal assistance of the Madonna of Good Counsel. The memory of both visits is perpetuated by inscriptions on marble slabs and by frescoes in the chapel of the holy image.

Right. A slab in the Basilica marks the place where lay the remains of Blessed Petruccia de Nocera, to whom Our Lady entrusted the task of building the shrine.

PAPA URBANO VIII

IL 21 OTTOBRE 1630
CELEBRAVA INNANZI A QUESTA
PRODIGIOSA IMMAGINE
IMPLORANDO LA CESSAZIONE
DELLA PESTE CHE SPOPOLAVA
L'ITALIA E ROMA

D O M

BEATA . PETRVCCIA . MVLIER . IENAZZANENSIS
INTER . DOMESTICAS . ORDINIS . S . AVGVSTINI . MONIALES
SANCTITATE . CELEBRIS
TEMPLVM . HOC . VETVSTATE . COLLAPSVM
IN . AVGVSTAM . MAIESTATEM . RESTITVIT . AERE . PROPRIO
ELEMOSINIS . ET . MVNIFICENTIA . POPVLORVM
VNDIQVE . CONFLVENTIVM
AD . SANCTAE . IMMAGINIS . APPARITIONEM
VISENDAM .
MORTEM . LAETA . OBIVIT . MCCCCLXX
SEPVLTA . SVB . ALTARE . CAPPELLAE . SANCTAE
IMMAGINIS . REMANSIT . IBI . VSQVE . AD . DIEM
XXVIII . IVNII . MDCCXXXIV .
RELIQVIAE . VERO . EIVS . EFFOSSAE . RECOGNITAE
NOVAQVE . ARCA . INCLVSAE . HIC . SVB . PAVIMENTO
EODEM . LOCO . REPOSITAE . SVNT . DIE . IX . MARTII
MDCCCLXXXII .

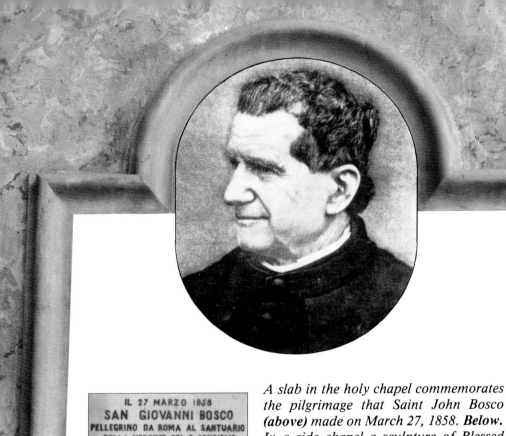

IL 27 MARZO 1858
SAN GIOVANNI BOSCO
PELLEGRINO DA ROMA AL SANTUARIO
DELLA VERGINE DEL B. CONSIGLIO
VI CELEBRAVA IL DIVIN SACRIFICIO
IMPLORANDO MATERNA ASSISTENZA
SULLA NASCENTE
CONGREGAZIONE SALESIANA
ANNO CENTENARIO 1958

A slab in the holy chapel commemorates the pilgrimage that Saint John Bosco (above) made on March 27, 1858. Below. In a side chapel a sculpture of Blessed Stefano Bellesini laying in state is venerated. He was the pastor of Genazzano from 1831 until his death in 1840 and was beatified by Saint Pius X in 1904.

and spent several hours in prayer. Today, a wall plaque in the church of Genazzano commemorates that blessed pilgrimage.

Some weeks later, when Saint John Bosco returned to Turin, several obstacles impeding the founding of the great Salesian congregation had been overcome and, further, the illustrious founder could now count on the help and protection of a great devotee of the Virgin of Genazzano: Pope Pius IX.

The Venerable Bartolomeo Menocchio, an Augustinian and a faithful companion of Pope Pius VII during his captivity in the hands of Napoleon Bonaparte, was also very devoted to the invocation of Good Counsel.

Blessed Stefano Bellesini

The order of the Hermits of Saint Augustine has in its ranks as many devotees to the Mother of Good Counsel as it has sons. One of them, Blessed Stefano Bellesini, shines like a precious pearl. His incorrupt body is kept in the Basilica at Genazzano.

Blessed Stefano was born in Trent in 1774, took the habit of his order in 1793, and made his profession in 1794. He studied philosophy and theology in Rome, Bologna, and Trent. During the Napoleonic invasion of the Pontifical States he suffered the proscription of the religious orders. For six years he was forced to live outside his monastery, separated from his brothers of vocation. When the papal monarchy was restored in 1814 and the possibility of religious life reopened, Blessed Stefano definitively left his hometown and rejoined the Augustinians (1817). His superiors designated Friar Stefano master of novices, first in the convent of Saint Augustine in Rome and afterwards in Città della Pieve.

In 1826, winds of stricter observance and greater fervor in religious life began to blow in the ranks of the Augustinians. Life in common was restored in some of the convents. Immediately, Father Bellesini asked to be admitted to that new degree of perfection. Thus, he transferred to the convent at Genazzano, the first place where the common life of the Hermits of Saint Augustine was reestablished. In 1831, he was appointed pastor of the shrine of Holy Mary of Good Counsel.

While in Genazzano, he always celebrated Mass on the altar of the Mother of Good Counsel and urged all the faithful to be devoted to her. To those who traveled or lived some distance from the shrine, he would distribute holy cards, oil from the sanctuary lamp, or anything that would remind them of the holy image. He was accustomed to consecrate to the Madonna of Good Counsel all the children he baptized, and he wished all his parishioners to be consecrated to her as well. He was very devoted to the Queen of Hearts and, among other pious practices, prayed the Rosary and the Litany of the Blessed Virgin Mary daily. When he was confined to bed because of an illness, one that would eventually bring about his death, the prior of the convent tried to spare him the fatigue of prayers. However, Blessed Stefano replied: "How do you expect me to appear before the Tribunal of God without having first prayed the Little Crown of Our Lady and the Rosary with its litany?"[114]

He was very obedient in life . . . and even after death. He asked his superior permission to present himself to God's Judgment on the feast of Mary's Purification, the feast of Our Lady of Good Success of Quito. The prior of the convent did not want to permit Stefano to die during this feast because of the blessing of candles and the large number of faithful who would come for the liturgical ceremonies. He feared that his death would inevitably disturb the solemnities. Blessed Stefano gladly yielded, saying: "When Our Lady's ceremony is over, mine will begin."[115]

At the end of vespers, the faithful in the church sang the last verse of the final hymn: "Mary of Good Counsel, bless us, the same as thy Son." With this the ceremonies were concluded. At four o'clock on the same day, Stefano surrendered his beautiful soul to God. It was February 2, 1840.[116]

During the process of his beatification, his body was exhumed in the presence of Cardinal Pedecini and numerous clergymen. The body was entire, incorrupt, and flexible. So it remains today. He was transferred to a new coffin which, unfortunately, was not well measured and turned out to be too narrow. The Cardinal addressed the deceased: "Father Bellesini, you who were so obedient in life, could you not arrange yourself so as to fit in this narrow coffin?" In view of all present, the body shrank just enough to fit into the coffin.[117]

This impressive miracle is shown to us by a model follower of the Queen of Heaven, who was also obedient throughout her life and with her *fiat* brought the Savior into the world.

The "Apple of the Eye" of the Order of Saint Augustine

The Shrine of Genazzano is considered to be the apple of the eye of the Order of the Hermits of Saint Augustine. Its superiors always zealously cared for the devotion to Our Lady of Good Counsel. This was very properly expressed by the Superior General, Nicol'Antonio Schiaffini, in the eighteenth century. He obtained from Pope Clement XII permission that the shrine depend directly on the General of the Order. When His Holiness asked him why he had such a great interest in that convent—which in reality was not one of the most important in the Order—Friar Schiaffini answered with these beautiful words related by the historian De Orgio: "Holy Father, Our Lady, who was in Scutari, Albania, came from that faraway country to Genazzano two hundred sixty-eight years ago; and she, of her own free will, gave and entrusted her holy image into the hands of the Augustinians. Consequently, it seems to me that it is a duty and a necessity, that I, as unworthy Superior General of the whole Order, have a special care, interest and zeal for that place, promoting by means of the clemency of your Holiness all the dignity, advantages, and honor of that shrine which, in my opinion, should be like the apple of the eye to me and to all my order."[118]

On October 11, 1967, during the commemoration of the five-hundredth anniversary of the miraculous transfer of the holy fresco, the Most Reverend Father-General Augustin Trape solemnly consecrated all the Order of the Hermits of Saint Augustine to the Mother of Good Counsel, asking her "with a moved and trusting spirit to be Mother, Queen, Advocate, and Counselor to all of the members of the Order."[119] May she also rule and guide us with motherly affection amidst the confusion and crises of this somber closing of the twentieth century.

Epilogue

WE have reached the conclusion of this brief history of the Mother of Good Counsel, who first appeared in Scutari seven hundred years ago and now is venerated in Genazzano. Throughout the ages, she has been an unshakable tower of help and protection for all those who have sought her aid. It was with great reason that Saint Bernard wrote in his pious prayer, the "Memorare," that "never was it known that anyone who fled to thy protection, implored thy help, or sought thy intercession, was left unaided." In Genazzano, she has given abundant and shining confirmations of these words of the Mellifluous Doctor.

Is it by mere coincidence that the reader has come to the final pages of this book? In truth, it was no accident but the pure hand of Mary that guided you. There are no accidents in the spiritual life as there are none in the relationship between God and men. Not one hair falls from one's head without the permission of the Heavenly Father (cf. Matt. 10:30). Divine Providence desired to guide your steps in such a way that you would know some of the marvels that His Mother performed in Genazzano.

Solicitude to protect you in all life's necessities was certainly the motive of this singular and loving Mother of Good Counsel. She is charitable. She is generous, helpful, protective, and caressing. She forgives, restores, and blesses. She calms the storms, solves the unsolvable, assists us in all dangers, and defends us from our enemies. Let us quote once again the most ardent Saint Bernard: "With her for guide, you shall never go astray; whilst invoking her, you shall never lose heart; so long as she is in your mind, you are safe from deception. Whilst she holds your hand, you cannot stumble; under her protection, you have nothing to fear; if she walks before you, you shall never grow weary; if she shows you favor, you shall certainly reach the goal."[120]

What does she ask in return for so many benefits? One thing only: that you remember her in all your difficulties.

To You, Dear Atheist

PLINIO CORRÊA DE OLIVEIRA

DEAR? This adjective may make readers wonder. After all, they have seen me, through my articles and other means, fight atheism for decades, especially the most actively imperialistic form it has assumed in the course of history, that is, Marxist atheism. How, then, can one justify the adjective "dear"? The explanation is this:

God wills the salvation of all men: of the good, so that they may receive the reward of their merits in heaven; of the bad so that they, touched by grace, may make amends and attain heaven. Therefore, from different standpoints and for different reasons, both the former and the latter are dear to God. Now, since they are dear to God, how could they not be so to a Catholic? Yes, dear, even when a Catholic fights against them in defense of the Church and Christendom. So, for example, at the very moment that a crusader fiercely fought a Mohammedan during the reconquest of the Holy Sepulcher, he could have addressed the Mohammedan in all sincerity as "dear brother."

The expression "dear atheist" is valid, therefore, and includes a range of different nuances; for there are nuances in atheism. Naturally, a specific sense of the word "dear" applies according to the nuance. Thus, there are atheists who rejoice to such an extent over their conviction that "God does not exist" that if some evident fact such as a spectacular miracle should convince them of the contrary, they might easily come to hate God and even to kill Him, if it were possible.

Other atheists are so mired in the things of the earth that their atheism consists not in denying the existence of God, but in being completely unconcerned about the matter. If the distinction is permissible, they are not "atheists" in the most radical sense of the word, but rather "a-theists," that is, laicists. God is not part of their conception of life and the world. Were it proven to them that God exists, they would see Him as a being with whom or without whom the world would go on just as it does. Their reaction would be to totally and perpetually banish Him from earthly affairs.

There is still a third kind of atheist who, crushed by the labors and disappointments of life, and seeing clearly, by bitter personal experience, that the things of this world are no more than "vanity and vexation of spirit" (Eccles. 1:14), desires that God exist. But hobbled by the sophistries of atheism, to which they had formerly opened their souls, and tied by rationalistic mental habits to which they had attached their minds, they are now groping in the darkness, unable to find the God whom they once rejected. When I meditate on that apostrophe of Jesus Christ, "Come to me, all you that labor, and are burdened, and I will refresh you" (Matt. 11:28), I think especially of this kind of atheist and feel especially inclined to call them "dear atheists."

This explains the kinds of atheists to whom these reflections are particularly addressed. Nevertheless, it is not only them that I have in mind, but many other readers who are much more dear to me: some brothers in the Catholic Faith, members, as I am, of the Mystical Body of Jesus Christ. Having read a reference I made to the spirituality of Saint Louis Marie Grignion de Montfort, they wanted me to say something more about the matter. So, I write this article for my brothers in the Faith, but with an eye toward the atheists.

Now I speak to the especially dear atheists, hoping to touch them to the depth of their souls, in the same text in which I speak to my very dear brothers in the Faith.

Imagine yourself, dear atheist, in one of those intervals of the daily life of yore in the calm of which agreeable and profound impressions—which the labor of the day, charged with the dust of triviality and the sweat of effort, had smothered in the subconscious—would rise to the surface of the spirit. Those were the ample moments of leisure in which the yearnings for a smiling past, the enchantments and hopes of a harsh but luminous present, and the so-often treacherous fantasies, would make an agreeable stereoscope for relaxing the soul, "put at ease . . . in that gay and blind deceit that fortune does not permit to long endure" (Camões, *Lusiadas*, Canto III, verse 120).

In today's scanty moments of leisure, on the contrary, it is the neurotic tumult of disappointments, worries, wild ambitions, and exacerbated weariness that rise to the surface. And over this tumult hovers an overwhelming, leaden, and obscure question: "What am I living for?"

* * *

Service, a Joy

IMAGINE, then, that to your spirit—bruised by life, calloused or even wounded, hot with fever—one of those figures appears about which your childhood innocence, dead now for many years, used to dream. A queen, all majestic and smiling, leads you by the hand into the rays of radiant, peaceful, rainbow-colored light surrounding her in an effort to help you. The atmosphere is of such purity that it seems fragrant with all the perfumes of nature: flowers, incense, or what you will. And you, dear atheist, let yourself be drawn. You walk gazing upon that figure even more beautiful than the lights enveloping her, and more aromatic than the perfumes flowing from her: magnificent gifts that she receives from an invisible but sovereign source not confounded with her but shining through her.

You recognize how much foolishness there is in the vast ocean of your bitterness. But now it is forgotten. You see that incommensurably beyond the daily sphere, in which your sorrows rage and multiply, there is a sublime and tranquil order of being which you will finally be able to enter. You perceive that only in this higher order will you find that happiness you sought among the worms but which really dwells beyond the stars.

More and more you gaze upon the Lady, and it begins to seem that you already knew her. You search her countenance trying to identify what it is that seems so profoundly familiar to you. In something about her gaze, in a certain loving note in her smile, in some of the assurance that she radiates—rich in implied expressions of affection—you recognize certain ineffable flashes of soul that you saw in the most generous motions of the soul of the earthly mother you had or, if one of the innumerable forms of orphanhood in today's world should have befallen you, of the mother you would like to have had.

You fix your gaze, and you see still more. Not just a mother, your mother, but someone—Someone—who seems to you the ineffable quintessence, the most complete synthesis of all the mothers that were, are, and will be, of all the motherly virtues that man's intelligence and heart can know. Even more, she seems the complete synthesis of degrees of virtue that only saints, flying on the wings of grace and heroism, know how to imagine and approach. She is the mother of all children and of all mothers. She is the mother of all men. She is the mother of *the* Man. Yes, of the God-Man, the God who became Man in her virginal womb, in order to redeem all men. She is a Mother defined by one word—*mare* (sea)—whence, in turn, comes a name, a name that is a heaven: MARY.

Through her come to you all graces and favors from the divine sun, infinitely superior but seeming to dwell in her (like the sun's rays seem to dwell in stained-glass windows). You beg, and you see yourself heeded. You want, and see yourself satisfied. From the depth of the peace beginning to anoint and envelop you, you sense a kind of happiness emerging that is the radiant opposite of that which, until a short while ago, you frantically sought after. This earthly happiness—if you did possess it—you finally cast aside as worn out, blasé, like a child pushing aside toys that are no longer entertaining.

Like a lily arising in a swamp or a spring welling up in a desert, something new begins to appear in the frustrated egoist that you were. This something new is not egoism, the exclusivistic love of yourself, but it is love; love of eternal principles, of fulgurant ideals, of lofty and spotless causes, that you see shining in the ineffable Lady and that you begin to desire to serve.

Behold the name of your new happiness: To serve, to dedicate yourself, to immolate yourself, and all that belongs to you. This happiness you will find in everything you formerly avoided: unrewarded good dedication, misunderstood goodwill, logic scorned by hypocrites or ignored by ears not wishing to hear; confrontation with calumny which at times howls like a hurricane, then discreetly hisses like a serpent, now, finally, lies like a lukewarm breeze loaded with deadly miasmas. Your joy now consists in resisting so much infamy, advancing and overcoming, even though you be wounded, rejected, or ignored. Everything for the service of the Lady "clothed with the sun, and the moon under her feet, and on her head a crown of twelve stars" (Apoc. 12:1). Yes, everything to serve her, and those who follow her.

You thought that happiness was to have everything. Now, on the contrary, you find that happiness consists in giving yourself completely.

Perhaps you fear that I may be dreaming and making you dream also as you read these lines, which, in your kindness, you may have imagined delectable. No, I do not dream, nor do I make you dream, nor are these lines magnificent. How colorless they are in comparison with the *True Devotion to the Blessed Virgin Mary*, by Saint Louis Grignion De Montfort. In this work, the famous missionary of the end of the seventeenth century and the beginning of the eighteenth (whose followers were the "Chouans," heroes of the fight against the atheistic and egalitarian French Revolution of the late eighteenth century) justified, through an impeccably logical reasoning founded on the most solid truths of the Faith, the profile of the sanctity of Mary. He deeply scrutinized the meaning of her virginal motherhood, her role in the Redemption of the human race, her position as Queen of Heaven and Earth, co-Redemptrix of men, and Universal Mediatrix of the graces that come to us from God as well as of the prayers of suffering mankind to Almighty God. In light of all this, the Saint analyzes the providence of Mary and shows how the Mother of the God-Man has each man in mind, loving each of us with greater love than all the mothers in the world could concentrate on one child.

It was to attract you to the consideration of these great treasures, these great thoughts, and these great truths, that I resolved to write to you. At the same time, I fulfilled the desire of several brothers in the Faith, who want nothing more than to have you in their midst, very close . . . to her.

If grace has deigned to bedew my words, you have felt within yourself something like a distant music, so consonant with yourself and with your liveliest aspirations that one would say it was composed for you, that you felt a thirst for harmony, and that you were born to give yourself to it.

In a word, you are ordered for her, and without her you are nothing but disorder.

And if, in the great harmony of the universe, even the most insignificant grain of sand, the most obscure drop of water, and the lowest and most contorted worm of the earth have their place and their function, will it not be the same with the order of the universe—or, rather, with its highest peaks—that is, the panorama of truths I have just presented to you through metaphors and that Saint Louis De Montfort deduces, with most sane and firm consistency, from the Catholic Faith, from that Faith which Saint Paul, in turn, defined as *"rationabile obsequium"* (Rom. 12:1)?

If this panorama that orders you and without which you are only chaos is false, then you, like every man, are out of place, a misfit, a—pardon my prosaism—a wart, an excrescence, a cancer, a catastrophe in this universe so supremely ordered. Can you imagine this being true of yourself, of us, of all men, who, as men, are in reality the royal apex of that order?

To believe that this is so, to believe in such a monstrous contradiction placed at the very apex of so perfect an order, is indeed, irrational. It is the apotheosis of absurdity.

*   *   *

Obey in Order to Be Free

NO, dear atheist. Giving a distant echo to the words of the Bishop Saint Remigius upon baptizing Clovis, the first Christian king of the Franks, I say to you: "Burn what you have adored and adore what you have burned." Yes, burn egoism, doubt, apathy, and, moved by the love of God, love and serve and fight for the Faith, for the Church, and for Christian civilization. Sacrifice yourself. Renounce yourself.

How? As they did throughout the ages, those who fought, for Jesus Christ, the "good fight" (2 Tim. 4:7).

And you will do it remarkably well if you follow the method defined and justified by Saint Louis De Montfort. It concerns the "slavery of love" to the Blessed Virgin.

Slavery . . . a harsh and strange word, especially for modern ears, accustomed to hearing at every moment about disalienation and freedom, and more and more inclined to the grand anarchy which, like the grim reaper with scythe in hand, seems to laugh sinisterly at men as it awaits them at the threshold of the exit from the twentieth century.

Now, there is a slavery that frees, and a freedom that enslaves.

A man fulfilling his obligations was formerly said to be a "slave of duty." In fact, he was a man at the height of his liberty, a man who, through a completely personal act of will, understood the ways that befell him to follow, deliberated with manly vigor to pursue them, and overcame the assaults of the disorderly passions that tried to blind him, weaken his will, and block the way he had freely chosen. Free was the man who, having gained this supreme victory, walked with a firm step in the proper direction.

On the contrary, he who allowed himself to be dragged by the unruly passions in a direction neither approved by his reason nor preferred by his will, was a "slave." These really defeated people were called "slaves of vice." By slavery to vice they had "liberated" themselves from the wholesome dominion of reason.

With his brilliant skill, Leo XIII explained these concepts of liberty and servitude in his encyclical, *Libertas*.

Today everything is inverted. A hippie going about aimlessly with a flower in his hand, or spreading terror at his pleasure with a bomb in his hand, is regarded as a model of a "free" man. On the contrary, whoever lives in obedience to the laws of God and of men is considered to be bound rather than free.

In the current perspective, free is one whom the law permits to buy the drugs he wants, to use them as he wishes, and, finally, to enslave himself to them. Enslaving and tyrannical is the law forbidding men to become enslaved to drugs.

In this cross-eyed perspective derived from an inversion of values, the religious vow by which a monk, in all awareness and in all freedom, renounces any step backward and surrenders himself to the abnegated service of the highest Christian ideals, is enslaving. In that act, in order to protect his decision against the tyranny of his own weakness, the monk subjects himself to the authority of vigilant superiors. Today, whoever thus binds himself to conserve himself free from bad passions is liable to be considered a vile slave, as if his superior imposed upon him a yoke that cut off his will. Instead, the superior serves as a handrail for elevated souls that aspire, freely and fearlessly—without yielding to the dangerous vertigo of the heights—to reach the top of the stairways of the highest ideals.

In brief, some consider him free who, with his reason fogged and his will shattered and driven by the madness of his senses, is capable of sliding voluptuously downward in the toboggan of bad manners. And he is a "slave" who serves his own reason, overcomes with his will power his own passions, obeys divine and human laws, and puts order into practice.

In that perspective, "slave," above all, is he who, in order to more completely guarantee his liberty, freely chooses to submit himself to authorities that guide him toward his goal. This is how far we are led by the present atmosphere, impregnated with Freudianism!

It was from another perspective that Saint Louis De Montfort devised the "slavery of love" to Our Lady, a slavery proper to all ages and to all states in life: layman, priest, religious, and so on.

What does the word "love" mean here, joined to the word "slavery" in a surprising way, since the latter is dominion brutally imposed by the strong upon the weak, by the egotistical upon the wretched whom he exploits?

In sound philosophy, "love" is the act by which the will freely wants something. In this way, also in current language, "to want" and "to love" are words that can be used in the same sense. "Slavery of love" is the noble apex of the act by which someone freely gives himself to an ideal or a cause, or, at times, binds himself to another.

The holy affection and the duties of matrimony have something that bind, that join, that ennoble. In Spanish, handcuffs are called "spouses." The meta-phor makes us smile; and since it alludes to indissolubility, it can bring a chill to those who believe in divorce. In English we speak of the "bonds" of matri-mony. More binding than the state of a married man is that of a priest. And, in a certain sense, still more binding is that of the religious. The higher the state freely chosen, the stronger the bond, and the more authentic the liberty.

So, Saint Louis De Montfort proposes that the faithful consecrate themselves freely to the Blessed Virgin as "slaves of love," giving her their bodies and souls, their goods, both interior and exterior, and even the value of all their good ac-tions, past, present, and future, so that Our Lady might dispose of them for the greater glory of God, in time and in eternity (cf. "Consecration to Jesus Christ, the Incarnate Wisdom, through the Blessed Virgin Mary"). In exchange, as a sublime Mother, Our Lady obtains for her "slaves of love" the graces of God that elevate their intellects to the most lucid understanding of the highest themes of the Faith, that grant their wills an angelic strength to rise freely to those ideals and to conquer all the interior and exterior obstacles that unduly oppose themselves to them.

But, someone will ask, how will a monk, already subject under vow to the authority of a superior, be able to begin practicing this diaphanous and angelic liberty?

Nothing is easier. If he is a monk through a call of God (vocation), it is therefore by the will of God that the religious obeys his superiors. The will of God is the will of Our Lady. In this way, whenever a religious is consecrated as a "slave of love" to Our Lady, it is as her slave that he obeys his own supe-rior. The voice of this superior is, for him, like the very voice of Our Lady on earth.

Calling all men to the heights of liberty afforded by the "slavery of love," Saint Louis De Montfort employs terms so prudent that they allow ample room for important nuances. His "slavery of love," so replete with special meaning for the persons bound by vow to the religious state, can be equally practiced by secular priests or laymen because, unlike the religious vows that bind for a certain period or for an entire life, the "slave of love" can leave this most elevated condition at any moment without ipso facto committing sin. And while the religious who disobeys his rule incurs a sin, the lay "slave of love" does not commit any sin by the simple fact of contradicting in something the total generosity of the gift he made. The layman maintains himself in this condition of slavery through a free act, implicitly or explicitly repeated each day, or better, at each instant.

The "slavery of love" is, then, for all the faithful that angelic and supreme liberty with which Our Lady awaits us at the threshold of the twenty-first century, smiling and attractive, inviting us to her reign, according to her promise in Fatima: "Finally, my Immaculate Heart will triumph."

Come, dear atheist, convert and walk with me, with all the "slaves of love" of Mary, toward that reign of supremely ordered freedom and of supremely free order, to which the Slave of Our Lord, the Queen of Heaven, invites you.

Turn aside from the threshold at which the devil, like the grim reaper with his macabre laugh, holds in his hand the scythe of supremely enslaving freedom and of supremely libertarian enslavement, the scythe of anarchy.

Appendices

Appendix 1
Historical Critique

THE historical actuality of the apparition of the image in Genazzano and of its transfer from Scutari, Albania, is based on uninterrupted and unchanging tradition over five centuries, documented files, contemporary authors, and monuments.

We must regret the loss of an abundant amount of documentation on the history of the holy image. Thus, Alexander VI, in 1502, calls those who stole valuable objects and documents from the shrine "children of iniquity." Other papers were lost at the end of the fifteenth century when a ship transporting them to Naples on orders of the famous Father Mariano of Genazzano sank near Pozzuoli.

Many documents were lost on account of wars: innumerable wars in the Genazzano region at the end of the fifteenth century and the beginning of the sixteenth century; the French invasion of the Pontifical States in the eighteenth century; the occupation of these States by Piedmontese troops in the reign of Pius IX. Finally, a fire in the eighteenth century destroyed part of the archives of Genazzano, resulting in a loss of records for the years 1460 to 1474 (including the year of the apparition, 1467).

In 1779, the Sacred Congregation of Rites submitted several documents about the apparition, presented by the postulator of the cause for a proper Office and Mass of Our Lady of Good Counsel, to the examination of two outstanding experts, Gaetano and Calisto Marini. The promoter of the Faith wanted to know if they could guarantee the authenticity of the proofs of the apparition so that they might serve as a basis for the Holy See to grant the requested Mass and Office. The two learned men made a thorough examination of the material, investigated the archives to resolve any misgivings, and traveled to Genazzano for on-site examinations of two inscriptions in the shrine. Their opinion, completely favorable, permitted the Congregation to approve the requested Mass and Office.

The Most Reverend Agostino Felice Addeo, O.E.S.A., titular bishop of Trajanopolis, assembled what one author calls a "mass of proofs" about the apparition of the image and of its origin and published them in the *Analecta Augustiniana* (vol. 20, January-December, 1946). That work, a fruit of great wisdom and learning, was later edited in book form and is priceless for those who study the history of Our Lady of Good Counsel of Genazzano.

Briefly, here are some of the documents assembled by Bishop Addeo.

I. REGARDING THE APPARITION IN GENAZZANO

a) Documents Contemporaneous with the Apparition (Fifteenth Century)

1. *IN DEFENSORIUM ORDINIS FRATRUM HEREMITARUM SANCTI AUGUSTINI.* A work published in 1481 by the General of the Order of the Hermits of Saint Augustine, Ambrosio Massari da Cori (or Coriolano), in answer to two canons regular of Saint Augustine who denied that the hermits had the Bishop of Hippo as a Patriarch. While demonstrating the flourishing of sanctity in his Order as a proof (among others) that it had its origin in the Holy Doctor, Coriolano wrote the most ancient extant narration of the miraculous event at Genazzano:

"The eighth was Blessed Petruccia of Genazzano, who sold all her possessions to build the church of our convent on the site of her own home, following the counsel of Christ: 'If thou wilt be perfect, go sell what thou hast, and give to the poor . . . and follow me.' And because her resources were insufficient to finish it she became the object of derision from all the people. She would, however, say: 'Do not worry, my children, because before I die (she was already very old), the Blessed Virgin and Saint Augustine will finish this church.' " The fulfillment of this prophecy was admirable, since scarcely a year later an image of the Blessed Virgin miraculously appeared on the wall of that church. All of Italy yearned to contemplate her—so much so that cities and villages went there in procession, resulting in indescribable signs, prodigies, and alms; and thus, while she was still living, not only a church but a beautiful convent was built. When she died, she was buried in the chapel of the aforementioned image during the time of our office as provincial."

Coriolano served as head of the Roman Province during two periods (1466-1468 and 1470-1476) and later became the General of the Order (1476-1485). The apparition occurred during his first period as provincial.

"The authority of Coriolano is very serious," writes the learned Gaetano

Marini, "due to his office and also because he was a contemporary author and eyewitness. Also important are the memoirs he left in his work written to refute the Lateran canons of the Congregation of Santa Maria Frisionaria. He obviously expected rebuttals and criticisms, for he prepared himself by relating things in his books that his enemies could not have easily refuted" (Addeo, pp. 89 and 130).

2. *VITA PAULI II*. Written in 1478 by the Most Reverend Miguel Canensio, bishop of Castro, and dedicated to the Cardinal D'Estouteville. It is considered the most important and complete of the contemporary biographies of that Pope (cf. Addeo, p. 10). Canensio says, in reference to the year 1467: "At that time, in the town of Genazzano, in the diocese of Palestrina, God performed numberless and admirable miracles by means of an image of the Blessed Virgin Mary; he [the Pope] appointed Gaucerio, bishop of Gap, and Nicolo, of the Church of Fara, for their examination" (Addeo, p. 10).

3. *LIBRI CAMERALES*. These are records of income and disbursements of the Apostolic Camera. This document refers to the payments made to the two prelates mentioned above for expenses incurred *"in eundo ad terram Jenazzani pro certa comissione eis facta per S. D. N. Papa"*; in another similar codex, in Italian, the payment on July 24, 1467, can be read *"per spese facte"* by the bishops *"in andare a Jenazzano mandati da nostro S."* (Addeo, pp. 11-13). That confirms the statement of the biographer of Paul II and indicates that the mission entrusted by the Pontiff to the two prelates was accomplished scarcely three months after the apparition of the image. As various authors record (Buonanno, pp. 56-57; Dillon, p. 155), Canesius then tells of the miracles performed during that time by two images, one in Viterbo (*Madonna della Quercia*) and another in Rome itself (*Madonna della Consolazione*) on the Capitoline Hill without any papal inquiries about the fact. This indicates the repercussion that reports of the apparition of the image in Genazzano must have had in Rome.

4. *CODEX BOMBACINUS* or *CODEX MIRACULORUM*. This is a 32-page volume bound in cordovan that relates details of the 161 miracles performed by the image from April 27, the second day after the apparition, until August 14, 1467. It lists the names of those favored, their condition and origin, the witnesses, and other circumstances of interest. It alludes to contemporary historical facts, easily verified through other sources, such as the cure of a soldier wounded seven years before during a campaign in the Marches. Precisely in 1460, Sigismund Malatesta fought in those provinces for Charles of Anjou, who claimed the throne of Naples. The handwriting, the style of the letters, the orthography, abbreviations, the manner of expression, in a word, everything

contributed to the confirmation of its authenticity. The previously mentioned Vatican archivists considered that piece both authentic and contemporary, having been written a few months after the apparition. "In a word," writes Gaetano Marini, "I say that there is in the *Codex* no defect, whether external or internal, which is what the diplomatic critique demands for such monuments" (Addeo, p. 123). (A summary of this *Codex*, undertaken by the historian De Orgio is transcribed in Chapter 7.)

5. ACTS OF THE NOTARY PUBLIC OF GENAZZANO. This is an octavo volume of 369 numbered pages in which the acts of the years 1465-1500 were recorded by the notary, Martino Antonio Rose. "It is truly a distinguished monument for the history of this shrine, especially in the first years, or rather, first months of the apparition of the holy image" (Addeo, p. 13). Among other documents contained therein is the will of Nicolaus Antonius Johannes Mance dated September 11, 1467. The testator asks that his body be buried in the church of Holy Mary of Good Counsel and leaves a certain sum for the then recently founded Confraternity of Blessed Mary (*reliquit fraternitati beatae Mariae nova inventa).*"

6. ACTS OF THE NOTARY STEPHANO URBANI DE PILEO. This codex contains the will of Joannes Spagnolus (1482) who also wished to be buried in the *"Ecclesia sanctae Mariae boni consilii"* and leaves two ducats to the *"Capela miraculorum in dicta Ecclesia sita et constructa sub vocabulo beatae Mariae virginis."*

7. *RETRACTUM PECUNIARUM RECIPIENDARUM CAPPELLAE B. MARIAE.* These are parts of a codex in which the offerings made by the faithful at the chapel of Our Lady are registered. Names that appear in other documents are recorded here, as, for example: Joannes Spagnolus; donations given by Antonio Colonna, Prince of Salerno and of Genazzano, mayor of Rome in 1458, and by his wife Imperiale Colonna. The mayor died in 1472. It is curious to find that a certain *"Ventura ebreus"* took his precious ducat to the Madonna.

8. *DIARIUM NEPESINUM* (1459-1468). This is a diary or chronicle of the city of Nepi written by Father Antonio Lotieri who held the offices of vicar of the bishop of his diocese, canon of the cathedral, and rector of the church of Saint Gratuliano. He was also a notary public. He narrates events that were told to him about the inhabitants of his city. The *Diarium Nepesinum*, describes processions and pilgrimages to Holy Mary of Genazzano in the year of the apparition. The *Codex Miraculorum* (see no. 4 above), mentions several cures of inhabitants of Nepi.

Octaua fuit beata petrutia de Genazano: que uenditis omnibus in domo sua ecclesiam nostri conuentus fabricauit:adimplés consilium christi.Si uis perfectus esse uade & uende omnia que habes:da paupi bus:& sequere me:& cum eius facultates ad ecclesiam complendā nō suffice nt uenit in derisum toti populo. Ipa autem dicebat. Nolite curare,filii mei:quia anteq moriar:cum tunc decrepita esset:beata uir go & Sanctus augustinus complebunt ecclesiam istam. Sed mirabil fuit prophetiæ adimpletio:q à prolatis uerbis uix transiuit annus:q dam ymago beate uirginis in pariete dictæ ecclesiæ miraclose apparu it.Ad quam uisendam tota italia sic commota est:ut processionaliter illuc opida:& ciuitates confluerent:cum signis:miraculis:& elemosi nis inexplicabilibus.& ita adhuc ea uiuente non solum ecclesia .Sed pulcherrimus conuentus factus fuit:& moriens in capella dictæ ima ginis tempore nostri prouincialatus sepelitur.

¶ NONa fuit beata Sancta etiam de Genazanoque sic in contemplatō ne supernorum eleuata erat:ut singulis diebusin spiritu raperetur im mo non solum semel:sed toties ouotiens de deo:& de passione chri sti.aut de uita beatorum aliquid audiret.

¶ TERTIVM CAPITVLVM HVIVS SECVNDE PARTIS.
In quo puilegiorum summaria describuntur.

Am tertiam partem huius secunde partis aggredientes sub alphabeto Romanorum pontificum preter ea que dicta sunt singula munera & indulta a Sede Apostoli ca huic sacratissimo ordini concessa sub quodam com pendio ponemus.¶ Imprimis igitur.
Alexander quartus concedit ordini sancti augustini infrascripta pri legia.Primum ordines sancti Guilielmi fratris iohann toni:de Fa bali:de Britinis:de penitentia iesu christi:unit habitui:& obseruanti is ordinisfratrum heremitarum Sancti Augustini:& q nō cogi tur ad accipiendum & retinendum proprietates possessionum.Et priuile gium incipit.Licet ecclesiæ catholice integritatem coŗ oris sui sincera

Right. Leaf 56 of what is considered the original manuscript of the Life of Paul II, written in 1478 by the Most Reverend Miguel Canensio, bishop of Castro. It provides information concerning the measures adopted by that Pontiff in response to the reports of the appearance of a miraculous image of the Blessed Virgin in Genazzano in 1467.

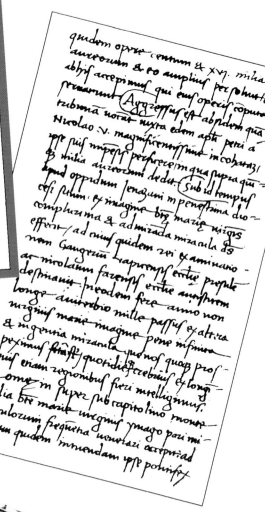

Left. Fifteenth-century tympanum of the main portal of the shrine of Mater Boni Consilii, one of the sections of the ancient "church of Blessed Petruccia" that have been preserved.

9. TWO INSCRIPTIONS. One, over the front of the chapel of the image, reads: *"Divinitus apparuit hec Imago A.D. MCLXVII XXV Aprilis"* (This image divinely appeared on April 25, 1467). The other inscription, over the main door of the church, reads: *"MCLXVII Sub annis Incarnati Dei Verbi festo Marci hora vesperi Dei Genetricis Mariae quam in hujus phani sacello marmoreo veneramini ex alto figura prospexit"* (At the hour of vespers, on the feast of Saint Mark, the year of the Incarnation of the Word 1467, the image of Mary, the Mother of God, that you venerate in the marble chapel, gazed from on high) (Addeo, p. 26). "Both inscriptions, carefully examined by experts, archaeologists, and custodians of the Vatican archives in 1779 by order of the Sacred Congregation of Rites, were recognized as authentic and contemporaneous with the apparition of the holy image" (Addeo, p. 26).

The latter inscription is the sole document of the fifteenth century that gives the hour of the miraculous event: the hour of vespers, that is, between four and five o'clock in the evening.

10. MARBLE ORNAMENT OF THE TYMPANUM OF THE MAIN DOOR OF THE CHURCH. The white marble tympanum represents, in sculpture, the Madonna and Child transported among clouds by angels. Like the inscriptions, it was considered by the aforementioned Vatican experts as contemporaneous with the miraculous apparition.

b) Documents from Shortly after the Apparition (Sixteenth Century)

1. *ACTA P. GENERALIS C. PATAVINI, AN. 1557.* In the general archives of the Order of the Hermits of Saint Augustine are two documents of the Prior General C. Patavino from the year 1557 with references to the apparition of the image of Our Lady in Genazzano and the miracles performed in the church of Holy Mary.

2. *INTROITO DAL 1567 USQUE 1647.* This is a volume kept in the convent of Holy Mary of Genazzano in which the ancient custom of donating money to the altar of the holy image on April 25 of each year in commemoration of the apparition can be confirmed.

3. *CHRONICON DE JERONIMO ROMAN* (Salamanca, 1569). This chronicles the apparition in virtually the same words as those of Coriolano.

4. *CRONICA ORDINIS FRATRUM EREMITARUM S. AUGUSTINI*, by Joseph Pamphilo, O.E.S.A. (Rome, 1581). This document also repeats Coriolano, adding the date and the hour of the miracle not found in that author.

5. WILL OF BARTOLOMEU BISCIA (1596). The testator leaves two hun-

dred coins for a lamp to be lit in front of the image of the "Most Holy Madonna of Genazzano, who divinely appeared in the locale of the Fathers of Saint Augustine."

These documents, although not belonging to the time of the miraculous event, are from a period relatively close to it and their authors, despite not witnessing the events narrated, could have heard of them from eyewitnesses.

However, it is only in the seventeenth century that histories, as such, appeared with all the details and circumstances surrounding the apparition. "But the want of such, in no way affects the mass of proof, traditional and historical, which exists, both for the wonderful apparition of the sacred image in Genazzano, and of its miraculous transfer from Scutari in Albania," comments Dillon (p. 146).

We conclude this part of our work with the words of Gaetano Marini, one of the Vatican experts who examined the documents on this subject: "We rejoice in the glorious image of Our Lady of Genazzano that had such illustrious and contemporary witnesses of her unexpected apparition and of the miracles performed then—from authors, the codex, and even the stones" (Addeo, p. 132).

II. REGARDING THE TRANSFER FROM SCUTARI

Regarding the transfer from Scutari to Genazzano, the silence of the archives is total. The writers of the day, Coriolano and Canesius, also omit that point. It is true that neither one wrote specifically a history of the apparition of the image but had other goals in mind: first, to prove that the Order of the Hermits was affiliated with Saint Augustine and, second, to narrate the life and acts of Pope Paul II. For these reasons, it is not surprising that they do not mention certain circumstances surrounding the event as, for example, the ringing of the bells, the heavenly choir, the arrival of the Albanian pilgrims, and the origin of the image.

The paucity of documents does not mean that evidence—clear, precise, and worthy of faith—did not exist long ago, since we have seen the vicissitudes the local archives suffered. If we do not have a written document about the transfer of the image, a constant and genuine tradition verifies it. Tradition is, for the historian, a source like any other, which, after due critique, deserves the same trust. "Any and every trace of the past capable of giving us information about a historical fact or event is called a document or source. . . . Documents are many and varied: they can be written texts, art objects, popular customs, oral traditions, and so on" (José Van Den Besselaar, *Introdução aos Estudos Históricos*, Coleção da Revista de História, 1956, p. 95).

Written documents as well as oral traditions rely on human testimony. In principle, it is true that every man can lie: *"Omnis homo mendax"* (Ps. 115:11). A person who gives an oral report can fool himself or lie just as can one who writes it down. But when it is a public event or a fact witnessed by a multitude, it is difficult that everyone would be equally deceived upon learning of it or would distort it in the same way when passing it on to posterity. Consequently, it is often the case that oral tradition is a surer source for the historian than an isolated written document. When facts reach us through different narrations—agreeing in their essential points (and this is precisely what happened in this case)—we can hold it as true since it is not probable that all the sources conspired to deceive us.

Having digressed a bit, let us return to our subject. Tradition regarding the arrival of the image in Genazzano from Albania was always very strong among the inhabitants of that town. The remembrance of this fact is also found among the Albanians, who always considered the Madonna of Good Counsel the same image that they formerly venerated in their country near Scutari.

First, let us examine the tradition of the image's presence in Genazzano and, then, the tradition persisting among the Albanian people.

a) The Tradition in Genazzano

To confirm the existence of the ancient tradition regarding the transfer of the image from Scutari to Genazzano we have:

1. THE GENEALOGY OF THE GEORGI FAMILY. According to tradition, two Albanians, Georgio and De Sclavis, followed the image of Scutari to Latium and set up residence close to the church chosen by her in Genazzano. Both were married there and left numerous offspring. The De Sclavis family line died out at the beginning of the eighteenth century. The Georgi (or Giorgi) family has continued until our time. Their family tree, put down in an orderly and legal way and based on notary documents, wills, and parish records, had its beginning in *"Georgius albanensis abitator Jenazzani,"* whose will was dictated to the notary Siciliani on February 25, 1512. This Georgius appears in many other documents with the denomination of *Contadinus, Albanensis, habitator* or *morans in Castro Genazzani* and even Schodrensis (of Schodra, = Scutari).

Among his descendants are several clergymen and religious, including a canon of the Lateran Basilica and many beneficiaries including outstanding figures in the public and social life of the city. Thus, together they form an uninterrupted chain, whose first link was the pilgrim Georgio, that has transmitted from father to son over five centuries the precious history of the translation.

2. TRADITION IN THE COLONNA FAMILY. The belief that the image had come from a remote region, transported by angels, always existed likewise among the princes of the house of Colonna, lords of Genazzano. A proof of this is the ex-voto offered to the chapel of the Madonna by the Constable Filipo Colonna, duke of Paliano, requesting the cure of his wife, Lucretia Tomacelli. It is a silver plaque depicting the duke on his knees and the duchess in her bed; the image of the Virgin is seen on high among the clouds, a clear reference to the miraculous translation. This piece dates from before 1622, the year in which that lady died.

Prince Giovanni, the son of Filipo Colonna, in a speech addressed to Pope Urban VIII when he visited the shrine in 1630, also comments on this fact when he affirms that the image was not transported by human hands and it came to Genazzano so that Latium would also have its Loreto. The Constable's secretary, Francisco Cirocco, was even more explicit when he stated that the painting had come from some remote country according to the "very old and deep-rooted tradition." A picture offered to the duchess of Paliano in 1648 shows the image upon clouds followed by the two Albanian pilgrims. All the details handed down to us by tradition are also related in a report by the Princess to Father Antonio Feroci on the same occasion.

3. TESTIMONY OF AGED INHABITANTS OF GENAZZANO IN 1778. In 1778, testimony of inhabitants of Genazzano nearing eighty years of age was presented to the Sacred Congregation of Rites. These declared having heard from their elders, who, in turn, had heard from their ancestors, that:

a) It is an ancient tradition that the image came from Albania, appearing on April 25, the feast of Saint Mark, between the hours of 4 and 5 in the evening and accompanied by an unexpected and miraculous ringing of all the bells in that place. As a remembrance of this, it is an old custom to have all the bells ring at that time of day during the Octave of the Feast;

b) It is an equally ancient tradition that this apparition was predicted by Blessed Petruccia;

c) Two Albanian pilgrims followed the image, one who was the head of the Giorgi family (still existing) and the other of the Sclavis family whose line has died out but whose last members the deponents knew personally;

d) Since time immemorial, the children of this city have sung these verses: "The Madonna of Good Counsel left Albania to come to my country. Long live the Madonna of Good Counsel";

e) They give evidence that they always heard their elders tell about the prodigies that took place at the shrine and the deponents were, themselves, witnesses to many in their time.

4. PRESENCE OF SEVERAL ALBANIANS IN GENAZZANO IMMEDIATELY FOLLOWING THE APPARITION. It was noted in the already mentioned *Codex Miraculorum* that during the first months after the apparition a great number of Albanians hastened to Genazzano. Three of them were favored with miracles in May and June of 1467. Three years later, with the conquest of Albania by the Turks, many Catholics from that country took refuge in Italy. They settled mainly in Venice and Calabria. Some, however, preferred Latium. The notary Rose records that at least six of them lived in Genazzano between 1487 and 1500. Why had they chosen that locality? Perhaps they wished to be close to the Madonna that they venerated in their own land. At any rate, they could have refuted the story told by their countrymen, Georgi and De Sclavis, had it been fraudulent.

5. DEVOTION OF THE ALBANIANS IN ITALY. A noteworthy circumstance as well as an argument of tradition that favors the fact that the image came from Scutari is that Albanians residing in Italy always showed devotion to the image, considering her as their patroness. The ardently apostolic priest Reverend Stefano Rodota was an Albanian by birth and a champion of that devotion in the eighteenth century. He referred to Our Lady of Good Counsel as the "Madonna of the Albanians."

b) The Enduring Tradition in Albania

A tradition analogous to that held by the Albanians residing in Italy existed among Catholics who remained in Albania after the Turkish invasion. Whoever is acquainted with the nature of the Turkish domination easily understands why no one went from Italy to Scutari to look into the truth of the matter about the two pilgrims, Georgio and DeSclavis. It was only in the eighteenth century, when Turkish religious intolerance softened somewhat, that it was possible to make any inquiries.

In a letter dated July 25, 1745, Captain Stephen Medin, an Albanian count, relates to a relative living in exile about the investigations he made in the Scutari region. The oldest inhabitants of the city stated that there was a church in the vicinity, almost in ruins, dedicated to Our Lady of the Annunciation where frequent miracles occurred. On the night of March 25, a lamp could be seen burning in front of the empty altar that was formerly occupied by the image of Our

Lady. Some felt that someone had taken the image away. However, the majority considered it a certainty that she had abandoned the church on her own. They added that the infidels had never been able to transform that church into a mosque, as was their custom, because impressive miracles always prevented profanation of the already ruined building. (This letter is reproduced in Chapter 10.)

In February 1748 an Albanian nobleman, Niccolo di Antonio Cambsi, who lived in Scutari and was a benefactor of the churches of the missionaries and bishops who had been sent to Albania by the Sacred Congregation of the Propagation of the Faith, testified under oath in Rome that a church greatly venerated by Catholics existed in his city and that there was a painting of the image on one wall of this church. That tradition was reinforced by the presence of the painting of two saints on either side of the place where the painting of Our Lady would have been. Niccolo was shown a copy of the image of the Mother of Good Counsel of the same size as the one venerated in Genazzano, and he stated that it corresponded to the empty space on the wall of the church in Scutari. He also told about the many punishments that fell upon the Turks who wanted to desecrate the church.

Catholics who lived in the neighborhood noticed that sometimes a light would descend over the ruins and burn in a miraculous way. Many Venetian citizens traveling to Scutari on business would customarily venerate the wall where the miraculous Virgin was. (Important passages of this declaration are transcribed in Chapter 10.)

In 1754, the Most Reverend Paulo Cambsi, bishop of Scutari, testified in the same manner—*"pro pura rei veritate"*—that according to ancient tradition, a church existed in the city from which an image of the Virgin Mary was divinely carried away and taken to other regions and that the faithful continued to receive many graces there, while the Mohammedans who tried to desecrate the venerable ruins were punished. He further declared that when he was in Genazzano, he celebrated Mass on the altar of the image and noticed that its colors were very similar to those of the paintings of the saints that remained in the church in Scutari. (Important passages of this declaration are transcribed in Chapter 10.)

In the last century, Father Pietro Belgrano, the Augustinian historian of the Genazzano shrine, received from Father Mariano de Palmanova, Apostolic Prefect of the Missions of Epirus, and from Monsignor Angelo Rodja, vicar-general of the archdiocese of Scutari, some interesting reports which confirmed that as late as 1878 the ancient tradition still existed among Albanian Catholics. (We have already quoted some of the passages of Monsignor Rodja's letter in

Chapter 10. Because of its documentary interest, Father Mariano de Palmanova's report was published in its entirety in the same chapter.)

In 1932, 340 Albanian pilgrims visited Genazzano at the invitation of the archbishop of Scutari. As a remembrance of that pilgrimage, a marble plaque was placed in the shrine inscribed in both Albanian and Italian as follows: "On June 2, 1932, Catholic Albania sent to this shrine under the direction of the Most Reverend Lazaro Mjedja, metropolitan archbishop of Scutari, together with six hierarchs from their Church, 340 sons and daughters—priests, religious and faithful—to pray with one voice and one soul: 'Return, O Lady of Good Counsel.' "

On June 25, 1967, Cardinal Ildebrando Antoniutti accompanied almost three hundred Albanian pilgrims to Genazzano who were refugees in Western Europe. He celebrated Mass close to the image "so that the Virgin [would] comfort them in their exile, clemently and piously assist their friends and relatives so far distant, and hasten the day of the liberation of their dear country" (*Madre del Buon Consiglio*, August-October 1967).

According to Monsignor Leone G. B. Nigris, Apostolic Delegate to Albania in 1946, even at that time there was great devotion to Our Lady of Good Counsel in that country, and there was not a Catholic home where her image was not found. She is the principal Patroness of Catholic Albania and the cathedral of Scutari is consecrated to her.

Monsignor Nigris, referring to the little church from whose walls the image of the Madonna of Genazzano was detached, states: "That church has not existed for a quarter of a century. In its place, a discreet church, still unfinished in its decoration, now rises. But a great error was committed: The wall with the rectangular space whence the fresco now in Genazzano detached itself was demolished without considering that a first-class document favoring tradition was being destroyed" (Addeo, p. 77). It was, indeed, an unfortunate error, for tradition has justly been called the "archive of truth, arbiter of doubts, treasurer of the years, and a highly esteemed gem of the Holy Church" (Francesco Cirocco, *Relazione del Ricevimento fatto in Genazzano della Santità di N. Sig. Papa Urbano VIII*, Foligno, 1633, in Addeo, p. 83).

*   *   *

Appendix 2
Documents

1 Italian text published in the magazine *Madre del Buon Consiglio* of Genazzano in its July-August 1985 issue, page 28.

"Da tempo eravamo sorpresi e amirati nel vedere spesso dei giovani stranieri raccolti en profonda preghiera nella cappella della Madonna. Um bel giorno abbiamo voluto conoscerli chiedendeo loro perché venivano così spesso a pregare nel nostro Santuario. Ci hanno detto che si sentivano molto attratti dalla bellissima Immagine della Madonna del Buon Consiglio, che se è manifestata con speciali favori al fondatore della loro Associazione: Plinio Corrêa de Oliveira. Abbiamo allora espresso il desiderio di poter avere una testimonianza del fatto, e gentilmente il Signor Plinio ci ha inviato dal Brasile la 'Dichiarazione' che pubblichiamo.

"Nel dicembre del 1967, avendo io 59 anni di età, fui colpito da una violenta crisi di diabete. Ne derivà una cancrena al piede destro, che indusse il chirurgo che mi curava a fare una amputazione delle quattro falangi minori.

"Tale misura non fu presa senza esitazione, poiché egli temeva profondamente che la cancrena si propagasse a tutto il piede, rendendo necessaria una amputazione più ampia.

"In questo caso, non sarebbe preferibile procedere in una sola volta a questa amputazione maggiore?

"Tuttavia continuai il ricovero con l'assistenza medica.

"Successe però, qualche tempo prima di questo fatto, che io avessi letto accidentalmente un libro intitolato 'La Vierge Mère du Bon Conseil', di Mons. George F. Dillon (Desclée de Brouwer, Bruges, 1885). Durante la lettura, sperimentavo nella mia anima una sensibile consolazione.

"Avendo viaggiato in Italia prima che mi ammalassi, il mio amico Dott. Vicente Ferreira, mi fece la gentilezza di portarmi da Genazzano una stampa rappresentante il venerato quadro di Nostra Signora del Buon Consiglio. Questa stampa

mi giunse nel momento di una prova spirituale che mi faceva soffrire molto più dell'infermità fisica.

"Dal 1960, ero presidente del Consiglio Nazionale della Società Brasiliana per la Difesa della Tradizione, Famiglia e Proprietà. Alcune circostanze, che non mi sembra il caso di menzionare, mi infondevano la certezza che fosse nei disegni della Providenza che questa associazione realizzasse una grande azione nel Brasile ed in tutta l'America del Sud, e anche in altri continenti, al servizio della Cristianità. D'altro lato, ero certo che la mia morte in quella situazione avrebbe portato alla rovina lo sforzo per l'opera che allora iniziava a fiorire con vigore, e che desideravo ardentemente portare a compimento per la maggior gloria di Nostra Signora prima di morire. A causa di ciò ero in uno stato di vera ansietà riguardo le incertezze sulla mia situazione clinica e chirurgica.

"Il giorno 16 dicembre, un altro amico, Dott. Martim Afonso Xavier da Silveira Jr., mi consegnò la suddetta stampa da parte del Dott. Vicente Ferreira.

"Quando la fissai, ebbi l'insperata impressione che la figura di Nostra Signora, pur non mutando in nulla, mi esprimesse una ineffabile e materna dolcezza, che mi confortava e mi infondeva nell'anima—non sò come—la convinzione che la Santissima Vergine mi prometteva che non sarei morto senza aver prima realizzato l'opera desiderata. Ciò mi infuse una grande soavità nell'anima.

"Anche ora conserva inatta la stessa convinzione. E, per il favore di Nostra Signore, questa opera ha prosperato ammirevolmente, avvalorando la speranza che la meta sarebbe stata raggiunta.

"Nell'occasione in cui fui beneficiato dalla grazia del sorriso promessa di Nostra Signora di Genazzano, non dissi nulla alle persone che mi erano intorno. Solo molto più tardi ne parlai agli amici. Due di questo, che mi tenevano compagnia in ospedale quando ricevetti la stampa, nell'udire la mia narrazione, affermarono di aver notato che la figura della Madre del Buon Consigilio mi fissava con molto compiacimento, il che attirò loro molto l'attenzione. Essi non avevano notato, tuttavia, il sorriso-promessa a cui alludevo.

"Essi sottoscrivono con me questa dichiarazione.

"Grazie anche alla Santissima Vergine, la mia salute all'epoca migliorò in modo tale da sorprendere il chirurgo. In conseguenza di ciò la seconda operazione non si rese necessaria.

"È con il cuore traboccante di amore e di gratitudine alla Madonna del Buon Consigilio di Genazzano che scrivo la presente dichiarazione.

Plinio Corrêa de Oliveira

San Paolo, 10 maggio 1985."

2 Italian text written on the back of the picture of Our Lady of Good Counsel that worked the stupendous miracle narrated in Chapter 9.

"Anno Domini 1796 Mense 7bris Die 4 hujus// Ad perpetuam rei memoriam. Si fa sapere a tutti i singoli che l'Imagine di Maria SSma. del Buon Consiglio, che qui avanti a questo picciolo Quadruccio, si vede in carta metà bruciata era prima attacata ad un muro nella Camera del Maestro di casa del Forno della Terra di Monte Compatri. Avendo voluto inbiancare detta camera si levò questa S. Immagine, quale senza avvedersene fu posta nel forno involta fra le fascine, che servirono a riscaldare il forno. Bruciate le fascine sudette, s'approssimò alla bocca del forno (cosa insolita) il Sig. Piero Settele, Direttore del medesimo, il quale si mise a tirare la carbonella, vidde una carta senza sapere cosa fosse, la rispinse affinchè bruciasse, dopo molto tempo vidde di nuovo la medesima carta, si levà dal fuoco, si guarda e si vede che era una carta rappresentante l'Immagine miracolissima di Maria SSma. di Genazzano, maravigliosamente preservata dalle fiamme incenditrice di quel forno, bruciata soltanto come si vede del basso dell'Immagine e di un lato. Maria ed il Suo SSmo. Figlio, non fu che toccata da qualche picola scintilla di fuoco, come si vede. Questo portentoso miracolo accaduto nel forno di Monte Compatri feudo di S. E. il Sig. Principe Borghese, si è registrato qui dietro a Detta SSma. Immagine, affinchè la memoria passi da Padre in Figlio, e da Figlio in Nipoti, e così in pertetuo, affinchè sempre mai viva si mentenga la Divozione a si cava Madre; il Sig. Pietro Settele a questo fine gli ha fatto fare il presente tabernacoletto, affinchè peretuamente si conservi, e ciò fece per sua particolar Divozione. //Piccola Orazione a Maria SSma. del Buon Consiglio // per impetrare la Sua protezione // Voi o Maria SSma. del Buon Consiglio, i cuori di tutti i vostri Divoti accendete voi tutti infiammateli affinchè tutti a voi ricorrino o gran Madre di Dio. Fate o gravi Signora, che tutti vi eleggono per Maestra, e Saggia consigliera della anime loro, essendo voi come dice S. Agostino; et consilium Apostolorum, et consilium omnium gentium. E così sia."

*   *   *

Appendix 3

The Cult of Our Lady of Good Counsel Through the Ages

AS we have seen, devotion to Our Lady of Good Counsel was never restricted to the inhabitants of Genazzano: Italy, Europe, the New World, and, truly, the whole world was the field chosen by Mary Most Holy to distribute her graces from Genazzano. Apostles of the cult of this holy fresco were not lacking, raised up by the Mother of Fair Love throughout the ages. Friar De Orgio, Father Belgrano, Father Buonanno, Monsignor Dillon, and others, wrote books about the Virgin of Good Counsel. Some, like Saint Alphonsus Mary De Liguori or Blessed Stefano Bellesini, were exalted to the honor of the altars. Others are less famous, though they are recognized by their contemporaries for their piety.

The Pious Union of Our Lady of Good Counsel

The great apostle of the devotion to Our Lady of Good Counsel in the eighteenth century was Canon Andrea Bacci. He satisfied every request made to him for pictures of the Madonna by "a great number of people from many distant provinces and kingdoms": Dalmatia, Portugal, Catalonia, America, and elsewhere, as he affirms in a letter dated 1748. Friar De Orgio wrote his history of Our Lady of Good Counsel, at his insistence. (Cf. Buonanno, pp. 245-256, and Dillon, pp. 386-396.)

However, this was not enough, for it was not possible for many of these devotees—even once in a lifetime—to go and kneel in front of the fresco in Genazzano. To satisfy those desires and enable them to participate in some way in the spiritual benefits so abundantly poured forth there, an association was founded to unite them. Thus was born the Pious Union of Our Lady of Good Counsel of Genazzano, a "daughter of the suffering that fills all of those who once visit the shrine and see the most pure face of this Mother and, afterwards, have to leave her" as Tomas, bishop of Salamanca, wrote in 1893. (Tomas, p. 105.)

The Pious Union was established in 1753 by Pope Benedict XIV with a solemn brief in response to the petition of Father Francis Xavier Vasquez, general of the Augustinians. His Holiness wanted to be the first member of the new association and inscribed his name in the register in his own hand. Following the Pope's example, the king of Spain and innumerable other princes and lords, as well as cardinals and bishops, joined the Pious Union throughout the centuries. Benedict XIV enriched it with many indulgences that were confirmed and augmented by his successors.

To belong to the association, it is necessary to be enrolled with the director at Genazzano or with a local director; to make a donation according to one's means; to pray three Hail Marys with the invocation *"Mater Boni Consilii, ora pro nobis"*; to carry on one's person a picture, medal, or scapular of the same Virgin; to celebrate or have a Mass celebrated every year or, if that is not possible, to receive Communion, the Mass or Communion to be offered for the spiritual benefit of all the members.

Members of the Pious Union may receive a plenary indulgence, with the usual conditions, on the following days:
—the day of enrollment;
—once a year, for those who visit the shrine of Genazzano;
—the feast of Our Lady of Good Counsel (April 26);
—the feast of Saint Monica (May 4);
—the feast of Saint Rita of Cascia (May 22);
—the feast of Saint Augustine (August 28);
—the feast of the Blessed Virgin Mary, Mother of Consolation (on the Sunday following the feast of Saint Augustine);
—the feast of the Nativity of Our Lady (September 8) for those who visit the shrine of the Madonna of Good Counsel in Genazzano on that day;
—the feast of Saint Nicholas of Tolentine (September 10). (See *Madre del Buon Consiglio*, nos. 1-2, January-February, 1987.)

The Liturgical Cult Through Time

The final and most significant seal that the Church places on a devotion is granting it a special liturgy and a proper feast. "How," Buonanno asks, "could she celebrate a fact without recognizing it as true?" (Buonanno, p.78; see also Dillon, pp. 415-416).

On July 12, 1727, the Sacred Congregation of Rites granted the secular and regular clergy of Genazzano the privilege of celebrating the feast of Our Lady of Good Counsel on the anniversary of the apparition of the image with the Mass and Office common to the other Marian feasts. Later on, this privilege was extended to the clergy of Palestrina, the diocese to which Genazzano belongs. Later yet, the feast was elevated to a Double of the Second Class, without an octave.

Subsequently, the Augustinian order asked the Sacred Congregation of Rites for the approval of a proper Mass and Office for Our Lady of Good Counsel. The Congregation submitted all the documents related to the apparition that had been gathered by the postulator of the cause for the proper Office and Mass for examination by two outstanding archaeologists and paleographers—Calistus and Gaetano Marini, custodians of the Secret Pontifical Archives. The result of the investigation by those experts (as mentioned in Appendix 1) was highly favorable. As a result, in 1779, the Sacred Dicastery approved for the Genazzano clergy the liturgy composed by the postulator himself, the Augustinian Father Daniel Marcolini. The Prior General of the Hermits of Saint Augustine extended that privilege to all his order with a decree of March 14, 1781. In 1789, the Congregation of Rites confirmed the concession of the proper Mass and Office of the feast of Our Lady of Good Counsel.

Pope Leo XIII, in turn, approved a new Office and Mass—with antiphons and lessons—more adequate to the invocation of Our Lady of Good Counsel. The hymns at Matins in this new Office—taken from the liturgy composed by Father Marcolini—invite the faithful to praise Mary, who chose Genazzano as the shrine for her miraculous image. The antiphons, taken from the Sapiential Books, are applied to the Blessed Virgin as the possessor and dispenser of the gifts of Counsel, Wisdom, and Knowledge: *"Accipe consilium intellectus et ne abjicias consilium meum"* (Take wise counsel, and cast not away my advice, Ecclus. 6:24); *"Via stulti recta in oculis ejus, qui autem sapiens est, audit consilia"* (The way of a fool is right in his own eyes, but he that is wise hearkeneth unto counsels, Prov. 12:15); and so on.

Later reforms of the liturgical books by Saint Pius X and Paul VI introduced small modifications in this Office.

For the city of Genazzano, the apparition of the holy fresco is celebrated on the day of the apparition, April 25; but in the rest of the Church, the feast is commemorated on April 26 since the 25th is consecrated to the Evangelist Saint Mark.

The Jubilee Year

April 25, 1967, was the five-hundredth anniversary of the holy apparition. An entire year of commemorations marked the sacred event. It began in Genazzano, in the name of and with a delegation of His Holiness Paul VI, by His Eminence Cardinal Benedict Aloisi Masella, bishop of the suburbicarian diocese of Palestrina.

Among the quinquennial celebrations, the series of conferences on the theme "The Holy Ghost and Most Holy Mary," promoted by the Executive Committee under the presidency of His Excellency Bishop Pietro Canisius van Lierde, sacristan to His Holiness, was outstanding.

During this jubilee year, crowds of pilgrims thronged the shrine. In the months of May, June, and July alone, close to 250,000 faithful venerated the miraculous image.

Notes

Chapter 1

1. Saint Bernard of Clairvaux, "First Sermon on the Virgin Mother," *St. Bernard's Sermons for the Seasons and Principal Festivals of the Year*, vol. 1 (Westminster, Md.: Carroll Press, 1950), pp. 64-65.

2. Saint Alphonsus De Liguori, "Acclamations in Praise of Mary," in *The Glories of Mary*, ed. Rev. Eugene Grimm, C.SS.R. (Brooklyn: Redemptorist Fathers, 1931), pp. 676-8.

Chapter 3

3. Fr. Thomas de Saint Laurent, *The Book of Confidence* (Crompond, N.Y.: America Needs Fatima, 1989), p. 11.

4. Raffaele Buoanno, *Memorie Storiche della Imagine di Maria SS. del Buon Consiglio che si venera in Genazzano*, 2d ed. (Naples: Tipografia dell'Immacolata, 1880), pp. 44-45.

5. Friar Angelo Maria De Orgio, Monsignor George F. Dillon, and Bishop Agostino Felici Addeo are authors who have published books of greater historical scope about the holy fresco of Genazzano.

The oldest of these works is *Istoriche Notizie della prodigiosa apparizione dell'Immagine di Maria Santissima del Buon Consiglio, nella Chiesa dei Padri Agostiniani di Genazzano*, published in 1748 in Rome by Friar Angelo Maria De Orgio, O.S.A. The author had access to innumerable original documents that had disappeared. (Regarding the disappearance of documents see Appendix 1.) Thus, his book became an indispensable reference for anyone studying the devotion to the Mother of Good Counsel of Genazzano.

A missionary in Australia, Monsignor George F. Dillon had to spend a long period in Italy to recover his health. During this time, he visited the shrine of Our Lady of Good Counsel in Genazzano and became a great devotee and promoter of this invocation. In Rome, in 1883, he wrote *The Virgin Mother of Good Counsel*, which received a laudatory letter of approval from the reigning Pontiff, Leo XIII. It is undoubtedly the most complete and well-documented work on the history of the devotion to Our Lady of Good Counsel. [Editor's note: While the author used the French translation of this work, prepared by the Benedictines of the Isle of Wight and reviewed by Monsignor Dillon himself, we have referred to the English edition published in Rome by Propaganda Fide in 1884. We have quoted exactly, save for some adjustments in punctuation to conform to modern style in cases where we believe clarity is thereby served.]

In addition to these works, the 1947 work of Bishop Agostino Felice Addeo, O.S.A., deserves mention as providing a precious collection of documents (some cited by Friar De Orgio, others first cited here) regarding the translation of the holy image from Scutari to Genazzano and the devotion to the Mother of Good Counsel in the two places. Under the title *Apparitionis Imaginis Beatae Mariae Virginis a Bono Consilio Documenta*, it appeared in *Analecta Augustiniana*, and the Tipografia Vaticana printed a separate of this study.

In the bibliography of the present volume, pp. 240-243, the reader will find a more ample list of publications on the theme of the work.

6. De Orgio, pp. 139-140.

7. Francisco Solimena, an Italian painter known as *Abate Ciccio*, was born in Nocera de Pagani on October 4, 1657, and died in Naples on April 5, 1747. A son of the painter Angel Solimena, his paintings are found in almost all European museums as well as in churches and palaces.

When already eighty years of age, he was commissioned to paint one of the eight pictures that would decorate the principal hall of the royal palace of Saint Ildephonsus in Spain. He also painted two pictures for King Philip V of Spain, which are now in the Prado, where there is also a self-portrait of the artist. Among his best works is a series of frescoes, depicting several stories of saints, painted for the church of Saint Paul in Rome. Naples, where he lived for most of his life, has many of his works. (Cf. *Enciclopédia Universal Ilustrada*, vol. 57 [Bilbao: Espasa-Calpe, 1927].)

8. For several centuries, the image was customarily veiled by a silver door and curtain which were opened only under certain circumstances.

9. Buonanno, pp. 196-200. See also Dillon, pp. 96-102.

10. Addeo, pp. 45-46

11. Monsignor Dillon, as previously noted, was a missionary in Australia.

12. Dillon, pp. 93-95.

13. Buonanno, p. 44.

14. Addeo, p. 120.

15. Ibid., pp. 121-122.

16. Ibid., p. 121.

17. Ludwig von Pastor, *The History of the Popes from the Close of the Middle Ages*, vol. 2 (St. Louis: B. Herder, 1923), p. 429.

Chapter 4

18. The official proclamation of Our Lady of Good Counsel as Patroness of Albania occurred only in 1895. However, according to the oldest traditions, the Albanians have considered her as their protectoress ever since the miraculous apparition in Scutari in the twelfth or thirteenth century. She was venerated under the title of Our Lady of Scutari, Our Lady of Good Services, or Our Lady of the Annunciation—the last name being derived from the ancient church on the banks of the Drin and the Bojana Rivers where the fresco was venerated.

In the magazine *Madre del Buon Consiglio*, published by the Augustinian friars of the Shrine of Genazzano (nos. 11-12, November-December 1985), Domenico Marcucci wrote in his article "Santuari Mariani dell'Albania": "The Blessed Virgin of Good Counsel was always deeply impressed in the hearts of the Albanians. In 1895 she was proclaimed Patroness of the nation. On the other hand, at the beginning of the present century, in the place where, according to tradition, the church of the Mother of Good Counsel was built, a new Marian shrine was erected with the same title.'' See further details of this in Chapter 10.

19. Pastor, ibid. Regarding the truth about the extraordinary life of Scanderbeg, Pastor, aside from quoting Barletius and Turkish sources contemporaneous with Scanderbeg, refers to studies by Hopf, Jirecek, Makuscev, Pisko, Caro, Kenner, Fallmerayer, Hertzberg, Petrowitsch, Pisani, et al. See also Johann Baptist Weiss, *Historia Universal*, vol. 8 (Barcelona: Tip. La Educación, 1927-1933). Among the historians of the shrine, see the works already quoted of De Orgio, Buonanno, Dillon, and Addeo.

20. Dillon, p. 106.

21. Weiss, vol. 8, p. 28 ff.; cf. Pastor, vol. 1, pp. 326 ff.

22. Dillon, pp. 126-127.

23. Dillon, p. 127.

24. Buonanno, p. 36.

25. Weiss, vol. 8, p. 89.

26. *"Ultra omnes catholicos principes de fide et religione christiana optimemeritum."* B. Llorca, S.J.; R. García Villoslada, S.J.; F. J. Montalban, S.J., *Historia de la Iglesia Católica*, vol. 3 (Madrid: B.A.C., 1960), p. 368.

27. Pastor, vol. 2, p. 434.

28. Weiss, vol. 8, p. 85.

29. Ibid., p. 90.

30. Historians differ about the exact year of the death, although not about the day. Some contend that it occurred in 1467; others hold that it was 1468. In this, we follow the opinions of Weiss, Rohrbacher, Dillon, and others.

31. Weiss, vol. 8, p. 92.

32. In the Ambras Collection at Vienna. Pastor, vol. 4, p. 90.

Chapter 5

33. About the proclamation of the Mother of Good Counsel as the Patroness of Albania, see note 18 in the preceding chapter.

34. Dillon, p. 106.

35. "And when Pharaoh had sent out the people . . . the Lord went before them to show the way by day in a pillar of a cloud, and by night in a pillar of fire: that he might be a guide of their journey at both times" (Exod. 13:17, 21).

36. The distance, in a straight line, from Scutari to Rome is 360 miles, of which nearly 200 are over the waters of the Adriatic. The shortest point between the Balkans and the Italian peninsula is 105 miles, much to the south of both Scutari and Rome.

37. Since the miraculous arrival of the holy fresco in Scutari in the twelfth century, the Albanians believed that the image came from some other region where she was not venerated with due piety and that she would move her lukewarm children to conversion by depriving them of her presence. The departure of the image from Scutari in 1467 did nothing short of affirming this conviction. Until this day, a verse of an old and well-known religious hymn sung by Catholic Albanians says: "Come back soon, O gracious Mother! Come back soon to Albania!"

38. Cf. Saint Augustine, *Basic Writings of Saint Augustine*, vol. 2, *The City of God* (New York: Random House, 1948), books 1 and 2.

39. See Dillon, pp. 58 and 64. This bas-relief is still kept in the shrine of Genazzano.

40. Cf. Elssio, O.E.S.A., *Encomasticon Augustinianum* (Brussels, 1654), pp. 558-559, in Addeo, p. 34; Choriolani, *In Defensorium Ordinis Fratrum Heremitarum Sancti Augustini* (Rome, 1481), in Addeo, p. 8.

41. Dillon, pp. 77-80.

43. Hvar, called Pharus in ancient times and Lesina in Italian, is an island located off the coast of Dalmatia, not far from Albania, presently in Yugoslavian waters.

44. See Addeo, pp. 10-12; Dillon, p. 153; Buonanno, pp. 55-58.

45. See Senni, *Memorie di Genazzano e de' vicini paesi* (Rome, 1838). See also Dillon, pp. 182-183, and Buonanno, pp. 44-45.

Chapter 6

46. Dillon, pp. 237-238.

47. Dillon, pp. 238-9. Monsignor Dillon published his book about Our Lady of Good Counsel in 1883. Some people affirm that the shrine of Lourdes today registers a greater number of miracles than Genazzano. Holy Mother Church does not advise making this kind of comparison. At any rate, the miracles of Lourdes, celebrated the world over, do not diminish the force of the affirmation made in 1883 by the great historian of the Queen of Good Counsel.

48. See Appendix 1 for the present state of the critical study of the documents referring to the Mother of Good Counsel.

49. Bishop Tomas of Salamanca, *María Madre del Buen Consejo* (Salamanca: Imp. Calatrava, 1893), pp. 66-67. Today innumerable ex-votos decorate the walls of the shrine. A museum was opened, occupying some rooms of the convent, to display documents and artworks attesting to the miracles. The pages of *Madre del Buon Consiglio*, a monthly publication, recount the pilgrimages and the gratitude of the faithful for graces obtained.

50. Unfortunately, the original documents on the 161 miracles cannot be found. Today we have only the substantial notes made by the historian De Orgio and the pontifical examiners. These are the object of the next chapter.

51. De Orgio, p. 27.

52. As mentioned earlier, for many centuries the image was customarily covered with a silver plate and curtain that were only opened under certain circumstances.

53. De Orgio, pp. 73-77.

54. De Orgio, pp. 55-57. In De Orgio's book, the Hungarian is called Marco (Mark) twice and later on, Nicola. We suppose the latter is a typographical error and so we have given Mark as the true name.

55. De Orgio, pp. 50-52.

56. Ibid., pp. 58-60.

57. Ibid., pp. 54-55.

58. Ibid., pp. 62-64.

59. Cf. ibid., pp. 60-61.

60. Cf. ibid., pp. 224-229.

61. Dillon, p. 269. See also Davide Perini, *Genazzano e suo territorio* (Rome: Ausonia, 1924), p. 135.

62. See the account of this pilgrimage in Chapter 11.

63. Dillon, pp. 270-1.

64. Ibid., p. 271.

65. Quoted by Dillon, pp. 271-2.

Chapter 7

66. Addeo, pp. 30-31.

Chapter 8

67. Pastor, vol. 3, pp. 325-326.
68. Plinio Corrêa de Oliveira, *Revolution and Counterrevolution*, 2d ed. (New Rochelle, N.Y.: Foundation for a Christian Civilization, 1980), p. 29.
69. Fr. Feliciano Cereceda, S.J., *Diego Lainez en la Europa religiosa de su tiempo: 1512-1565* (Madrid: Ed. Cultura Hispánica, 1945), p. 175. As regards that decadence, we can also consult Pastor, vols. 2-8; Weiss, vols. 6-7; J. Lucas-Dubreton, *La renaissance italienne* (Paris: Amiot, 1953); Paul Faure, *La renaissance*, 5th ed. (Paris: Puf, 1969); Franz Funck-Brentano, *The Renaissance* (New York: The Macmillan Company, 1936); Louis Batiffol, *Le siècle de la Renaissance* (Paris: Hachette, 1924); Abel Lefranc, *A vida quotidiana no tempo do Renascimento* (Lisbon: Ed. Livros do Brasil, 1962).
70. Pastor, vol. 9, pp. 134-135. That panorama of generalized decadence described by contemporary pontifical documents is also depicted by highly regarded historians of our time.
71. Corrêa de Oliveira, pp. 28-38 and pp. 61-70.
72. In the Bull *Exsurge Domine*, of June 15, 1520, Pope Leo X condemned this abominable affirmation together with forty other errors of the German heretic. Cf. Heinrich Denzinger and Adolphus Schoenmetzer, *Enchiridion Symbolorum*, no. 1484 (previously no. 774).
73. Cf. Dillon, pp. 135-139.
74. Ibid., pp. 139-140.
75. Cf. Deut. 32; Joshua 7; Judges 2:1-23, 3:7-15, and others.
76. Buonanno, p. 135
77. Dillon, p. 142.
78. Fabio Mariano and Cesare Panepuccia, *Genazzano, storia e architectura* (Rome: Ed. Kappa, 1985), pp. 45-46.
79. Cf. Weiss, vol. 11, pp. 527, 552 and 556.
80. Cf. Dillon, pp. 142-3, 325.
81. In this regard, see the impressive account of a witness of the crowning in Chapter 3.
82. Weiss, vol. 11, p. 540.
83. Ibid., p. 899.

Chapter 9

84. Manzini, *Vita e miracoli de B.L.G.* (Brescia: 1701), L. I, c. 7, p. 75; L.3, c. 4, p. 338, in Fr. Maurice Meschler, S.J., *St. Aloysius Gonzaga: Patron of Christian Youth* (London: B. Herder Book Co., 1911), p. 80.
85. Dillon, pp. 300-301. The picture was glued to a piece of wood, on the back of which was placed a written declaration of the miracle. An English translation of it may be found in Appendix 2.
86. Manoel Altenfelder Silva, *Brasileiros Heróis da Fé*, vol. 2 (Petrópolis: Vozes, 1949), p. 73.

Chapter 10

87. Dillon, p. 151.

88. Dillon, pp. 183-189.

89. Dillon, p. 217. This document is from the nineteenth century. Actually, those churches no longer exist today. See also Addeo, p. 70.

90. Cf. Addeo, loc. cit.

91. Dillon, pp. 202-204.

92. De Orgio, pp. 4-6.

93. Addeo, pp. 59-61.

94. Addeo, pp. 61-62.

95. Addeo, pp. 63-68.

96. Addeo, p. 77.

97. Addeo, pp. 77-78.

98. Gjon Sinishta, *The Fulfilled Promise: A Documentary Account of Religious Persecution in Albania* (Santa Clara, Calif.: H & F Composing Service—Printing, 1976), pp. 68-69; Anton Gaspri, "Mother, Do Not Weep for What You See Now. Weep for What Is to Come: A Testimony of Bishop George Volaj of Sappa—His Sufferings and Death," in Sinishta, pp. 95-98.

99. Prof. Karl Gurakuqi, "Madonna of Shkodra—A Holy Legend," in Sinishta, pp. 206-209; Gaspri, p. 97.

100. *Der Fels*, Regensburg, March 1986, p. 82.

101. Gaspri, p. 97.

102. This is how the famous document of the Sacred Congregation for the Doctrine of the Faith, signed by Cardinal Ratzinger describes the communist regimes. See *Instruction on Certain Aspects of the "Theology of Liberation,"* August 6, 1984 (Boston: St. Paul Editions, 1984), XI, p. 32.

103. *TFP Newsletter*, vol. 4, no. 15, 1985.

Chapter 11

104. In his famous encyclical *Pascendi Dominici Gregis*, Saint Pius X declared modernism to be the "synthesis of all heresies."

105. Rafael Cardinal Merry del Val, *Memories of Pope Pius X* (Westminster, Md.: The Newman Press, 1951), pp. 2-3.

106. Cf. Virgilio Caselli, *Ricordi di un itinerario: Visite a Maria in centoundici chiese Romane* (Rome: Benedittine di Priscilla, 1957), p. 246.

107. In those days, a decree of the Curia forbade the construction of churches or chapels that had their inspiration in "apparitions" not recognized by the Church as authentic. See Chapter 7 for more details about this pontifical inquiry.

108. See Chapter 8.

109. See Appendix 3 for the history of the Pious Union of Our Lady of Good Counsel. Commenting on the brief of approbation of Benedict XIV, Monsignor Dillon writes: "Certainly no Pontiff ever lived who could be more careful in the examination of the claims to sanctity of persons, or places, or things, than Benedict XIV" (p. 451); and later, he qualifies this Pope as the greatest "enemy of anything like exaggeration in the narration of supernatural occurrences" (p. 194).

110. *Insegnamenti di Giovanni Paolo II — 1978*, vol. 1 (Lib. Ed. Vaticana, 1979), p. 63.

111. Dillon, p. 123.

112. Belgrano, "Giornale del Pellegrino," in Addeo, p. 85.

113. Cf. Giovanni Battista Lemoyne, *Memorie Biografiche del Venerabile Don Giovanni Bosco*, vol. 5 (Turin: Buona Stampa, 1905), pp. 898-899, extra commercial ed.; *Vita di San Giovanni Bosco*, vol. 1 (Turin: Sta. Ed. Internazionale, 1941), pp. 543-553.

114. Attilio Borzi, *Um uomo per gli altri: B. Stefano Bellesini* (Genazzano: Santuario Madre del Buon Consiglio, 1973), p. 155.

115. Borzi, p. 167.

116. Father Stefano Bellesini was beatified by Saint Pius X on December 27, 1904. The Church celebrates his memory on February 3 so as not to conflict with the feast of Our Lady.

117. Tomas, pp. 93-94.

118. De Orgio, p. 152.

119. *Catolicismo*, nos. 208-209, April-May 1968.

Epilogue

120. Saint Bernard, "Glories of the Virgin Mother," *Missus Est*, homily 2,17, from Ailbe J. Luddy, O.Cist., *Life and Teaching of St. Bernard*, 2d ed. (Dublin: M. H. Gill & Son, 1937), p. 92.

Bibliography

Addeo, O.E.S.A., Fr. Augustinus Felix. *Apparitionis Imaginis Beatae Mariae Virginis a Bono Consilio Documenta.* Typis Polyglottis Vaticanis, 1947; excerptum ex *Analecta Augustiniana,* vol. 20, January 1945-December 1946.

Alphonsus De Liguori, Saint. *The Glories of Mary.* Brooklyn: Redemptorist Fathers, 1931.

Augustine, Saint. *Basic Writings of Saint Augustine.* Vol. 2. *The City of God.* New York: Random House, 1948.

Altenfelder Silva, Manoel E. *Brasileiros Heróis da Fé.* Petrópolis: Vozes, 1949.

Aubron, S.J., Pierre. *L'Oeuvre Mariale de Saint Bernard.* Paris: Ed. du Cerf, 1936.

Batiffol, Louis. *Le siècle de la Renaissance.* Paris: Hachette, 1924.

Bernard, Saint. *St. Bernard's Sermons for the Seasons and Principal Festivals of the Year.* Westminster, Md.: Carroll Press, 1950.

Besselaar, José Van Den. *Introdução aos Estudos Históricos.* Coleção da Revista de História, 1956.

Borzi, Attilio. *Um uomo per gli altri: B. Stefano Bellesini.* Genazzano: Santuario Madre del Buon Consiglio, 1973.

Buonanno, Raffaele. *Memorie Storiche della Immagine di Maria SS. del Buon Consiglio che si venera in Genazzano.* 2d ed. Naples: Tipografia dell'Immacolata, 1880.

Caselli, Virgilio. *Ricordi di un itinerario: Visite a Maria in centoundici chiese Romane.* Rome: Benedittine di Priscilla, 1957.

Cereceda, S.J., Fr. Feliciano. *Diego Lainez en la Europa Religiosa de su tiempo: 1512-1565.* Madrid: Ed. Cultura Hispánica, 1945.

Chevalier, Bernard. *L'Occident de 1280 à 1492.* Paris: Armand Colin, 1969.

Choriolani, Ambrosii. *In Defensorium Ordinis Fratrum Heremitarum Sancti Augustini.* Rome: Georgio Herolt, 1481.

Cirocco, Francesco. *Relazione del Ricevimento fatto in Genazzano della Santità di N. Sig. Papa Urbano VIII.* Foligno, 1633.

Corrêa de Oliveira, Plinio. *Revolution and Counterrevolution.* 2d ed. New Rochelle, N.Y.: The Foundation for a Christian Civilization, Inc., 1980.

De Orgio, Fr. Angelo Maria. *Istoriche Notizie della prodigiosa apparizione dell'Immagine di Maria Santissima del Buon Consiglio, nella Chiesa dei Padri Agostiniani di Genazzano.* Rome: Stamperia di S. Michele, 1748.

Denzinger, Henricus, and Schönmetzer, Adolfus. *Enchiridion Symbolorum.* Rome: Herder, 1965.

Dillon, Msgr. George F. *The Virgin Mother of Good Counsel.* Rome: Propaganda Fide, 1884.

Elssio O.E.S.A., *Encomiasticon Augustinianum.* Brussels, 1654.

Faure, Paul. *La Renaissance.* 5th ed. Paris: PUF, 1969.

Feroci, M. *Breve racconto della miracolosa apparizione di Maria del Buon Consiglio e del prodigioso portento della Sacra Effigie di Gesù Crocifisso.* Palestrina, n.d. (circa 1717).

Fossier, Robert. *Le Moyen Age.* Paris: Armand Colin, 1983.

Funck-Brentano, Franz. *The Renaissance.* New York: The Macmillan Company, 1936.

Gaspri, Anton. " 'Mother, Do Not Weep for What You See Now. Weep for What Is to Come': A Testimony of Bishop George Volaj of Sappa—His Sufferings and Death," in Sinishta, pp. 95-98.

Gurakuqi, Karl. "Madonna of Shkodra—A Holy Legend," in Sinishta, pp. 206-209.

Hale, J.R. *La Europa del Renacimiento, 1480-1520.* Siglo Veintiuno Editores.

John Paul II. *Insegnamenti di Giovanni Paolo II — 1978.* Libreria Editrice Vaticana, vol. 1, 1979.

Lefranc, Abel. *A vida quotidiana no tempo do Renascimento.* Lisbon: Ed. Livros do Brasil, 1962.

Lemoyne, Giovanni Battista. *Memorie Biografiche del Venerabile Don Giovanni Bosco.* Turin: Buona Stampa, 1905, ed. extra comercial; *Vita di San Giovanni Bosco.* Turin: Sta. Ed. Internazionale, 1941.

Llorca, S.J., Bernardino; García Villoslada, S.J., Ricardo; Leturia, S.J., P. de; and Montalban, S.J., F. J. *Historia de la Iglesia Católica*. Madrid: B.A.C., 1953-1960.

Lucas-Dubreton, J. *La Renaissance italienne*. Paris: Amiot, 1953.

Luddy, O.Cist., Ailbe J. *Life and Teaching of St. Bernard*. 2d ed. Dublin: M. H. Gill & Son, 1937.

Manzini. *Vita e miracoli de B.L.G.*, Brescia, 1701.

Mariano, Fabio, and Panepuccia, Cesare. *Genazzano, storia e architettura*. Rome: Kappa, 1985.

Merry del Val, Cardinal Rafael. *Memories of Pope Pius X*. Westminster, Md.: The Newman Press, 1951.

Meschler, S.J., Father Maurice. *St. Aloysius Gonzaga: Patron of Christian Youth*. London: B. Herder Book Co., 1911.

Parente, Card. Pietro, et al. *Lo Spirito Santo e Maria Santissima*. Typ. Pol. Vaticana, 1976. Seven studies on the occasion of the 500th anniversary of the apparition in Genazzano.

Pastor, Ludwig von. *The History of the Popes from the Close of the Middle Ages*. St. Louis: B. Herder, 1923.

Perini, Davide A. *Genazzano e suo territorio*. Rome: Ausonia, 1924.

Philipon, O.P., M. M. *Los dones del Espíritu Santo*. Madrid: Ediciones Palabra, 1983.

Ratzinger, Joseph Cardinal. *Instruction on Certain Aspects of the "Theology of Liberation."* Boston: St. Paul Editions, 1984.

Riccardi, Balilla. *Guida del Santuario di Genazzano*. Rome: Tip. Pallotti, 1953.

Riccardi, Fr. Duilio. *Un Santo tra poveri e ragazzi: Vita del B. Stefano Bellesini*. Milan: Editrice Ancora, 1970.

Rodríguez Villar, Ildefonso; Bandera, O.P., Armando; and Martinez, O.P., Constantino. *Conoce a tu Madre: Mariología en diálogo*. Madrid: Editorial Fernando III el Santo, 1987.

Rodríguez y Rodríguez, O.P., Fr. Victorino. *Temas-Clave de Humanismo Cristiano*. Madrid: Speiro, 1984.

Roschini, O.S.M., Gabriel. *Instruções Marianas*. São Paulo: Ed. Paulinas, 1960.

Royo Marín, O.P., Fr. Antonio. *The Theology of Christian Perfection.* New York: The Foundation for a Christian Civilization, 1987.

Saint Laurent, Fr. Thomas de. *The Book of Confidence.* Crompond, N.Y.: America Needs Fatima, 1989.

Senni, G. *Memorie di Genazzano e de' vicini paesi.* Rome, 1838.

Sinishta, Gjon. *The Fulfilled Promise: A Documentary Account of Religious Persecution in Albania.* Santa Clara, Calif.: H & F Composing Service—Printing, 1976.

Stella, Vico. *Il Beato Stefano Bellesini.* Santuario Madonna del Buon Consiglio, n.d.

Tomás, Bishop of Salamanca. *María Madre del Buen Consejo.* Salamanca: Imp. Calatrava, 1893.

Vannutelli, L. *Cenni storici sul Santuario di Maria Santissima del Buon Consiglio di Genazzano.* Rome, 1839; *Notizie e istrumenti del Convento di S. Maria del Buon Consiglio in Genazzano,* Arquivo Conventual de Genazzano, n.d.; *Ricordi del suolo nativo, Genazzano,* Isola del Liri, 1936.

Weiss, Johann B. *Historia Universal.* Barcelona: Tip. La Educación, 1927-1933.

*   *   *

Catolicismo, São Paulo, nos. 208-209, April-May 1968; and no. 424, April 1986.

Der Fels, Regensburg, March 1986; February 1988.

Enciclopedia Universal Ilustrada. Madrid-Barcelona: Espasa-Calpe, 1910-1919.

Madre del Buon Consiglio, magazine from the shrine of Genazzano, August-October 1967; July-August 1985; November-December 1985; January-February 1987.

Santuario Madre del Buon Consiglio — Genazzano. Subiaco: Tipografia Editrice S. Scolastica, n.d.

TFP Newsletter, vol. 4, no. 15, 1985.

Picture Credits

Addeo, O.E.S.A., Msgr. Agostino Felice, 93 (top), 166, 217.
Albrecht, Dr., 145 (second from top), 154, 155.
Alcasid, José Maria, xv (bottom), 16 (bottom), 125 (bottom), 145 (bottom left).
American Society for the Defense of Tradition, Family and Property, xxiv (top left), 55.
Benziger Brothers, *La Madonna del Buon Consiglio* (1888), 43, 49, 71, 145 (third from top).
Brazilian Society for the Defense of Tradition, Family and Property, 122, 174, 199, 209.
Campos, Siqueira, xi, 211, back cover.
Clá Dias, João S., front cover, iii, v, xiii, xv (top), xvi, xxiv (bottom), 1, 6, 7 (top), 9, 11, 15-25, 27, 33 (top), 81, 83, 98, 103 (bottom), 113 (bottom), 125 (top left), 161 (top), 181, 190, 191 (bottom), 195.
Dias Tavares, José R., 7 (bottom).
Felici, G., 186 (left).
Historisches Bildarchiv Handke-Bad Berneck, 45.
Historisches Museum der Stadt Wien, Copyright, 142-143 (bottom).
Jesuit Fathers of Colegio São Luis, São Paulo, Brazil, 145 (top left), 152 (top left), 159.
Koninklijke Smeets Offset, Weert, 58.
Mariano, Fabio and Cesare Panepuccia, Edizioni Kappa, Rome, 93 (bottom), 121, 145 (bottom right).
Museum of Santa Cruz, Toledo, 136 (left).
Patrimonio Nacional (Spain), photograph granted and authorized by, 136 (right).
Postulação Fatima, xxiv (center).
Santuario Madre del Buon Consiglio-Genazzano, Subiaco, 33 (bottom), 38, 39, 65, 76-77, 99, 103 (top), 133 (top), 137 (bottom).